The History of St. Louis Writers Guild

CELEBRATING A CENTURY

Brad R. Cook
HISTORIAN AND PAST-PRESIDENT

The History
of
St. Louis Writers Guild

Celebrating a Century

Brad R. Cook
Historian and Past-President

founded in 1920

The History of St. Louis Writers Guild
Celebrating a Century
Brad R. Cook

Copyright 2020 © Brad R. Cook

All Rights Reserved

Published in the United States by
Broadsword Books L.L.C.

In accordance with the U.S. Copyright Act of 1976, no part of this book maybe reproduced, scanned, or distributed in any printed or electronic form without written permission from the publisher. Except as permitted for review purposes. Please do not participate in the piracy of copyrighted materials and thank you for supporting author's rights.

All rights reserved under international and pan-american copyright conventions. No part of this book may be used or reproduced in any manner without written permission.
ISBN: 978-0-99964333-4

www.bradrcook.com
@bradrcook

Stlwritersguild.org

Book Cover and Interior Layout by Brad R. Cook
Arch Photo by James Roblee
Used with permission from Shutterstock.com.
Color enhancement and cover design by Brad R. Cook.
SLWG Logos used with permission
Edited by Mary Ward Menke - Word Abilities

For

The Past, Present, and Future
Members of St. Louis Writers Guild

- 100th Anniversary Logo

1 |
My Introduction to
St. Louis Writers Guild

I discovered St. Louis Writers Guild, like many new writers, because I had written a lot of words but didn't know what to do with them.

I finished my first manuscript in December of 2006 and was trying to figure out how to become an author. My wife was online one day, and found the website for St. Louis Writers Guild. She called me in. I read about their upcoming meeting. Not certain if I could become a member, or if St. Louis Writers Guild could even help, I thought I would check it out. It was a step in the right direction; if nothing else, a place to learn more about the publishing industry.

In the days leading up to the meeting, I debated whether or not to even go. I kept thinking . . . who am I? I'm not really a writer. I'm only trying to be a writer. Sure, I'd written several pieces but I wasn't significantly published. Would anyone even like this book, an epic fantasy only three years after *The Lord of the Rings*? Writers were smart people who could break down characters, plots, and English-teacher-levels of meaning in the words. I was a guy who liked to read, liked to create stories, and happened to write a few down.

Yes, of course I had done more than that, but not in my mind. I wasn't a success. I'd written assignments in school that had attracted attention. My first was in elementary school. For not turning in an assignment, I had to write an essay on why I hadn't. My piece, "Why Homework Shouldn't be Late" went on to be published in the school's newsletter. My first book was in elementary school, a little picture book for creative writing class. By high school, my play was chosen to be performed by the playwriting teacher.

BUT it's not like I was a real writer or anything . . . it was only a dream. (*If you haven't read through the sarcasm, this is a common thread I hear in writers including myself—"I'm not yet a writer"—afraid not. If you write, you're a writer.*)

I decided to jump in. If nothing else, I'd stay for a moment, and slip out the back. Nervous and figuring I would never fit in, I took a notebook, and jumped in my car on a mild January morning.

Saturday, January 6, 2007, the weather was cold, but I don't remember tons of snow. At that time, St. Louis Writers Guild met in a large room, the Community Room, in the back of the Crestwood Barnes & Noble on Watson Road. Worried about being late, I arrived thirty minutes early. To pass the time, I wandered through the stacks, and slowly made my way to the back room.

Laughter seeped around the door which sat slightly ajar. Taking a deep breath, I stepped inside. Three women arranged rows of chairs and a couple of large tables at the front. The rectangular room stretched far to the back of the store and the chairs were lined up to face one of the long walls. A thin-framed woman with short hair approached with a smile and said, "Welcome, we're still setting up, if you can give us a minute."

Her warm smile instantly put me at ease. From her nametag, I learned her name was Marianne Blake, the Membership Coordinator at that time. I responded with an, "Of course. Sorry. I know I'm a little early."

To be honest, I don't really remember the rest of that conversation. I was trying to take in everyone and everything. It's a bit of a blur, but she wouldn't let me leave. As we spoke, she laid out name tags. She had a large box or book that stored each member's name tag. A white card in a plastic holder with a pin back. Next to the rows of nametags, Marianne set a pile of sticky nametags and a couple of Sharpies.

Taking a sticky-back nametag, I wrote Brad Cook, peeled the back off and placed it on my blazer. I wore a blazer, tried to casual it up with jeans, but thinking back it was probably a look-the-part kind of thing. Now as an author, I can say, there isn't really much of a uniform.

The other two women paused their work and approached. The taller of the two said, "Hi, I'm Robin. Welcome to St. Louis Writers Guild." She motioned to the other woman, "That's Mary."

The woman with short brown hair waved her hand, "Come on in."

Their warmth and openness put any fears I had at ease. I smiled, said hello, and added, "I think I'm supposed to pay five dollars?" That was the cost for a non-member to attend the workshop. All three chuckled and nodded. I remember Marianne thanking me and telling me how it could be applied to membership if I joined in the next thirty days. I wasn't certain if I was joining yet, so I thanked her.

Robin asked, "Is this your first meeting?"

"Yes," I replied and wondered what it meant. "I wrote a manuscript." I thought I was cool using publishing terminology, but I couldn't yet say I had written a book.

Mary instantly added, "You've come to the right place."

Not wanting to be in the way, I stepped out to get something to drink. (*Snapple Apple, if you were wondering.*)

Soon, a flood of people flowed into the room; my nerves took over and I wanted to bolt. Once the room began to fill up, I stepped back inside and took a seat toward the back.

I didn't know what to do other than sit, but most of the room was really friendly. Several people asked if it was my first time, and what I wrote. My answer of, "Yes, and I've written a fantasy novel," was met with excitement.

Robin Moore Theiss, the president at that time, talked to almost everyone who stepped in the room. In fact, something truly terrifying was how many of these people knew each other. My first glimpse of St. Louis' literary community. Little did I know, I'd just met my people.

Over by the door, Mary spoke to several other members,

including a young woman with curly hair. Later I'd learn her name was Alicia, and she was treasurer at that time. Name tags were a wonderful thing. A man ran around with a camera, snapping photos of the event, but I never did learn his name. The room mixed all ages and genres. At that time, memoirs were all the rage, so much of the room was writing their life story. However, I met people writing articles for journals, stories for anthologies and collections, and even several novelists like me.

Not knowing who to approach or talk to, I took a seat. To be honest, I was still trying to soak it all in. I'm a people-watcher who likes to sit back and observe a room like a naturalist in the wild. However, a man came up and sat next to me. He wore a floppy brimmed hat that revealed a ring of white hair when removed. With the friendliest demeanor, he extended his hand, and said, "Hi, Peter Green. First time here at St. Louis Writers Guild?"

"It is." I shook his hand.

"I'm new here too," he replied, but it wasn't his first meeting. Little did I know who the universe had dropped in front of me. Peter turned out to be a friend that I worked with on the board for the next several years. Peter was writing a mystery novel and a memoir about his father (*Ben's War with the U.S. Marines*, if anyone else might be interested). An intriguing tale: his father scooped the end of World War II as a radio operator in the Pacific. The book was about the letters his mom and dad shared during the war, and as a history buff, I was hooked. We would have spoken more, but Robin took the center of the room.

"Welcome," she began. "I'm Robin Theiss, President of St. Louis Writers Guild, and we have a few announcements to go over before we get to our presenter. Did everyone get a calendar?"

I hadn't. In all my confusion, I hadn't grabbed one of the two-month calendars handed out at each meeting. Peter showed me his. Robin went over the events held that month and what the program would be the following month. At the time, St. Louis Writers Guild had as many four events a month, the workshop on the first Saturday, two open mic nights, and the lecture which was held on the evening of the third Thursday.

Then Robin asked, "Who here submitted for publication in

the last month?" A number of people raised their hands, and she added, "who received a rejection in the last month?" Many kept their hands up, as others lowered their arms. Everyone applauded their efforts and she asked, "Who received an acceptance?" Several people raised their hands. One woman announced she would be published in an anthology. A gentleman stated his article appeared in a national magazine. I was impressed. The people sitting in this room were doing what I wanted to do. Plus, they applauded rejection, something that terrified me. I decided to join. The memory of that moment remains so vivid in my mind, even all these years later. I had been deciding if writing was the right path for me, but from the announcements, I knew I'd found something I wanted to try.

The workshop, about setting writing goals was informative, and I took so many notes. Two hours passed in the blink of an eye and the event was over. Peter and I talked on the way out, and he asked if I would be back. I said yes. We shook hands, and Peter said, "Hope to see you next month."

I went home and didn't stop talking about the workshop. Next month, I returned, and I ended up attending every workshop that year. Within that time, the true novice who had stepped in that back room transformed to a well-informed writer. The following year I joined the board, and in 2011, I became president, a position I held for three and a half years.

What follows are personal accounts and matters of historical record, mixed with a bit of legend and lore. St. Louis Writers Guild (hereafter referred to as SLWG or the Guild) has had a few historians over the years, and as the organization turns 100 years old, it is time to collect all these tales into one place – *somewhere that is not my brain* – so it can be accessed by anyone who wishes or needs it.

I hope you enjoy!

The History of St. Louis Writers Guild

Shirley Seifert's House, SLWG's 1st Meeting Place
Thursday, October 28, 1920

2 |
Life in 1920

St. Louis in 1920 was a city on the rise. What had been the last stop before heading into the Wild West had become the center of trade moving north and south along the river and east and west along road and rail. A city of wood transformed into a city of brick and became a foundation of the Midwest.

To put the world in perspective, in 1920 . . .

- Babe Ruth was traded by the Red Sox for $125,000, the largest sum ever paid for a player at that time ($1,532,000 in 2019).
- The Eighteenth Amendment to the Constitution started Prohibition in the United States.
- The US Silver Dollar was still in circulation.
- Streetcars cost a dime to ride ($1.20).
- A new Ford cost $750 ($9,192).
- A postage stamp cost $0.02.
- The United States Post Office Department ruled that children could not be sent via parcel post.
- The first domestic radio set, the Westinghouse radio, appeared in the United States. A Westinghouse radio cost $10 ($125).
- On January 9, thousands of people watched George Polley, "The Human Fly," climb thirty floors of the Woolworth Building in New York City before being arrested.

The History of St. Louis Writers Guild

- World War I officially ended on January 20 when the Treaty of Versailles went into effect.
- The League of Women Voters was founded on February 14 in Chicago.
- On February 17, Anna Anderson tried to commit suicide in Berlin, and was taken to a mental hospital where she claimed to be the Grand Duchess Anastasia of Russia.
- The Summer Olympics opened on April 20 in Antwerp, Belgium, and it was the first time the symbol of the five interlocking rings were displayed.
- The Nineteenth Amendment to the United States Constitution guaranteeing women's right to vote was passed on August 26.
- The National Football League (NFL) was established on September 17 as the American Professional Football Association.
- Republican U. S. Senator Warren G. Harding defeated Democratic Governor of Ohio James M. Cox on November 2 to become President of the United States. It was the first national election in which women had the right to vote.
- It was a leap year.
- Top three songs in the USA were
  - *Whispering* by Paul Whiteman & His Orchestra
  - *I'm in Heaven When I'm in My Mother's Arms* by William Robyn
  - *A Young Man's Fancy* by Art Hickman & His Orchestra

Meanwhile, in St. Louis . . .

- St. Louis, The Gateway to the West, and midway point on the Mississippi River, was transforming into a city of brick.
- The city was nicknamed Mound City, for the grass-covered hilltops of the mound-building cultures which dotted not only the downtown and riverfront but much of the surrounding counties. By this point, most had been destroyed.
- The Chase Hotel was built.
- There were 772,897 people living in the city, the sixth largest population in the country.

- The Bear Pits at the St. Louis Zoo were completed in 1919.
- Three newspapers existed in the city, the *St. Louis Star-Times*, the *St. Louis Globe-Democrat*, and the newest paper, the *St. Louis Post-Dispatch*.

St. Louis Writers Guild held its first meeting on Thursday, October 28, 1920 at 8 p.m. An announcement was placed two days earlier on the twenty-sixth, in the *St. Louis Post-Dispatch*, the youngest of the newspapers at that time. The announcement also appeared in the *St. Louis Globe-Democrat*, and the *Star-Times* as well. A clipping was even in St. Louis Writers Guild's archive at the Central Public Library.

The article in the *St. Louis Post-Dispatch*, "St. Louis Story Writers And Dramatists To Meet," was a call for writers, an invitation to hear a "novel literary program." As Shirley Seifert explained in her invitation, "This meeting is primarily intended to bring together for recreation all local members of the Missouri Writers' Guild. The Guild, through its annual spring meeting at Columbia, Missouri, and its annual fall outing in the Ozarks, has demonstrated that writers can gain much from meeting each other." Shirley continued, "For that reason St. Louis members of the Guild have prevailed upon me to call the first meeting. It is planned to hold monthly meetings hereafter at the homes of other members."

Just as today, a few dedicated volunteers were the heart of St. Louis Writers Guild. In the beginning, six founders created and formed the organization. From newspapermen to short story writers and novelists, each was a professional writer.

The six founders were Sam Hellman, Shirley Seifert, Ralph Mooney, Jay Gelzer, William Brennan, and Leonora McPheeters. They came from different areas of the literary world but understood writers could benefit from community support. Along with a number of Charter Members and the first SLWG members, they established the foundation of the organization.

The spark that inspired the idea of St. Louis Writers Guild ignited four years earlier at the 1916 Missouri Writers Guild retreat.

The History of St. Louis Writers Guild

This event was an affair to remember and was mentioned several times in the early days of St. Louis Writers Guild.

Seventy-five Missouri writers met from September 23 to September 30, 1916 at Lake Taneycomo in the Ozarks. They fished, boated, hiked, rode horses, and swam as well as talked about writing and books. The idea was to foster a fellowship among the authors of the state. Apparently, friendships were forged, and several in attendance became well-published in the following years. A few informal meetings were held with St. Louis writers but never regularly or beyond a few friends gathering to write and talk about writing.

Missouri Writers Guild was founded in 1915 because the professional writers of the state wanted to gather for camaraderie and to support one another. On May 4, 1915, MWG was officially organized at the University of Missouri in Columbia, Missouri. The newly formed Missouri Writers Guild met twice a year. In the spring, a meeting was held on the last day of Journalism Week at the university in Columbia, Missouri. The second meeting occurred each fall and was required by the MWG by-laws to be in a more picturesque spot. Often, Lake of the Ozarks was selected, but other locations were chosen, like the Tennessee River valley. Without a highway system, arriving at the meeting meant taking Clayton Road to Jefferson City, then south to the Ozarks. Several writers packed into a 1920s automobile, bouncing along the dusty dirt roads that gangsters like Bonnie and Clyde or John Dillinger made famous.

Let's hope there was also a train.

By 1920, twice a year was not enough, and after returning from the autumn meeting, several St. Louis members of the Missouri Writers Guild wanted to capture the feeling of those meetings. In September, Mrs. Cecil T. Fennell hosted an evening at her house on Julian Avenue for about a dozen St. Louis area authors. They recounted what had been discussed at the annual Missouri Writers Guild event and decided that more meetings should be held.

A month later, they gathered together to hear a discussion of novels—a tradition St. Louis Writers Guild continues to this day.

Most members of St. Louis Writers Guild lived in the area between the Central West End and Washington University, and a few lived on the south side of the city. Big Bend represented the western border of St. Louis, and roads like Lindell, Olive, and Market were the main thoroughfares of the city. Places like Webster Groves and Kirkwood were miles outside the city.

Shirley Seifert lived with her parents in a house that still exists in the five thousand block of De Giverville Avenue. It's a lovely two-story house with a small porch, on a short cul-de-sac in the Skinker/DeBaliviere neighborhood.

Thirty people attended the first meeting, which featured food and a presentation on novels. Known to have attended were Sam Hellman, Temple Bailey, Louis Dodge, Elinor Maxwell, Ralph Mooney, Margaretta Lawler, Capt. Donald Wright, Susan Boogher, and Robertus Love.

If I could travel back in time, this meeting would be one of my first stops. The women in fine gowns and the men all in suits, gathered in a living room with not enough chairs or space. Friends and acquaintances, all of them writers, formed a closely connected literary community. St. Louis always had that small-town feel, much more like Main Street than a sprawling city.

Let's meet the founders…

The History of St. Louis Writers Guild

Sam Hellman, First President
1929 *St. Louis Globe-Democrat*

3 |
Sam Hellman,
Founder and First President, 1920

Sam Hellman became the first president of St. Louis Writers Guild in 1920 and was instrumental in the founding and formation of the organization. He was most likely elected, but it could have been his sheer force of personality and drive that brought him to the helm. A bit of a local celebrity, Sam was a newspaperman who went on to pen much of Hollywood's Golden Age. A man of wit, intelligence, cunning, and intensity, his stories, and movies captured the era of the 1920s and 1930s. His genius as a writer was defined by the pace and slang in his dialogue.

Born in San Francisco, California on July 4, 1885, Sam Hellman moved to St. Louis after college. A bout with typhoid in 1906 caused him to leave California. He became a newspaper columnist who wrote articles and short stories, at first for the *St. Louis Star-Times*, before switching to the newest paper on the block – The *St. Louis Post-Dispatch*. He eventually served as the *Post-Dispatch's* managing editor.

Though the first edition of the *St. Louis Post-Dispatch* dropped on December 12, 1878, the *St. Louis Globe-Democrat* was the longstanding juggernaut which had been around since 1852. The third major paper of the day was The *St. Louis Star*.

Sam Hellman wrote articles and advertisements for the *Post-Dispatch*, but starting in 1916, the paper started buying his short stories. Soon his stories were being published in major magazines and in newspapers across the country. The tales ran the gamut from humorous to salacious, but always with an underlying message and a devilishly wonderful sense of language. Sam had a legendary wit and used slang to make it razor sharp. His good friend and future St. Louis Writers Guild president, Mrs. Elinor Maxwell McCord, described him this way: "Mr. Hellman is a riot in conversation. It was better listening to him than reading one of his stories. He keeps a running chatter of conversation, couched in the most marvelous slang imaginable, and some unimaginable."

Sam married the love of his life, Selma Schwartz, and together they had two daughters, Verna and Emmy Lou. Rising to the heights of St. Louis society, they lived on Pershing near Washington University. The house even had a radio, a luxury at the time, and one that was noted in the census.

An article in the *St. Louis Post-Dispatch* from 1920 reports on an incident involving the theft of Mrs. Hellman's jewelry. At the time, Sam and Velma lived on Westminster Place in St. Louis. While attending a fitting, Mrs. Hellman set a platinum bar pin set with twenty-one diamonds on the counter of Louis Schmidt's tailor shop on Delmar Boulevard. She removed the bar pin while being measured for dress alterations, and when she went to put it back on, the pin was gone. Mr. Carl Larsen, the tailor's chauffer, was arrested after extensive questioning by Mr. Hellman and the police. Mr. Larsen had taken the center diamond valued at $500 ($6,100) and thrown the rest of the pin, valued at $700 ($8,900) in the refuse. Mr. Hellman hired a man for $25 ($300) to search the dump; that man sublet the job to five Italian laborers who spent the day going through the dump. The pin was never found, and Sam Hellman decided not to press charges against Mr. Larsen.

In 1929, newspaperman Hamilton Thornton described Sam in an article about St. Louis Writers Guild in the *St. Louis Globe-Democrat*. He wrote, "Sam Hellman is a wise cracker par excellence. As even the most casual readers of nationally popular magazines know, he can string pithy pundits together into yarns that move along in the aura of the highest-powered slang."

Sam Hellman was a fixture at many events. His presence was often described as intense—he was 6 ft., 2 in. tall, with broad shoulders and a full head of dark hair that swirled atop his head—

he often sat in a high-backed chair, listening to the evening's story, and then having a clear opinion on the piece that he would be certain to share.

Sam Hellman passed away on August 11, 1950 at the age of 65 in Beverly Hills, California and left a legacy matched by few other presidents. Between the articles he wrote for the newspapers, his witty short stories, and the movies he made, there is a library of material to sort through. Spend a couple of nights engrossed in Sam Hellman's filmography, then read his stories, and not only would one be entertained, but eventually the real man, the writer behind the words emerges.

The Golden Age of Hollywood's Silver Screen

Sam worked on his first film in 1924, and eventually, he and his family departed St. Louis and returned to California where he became an established writer for 20th Century Fox. In the 1940s, he switched to Warner Brothers. Sam penned over forty films during Hollywood's golden age of cinema, writing witty lines of dialogue for acting legends like Spencer Tracey, Will Rodgers, and John Carradine, as well as being responsible for several Shirley Temple movies including *Poor Little Rich Girl* (1936) and *Captain January* (1936).

A few of his notable hits include *Flying Fists* (1924, writer), *The Lottery Lover* (1935, writer), *Stanley and Livingstone* (1939, historical research and story outline), *The Doughgirls* (1944, writer), *My Darling Clementine* (1946, story), and his final film, *Powder River* (1953, writer).

Sam Hellman co-authored the screenplay for *Slave Ship* with William Faulkner. The film was released in 1937 and starred Jim Lovett, Elizabeth Allan, and Mickey Rooney.

Success on the silver screen made the Hellmans a fixture of Long Island, New York society. Avid bridge players, they often entertained at their home.

Sam Stuck to his Guns

Sam was never one to shy away from controversy or criticism. In 1906 while editor of the Student Newspaper at

Berkley University, he agreed at a meeting to not run an article about a certain powerful individual; however, after the meeting Sam ran the story. The man stormed the campus, demanding Sam come forth. He made many threats but eventually was forced to leave the campus. Sam Hellman never ran a retraction. In fact, it became a bigger story.

In August 1939, critics were angered by Sam's latest movie. He'd written the screenplay for a story of Wyatt Earp based off a recent book but had changed certain details of the shootout at the OK Corral. Sam appeared to be unaffected by criticism and explained it off as being part of the movie making business.

Samuel Hellman Filmography

Powder River (1953) (writer)
Sorrowful Jones (1949) (adaptation)
Pirates of Monterey (1947) (writer)
My Darling Clementine (1946) (story) ... a.k.a John Ford's My Darling Clementine (USA: complete title)
The Dark Horse (1946) (story)
The Runaround (1946) (writer)
The Horn Blows at Midnight (1945) (writer)
The Doughgirls (1944) (writer)
Shine on Harvest Moon (1944) (screenplay)
The Return of Frank James (1940) (original screenplay)
He Married His Wife (1940) (screenplay)
Day-Time Wife (1939) (contributor to screenplay) (uncredited)
Here I Am a Stranger (1939) (writer)
Stanley and Livingstone (1939) (historical research and story outline)
Frontier Marshal (1939) (screenplay)
The Three Musketeers (1939) (screenplay) ... a.k.a The Singing Musketeer (UK)
We're Going to Be Rich (1938) (writer)
The Baroness and the Butler (1938) (screenplay)
Slave Ship (1937) (writer)
Reunion (1936) (writer)
Poor Little Rich Girl (1936) (writer)

Captain January (1936) (writer)
A Message to Garcia (1936) (writer)
In Old Kentucky (1935) (writer)
Two-Fisted (1935) (writer)
The Daring Young Man (1935) (writer)
It's a Small World (1935) (writer)
George White's 1935 *Scandals* (1935) (contributing to treatment) (uncredited) (story)... a.k.a George White's Scandals
The Lottery Lover (1935) (writer)
The County Chairman (1935) (writer)
Little Miss Marker (1934) (screenplay) ... a.k.a The Girl in Pawn (UK)
Murder at the Vanities (1934) (dialogue)
Thirty Day Princess (1934) (adaptation)
Good Dame (1934) (writer)... a.k.a Good Girl (UK)
Search for Beauty (1934) (dialogue)
Casey at the Bat (1927) (titles)
A Kiss in a Taxi (1927) (titles)
Fighting Hearts (1926) (writer)
Flying Fists (1924) (writer)

From www.imdb.com

Shirley Seifert, Second President
1938 *St. Louis Globe-Democrat*

4 |
Shirley Seifert, Founder and Second President
1921 and 1923

Without a doubt, Shirley Seifert was one of the driving forces that created St. Louis Writers Guild. Her fire and passion for not only the written word, but also her fellow writers and the greater writing community was what forged the writers' guild. She remained a guiding light and continued to influence the modern day.

Born in St. Peters, Missouri in 1888, her father, Richard Seifert, was an electrical engineer who emigrated from Germany. Her mother, Anna Sanford, had roots in Massachusetts that traced back to 1634. Shirley was officially announced to St. Louis in 1919 when the *St. Louis Post-Dispatch* introduced her to the world as the preeminent author of her day. The article, which ran on September 22, 1919, titled "Here Is Latest St. Louis Writer To 'Arrive'—Shirley Seifert, Once She Got Started, Made Rapid Headway in the Big Magazines," introduced her like a debutante, and showcased her writing and publications.

At Central High School, Shirley credited several teachers and a "wonderful world of books" for her love of the written word. While attending Washington University, she majored in classical and modern languages. She turned this love of language and history into a job teaching English, Latin, and history. Shirley soon found her passion lay in the words and not in the classroom. At the urging of her journalism professor, she pursued her writing, which led to her first article in *Popular Science Monthly*. She was paid $3.

The History of St. Louis Writers Guild

Seifert wrote, "The Girl Who Was Too Good Looking" in 1919, earning $100 from *American* magazine. She would also be published in *Redbook, McCall's, Ladies Home Journal,* and *New York Herald-Tribune Magazine.*

Shirley's home on De Giverville Avenue was a quaint Urban Craftsman style with two sets of steps that lead from the sidewalk to a small porch with a pair of columns holding up the roof. Stone at the base, with brick walls, the two-story home had a basement and an attic dormer. This was a common style of home in many historic St. Louis neighborhoods.

In January 1921, Shirley was elected president of St. Louis Writers Guild. She was the first female president and one of the youngest at 33 years old. She was elected again in 1923. She remained active in the Guild throughout the twenties and thirties.

Shirley Seifert's literary career focused on historical fiction. Many of her novels featured ordinary people living extraordinary lives set in the American Midwest. Drawing from old records, letters, newspaper clippings, and diaries, she developed the factual information for her stories. Though she featured the hardships of life in the United States, her stories retained a positive outlook for the future. She was fond of saying, "I am no defeatist. When I am doing research for a novel, I see how America will work out of its present crisis."

Shirley wrote a novel about every two years, fifteen in all, and earned a noteworthy place in American literature, as her novel *The Wayfarer* was nominated for the Pulitzer Prize.

Named a "St. Louis Woman of Distinction" twice, she loved and remained a devoted citizen of St. Louis throughout her life. In regards to this city she said, "…recognizing all its faults and liking even those, if you press me too hard." She was vocal about her opinions, and often wrote the editors of newspapers stating her opinions. One of these letters focused on the newly forming suburbs, and what a blight they were to the city.

An avid traveler, gardener, and seamstress, Shirley filled her life with more than books. She wasn't the only literary talent in her family either. Both her sisters, Adele Seifert and Elizabeth Seifert Gasparotti, were accomplished authors and members of St. Louis

Writers Guild. Adele authored several mystery novels and even collaborated with Shirley on a couple of books. Elizabeth focused on medical stories about doctors. She had been interested in pursuing medicine at one time but ended up publishing twenty-four novels over her lifetime. St. Louis Writers Guild celebrated Mrs. Elizabeth Gasparotti and her two sisters at a dinner event at the Park Plaza Hotel in April of 1939. By then, Shirley and her sister Adele had moved to Kirkwood with their parents. They held a held a tea party after the event in honor of the occasion and invited all their friends over.

A tireless advocate for writers, Shirley not only served St. Louis Writers Guild for years, she also traveled throughout the region giving talks and encouraging writers. In 1924, while attending the Anti Rust Society's annual meeting, she was asked "if a writer of the small town had as good a chance to win success as a writer of the great city." Miss Seifert replied,

The story is the thing, whether it comes from Prairie Dell or London. But the writers in the smaller places will only succeed when they stick to the environment they know best. There is no reason why they should not. 'The Mill on the Floss' was a great story in a rural setting. The forest, the river, the mountains, and the prairie wilderness have dramatic potentialities greater than along the route of the clanging trolley. It's not where you are that makes the writer — it's you. And right here I want to say if there is any well-oiled roadway to success in fiction writing it has been outside my chart. Recognition only comes from hard and painstaking effort. You have to do something better than 'just fairly good.' Your work must stand out in order to give a reason for its being printed. And it is well. When your name appears with a story you want to feel you've done your best, and that those who read what you have written have derived pleasure and inspiration from it.

Shirley Seifert passed away in 1971 at the age of 83, at her house on North Clay Avenue in Kirkwood, Missouri. Her sister Elizabeth died in 1983, and Adele followed in 1986. All three are remembered and admired by St. Louis Writers Guild; however, because of Shirley Seifert's establishment of this literary organization, her body of work, and her commitment to the city she loved, will always be a pillar of St. Louis Writer's Guild's legacy.

Booklist of Shirley Seifert

Land of Tomorrow; A Legend of Kentucky, 1937
The Wayfarer, 1938
Death Stops at the Old Stone Inn, 1938
River Out of Eden, 1940
Waters of the Wilderness, 1941
Those Who Go Against the Current, 1943
Captain Grant, 1946
The Proud Way, 1948
Turquoise Trail, 1950
Three Lives of Elizabeth, 1952
Farewell My General, 1955
Let My Name Stand Fair, 1956
Destiny in Dallas, 1958
Grace Church, Kirkwood, Missouri: Its Story, 1959
Look to the Rose, 1960
By the King's Command, 1962
Key to St. Louis, 1963
The Senator's Lady, 1967
The Medicine Man, 1971
Never No More, 1976

Brad R. Cook

The History of St. Louis Writers Guild

Ralph Mooney, Founder and President
1929 *St. Louis Globe-Democrat*

5 |
Ralph E. Mooney,
Founder and President 1924 & 1941

Ralph E. Mooney, the youngest of the St. Louis Writers Guild founders, became president in 1924 and again in 1941, which demonstrates exactly how many decades he was a part of St. Louis Writers Guild. For many of those years, he served on the board performing various duties, but most of them as SLWG Secretary. Along with being instrumental to the organization's operations for decades, Ralph also had a long and varied writing career. He was known for opening his home on Sunday afternoons to any writer who might want to drop by to write and discuss their manuscript issues.

Ralph was born in 1891, and by the 1920s, he began writing short stories for major magazines like the *Saturday Evening Post, Argosy All-Story Weekly, The Popular Magazine, Munsey's, American Magazine*, and *People's Favorite Magazine*. This included his most well-known stories, "Look like a Million," in American Magazine in 1921, and "Polysynthetic Football," published in *The Saturday Evening Post* in 1922. For a time, he was a newspaper reporter with *The Star*.

In December of 1921, members of St. Louis Writers Guild told ghost stories while sitting around a roaring fire. The event was held at Dean Hefferman's house on Clemens Avenue. Ralph Mooney, Mrs. Cecil G Fennell, Mrs. Corrine Harris Markey, and Harold Shumate read original works about their personal experiences.

The History of St. Louis Writers Guild

In September of 1923, Ralph had another of his humorous football stories, "The Sheik of the Hard-Boiled League," published in the August 10, *Short Stories Anthology*.

"The Solid Thing" was published in the January 1924 *Munsey Magazine*, and told the tale of "a fine old fireman who couldn't be anything else."

During his presidency in 1924, Ralph continued the writing installments. At the time, SLWG wrote a story in pieces with members contributing each month. He read the latest installment at the meetings. In September 1928, he presented "Correcting the Manuscripts" at the annual Missouri Writers Guild Meeting at the Lake of the Ozarks.

Ralph Mooney was a member of the Advertising Club of St. Louis.

His first novel, *David Rudd*, was published in 1927 by Henry Waterson, New York. The novel was often called a memoir and was described as a romance of the Mississippi River. He followed it up with his second novel, *Mr. Pelly's Little Home*. A tragedy based on real events; it was published in 1936. On March 8, 1936, the *St. Louis Post-Dispatch* wrote a review of the "notable novel," and an announcement for the novel's release was found in the April 3, 1936 edition of the *Alton Evening Telegraph*.

Ralph Mooney also wrote for the theater with his friend, C. Eugene Smith. In 1914, they penned a three-act operetta, *The Love Star*, which was produced by W. Gus Hanschen, with words and music written by Mooney and Smith. The instrumental ensemble for the chorus and piano was produced by the Quadrangle Club of Washington University.

Not one to hide his opinion, several of his pieces were listed in "Letters to the People," a column in the *St. Louis Post-Dispatch*. In 1916, he wrote an article about how every American should engage in civil service, calling it Universal Service, and declaring that as a man of 25, he could think of no greater way to spend his life at that moment.

Between writing for the *Argosy*, *The Saturday Evening Post*, and brushing shoulders with greats like Frank Munsey and Norman Rockwell, Ralph hosted many of SLWG's earliest meetings at his home on Forest Park Boulevard or later on McPherson Avenue or Washington Avenue. He lived there with his wife Margaret Sharp Mooney, their daughter Margaret, a second daughter, and a son, Terrance.

Mrs. Margaret Anna Mooney, a graduate of Mary Institute and Washington U, was a librarian with the St. Louis Public Library, and active in the Girl Scouts and the church.

In Hamilton Thornton's 1929 *St. Louis Globe-Democrat* article about the Guild (see Chapter 10, "The Globe-Democrat Article in 1929") Ralph explained that he and his wife "have evolved a system of their own for keeping the dew on the butterfly and the moss on the rose. The secret is this: they see each other only once a day—that is, except when it is necessary for Mooney to go downtown or leave the house for some reason."

He worked for Southwestern Bell for many years, before moving to Chicago in 1946. He was historian for the American Telephone and Telegraph Company in New York and was the editor of the Southwestern Telephone News the magazine for the Southwestern Bell Telephone Company.

Ralph Mooney dedicated his life to writing and encouraging others to write. He passed away in Redding, Connecticut in August 1958, at the age of 65.

His wife Margaret Anna Mooney, passed away on May 3, 1973 in Mequon, Wisconsin, after a long illness. She was 81.

Articles and Stories by Ralph Mooney
"Currents of Fate"
"Like a Million" *American Magazine*
"The Master Law" a series featured in *Detective Stories.*
"Improbably" *The Saturday Evening Post*
"Tire Jockey" *The Saturday Evening Post*
"Miss Kent Understands" *The Saturday Evening Post*
"Polysynthetic Football" *The Saturday Evening Post* in 1922
"The Sheik of the Hard-Boiled League" *Short Stories Anthology* in 1923
"The Solid Thing" *Munsey Magazine*, in January 1924
"The Love Star" three-act operetta

Books by Ralph Mooney
David Rudd, 1927
Mr. Pelly's Little Home, 1936

Brad R. Cook

Louis Dodge, Third President
1929 *St. Louis Globe-Democrat*

6 |
Jay Gelzer,
Founder of St. Louis Writers Guild

Born in England (though some sources list her birthplace as Buffalo, New York) in January of 1889, Jay immigrated to the United States in her youth. She married Jennings Gelzer, an electrical engineer in Chicago, and they had two sons, Philip and John. By the 1920s, she was an established author and had moved to St. Louis. She published many short stories in popular magazines, including *Good Housekeeping*, *Woman's World*, and *Cosmopolitan*. Jay Gelzer's story "Redhot Blues" ran in Collier's. Her first book was a collection of short stories titled, *The Street of a Thousand Delights* and was followed by *Compromise: A Novel*.

In 1924, she copyrighted a dramatic comedy screenplay called Lonely Woman, and the 1929 film, *Broadway Babies* was based on one of her stories.

Jay Gelzer shared not only her stories but also her opinions. She often appeared in the newspaper, and in November 1924, *The Montrose Tidings* ran her piece, "Square Deal Key to Success in Marriage." From an article originally shared in *Hearst International*, Mrs. Jay Gelzer said, "I told myself that marriage needn't be the end of personal achievement for a woman. That it might, instead, serve as the beginning. . . . I must manage somehow to achieve more, to be smarter, to work harder than mothers are usually called upon to work."

In the Street of a Thousand Delights was a collection of eight stories released in 1921, and set in Melbourne, Australia. Based loosely on a collection of English stories called *Limehouse Nights*, each tale was tragic but with a theme and treatment which made the stories more pleasing. All were about intermarriage, and Jay Gelzer apparently handled this subject sensitively considering how the racial antagonism and misunderstandings were construed. Her second release was *Compromise: A Novel*.

Jay Gelzer passed away in San Diego, California on June 15, 1964 at the age of 75.

Brad R. Cook

Temple Bailey, Charter Member
1929 *St. Louis Globe-Democrat*

7 |
William Brennan and Leonora McPheeters

I wish I knew more about William Brennan and Leonora McPheeters. Unfortunately, not all of us leave tracks in history. I've dug through census records, old newspaper clippings, and countless records, but William Brennan is a common name of the time, and didn't leave much to find. There was even less to find about Leonora McPheeters, until I came across the announcement of the board of directors in 1958. It listed her as Mrs. Chester McPheeters, which allowed me to locate her records from the 1920s and 1930s.

William Brennan

William Brennan was a newspaperman. He wrote stories for the *Saturday Evening Post*, and eventually worked on movies as a screenplay writer. He was not William Brennan the carpenter, William Brennan the shoemaker, Justice William Brennan, or even the boxer Bill Brennan, all of whom lived in the 1920s. There is even the possibility the name William Brennan could refer to Frederick Hazlitt Brennan, who was a member in the 1920s and 1930s; however there is no evidence that Frederick Brennan was a founder of St. Louis Writers Guild.

Leonora McPheeters

Leonora Woodward married Lieutenant Chester McPheeters in 1917 in Baltimore Maryland, where he was stationed. They

The History of St. Louis Writers Guild

returned to St. Louis the following year after he was discharged from aviation service. She was co-chairman of "Efficiency in Government" for the Missouri League of Women Voters. Leonora McPheeters wrote short stories. She was deeply involved with St. Louis Writers Guild. In 1931, she gave a constructive analysis of her short story at a meeting, and also was one of the writing contest coordinators. In 1958, she served on the board as Secretary, which meant she had been involved with St. Louis Writers Guild for over thirty years, maybe forty.

Note: I cannot explain why neither Leonora or William appeared in Louis Dodge's history of SLWG in 1921, Hamilton Thornton's article in the *Globe-Democrat* in 1929, or in Robert Hereford's historical account in 1946. The first official listing of them as founders comes from Marcella Thum and King McElroy's accounts for the 50th Anniversary.

If you have any information about either of these writers, please let me know; you can find my contact information in the back of the book. I would love to know more about these two individuals who were such an important part of St. Louis Writers Guild.

Brad R. Cook

May Wilson Todd,
Charter Member

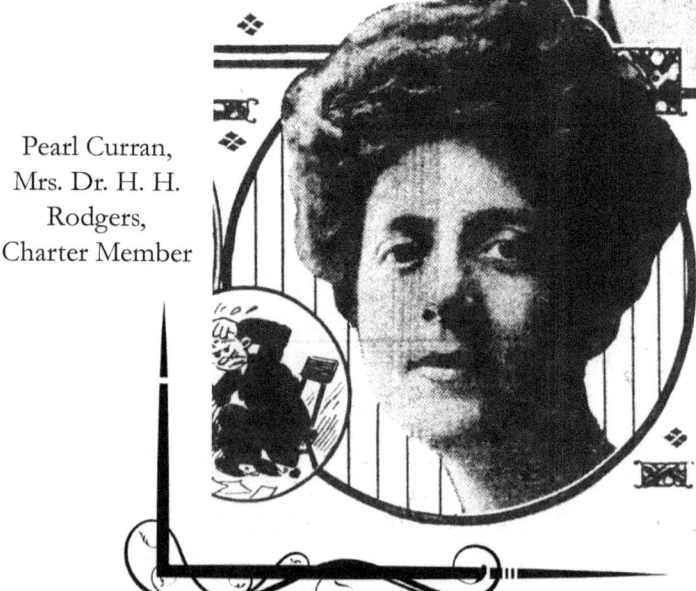

Pearl Curran,
Mrs. Dr. H. H.
Rodgers,
Charter Member

8 |
The Writers Guild of St. Louis in the 1920s

In the 1920s, St. Louis Writers Guild created a number of programs, a format for the organization, that became the foundation which survived to this day. One thing discovered during the research of this book, many of the programs, events, and contests St. Louis Writers Guild still held were rooted or had their origins in these early days of the organization, including writing contests, which were started in the beginning. Events like the 5+5 Critique Workshops, the readings at the open mics, authors talking about writing—some of the workshop titles are even the same—all have a foundation in the early days of St. Louis Writers Guild.

On one level, this shows that the lessons and skills writers need never change. Workshops on world building, editing, and copyright law will still be taught a century from now. Second, showcasing St. Louis writers and allowing them to read mean open mics will continue in varying forms. There was, however, something else that emerged from the research, and that was how much had been passed down through the decades. The 5+5 Critique Workshop is an old staple of St. Louis Writers Guild, which for years was the go-to workshop if nothing had been planned, or by the 2000s, a workshop for when a speaker cancelled last-minute. It turns out this workshop actually replicated what had been done at those earliest meetings. Even a large writers' conference, like the Gateway to Publishing Conference & Convention, had its origin long ago.

The History of St. Louis Writers Guild

The First Meetings of St. Louis Writers Guild

The early meetings established a format for St. Louis Writers Guild that lasted for about a two decades, and influenced many events in the future. Meetings were held in the evening. In the beginning, they met on Thursday, but that quickly switched to Tuesday, and by the 1950s switched to Wednesday, before settling on Saturday in the 2000s.

Members gathered for dinner or a picnic of some form. Often the dinner was set outside in the garden or on the lawn. Over food and drinks, part of a novel, a scene, a short story, or poem was read aloud by the president or the chairman who presided over the meeting, and then the work was discussed. Sam Hellman, the first president, was known for sitting back in his chair, listening intently, and then giving his opinion. Sometimes a visiting or local author presented a short lecture on a topic of interest to writers. It could be about novels, characters, or even capturing rural America in words. A social hour followed each meeting.

Roll was called, allowing each member to mention any literary accomplishments they had recently obtained. Today, SLWG continues this tradition. At the start of every meeting the president asks, "Who here submitted in the last month?" and several people will raise their hands. The audience applauds. "Who received a rejection in the last month?" Several will keep their hands up, and one or two more may join in. This is met with thunderous applause. Rejection has always been part of the writing process, and SLWG celebrates each attempt to reach the dream. Lastly, the president or chairman asks, "Does anyone have an acceptance or other good news?" Usually a couple of members will have some new publication, book signing event, or request from an agent to announce. This too is applauded, as SLWG encourages members to support one another's events and projects.

In July 1921, a picnic supper was served on the lawn of Mrs. M.F. Watts' home on Cabanne Avenue before the meeting. She was the mother of Guild member, Mrs. J.J. Frey. Short stories and poetry followed.

These dinner events were attended by twenty to thirty members and guests. Sam Hellman, Shirley Seifert, and then Louis Dodge presided over these early meetings.

The Charter Members of St. Louis Writers Guild

A mysterious term to say the least, the Charter Members were mentioned in the early days of the Guild. The names of a few were known, along with one account that they numbered about thirty, but nothing else, only the mention that St. Louis Writers Guild began with the six founders and the charter members. Twice, people have claimed to have found the list. In each case, they had found the incorporation letters filed with the state of Missouri, usually in modern times, for tax purposes. St. Louis Writers Guild was not always an official 501(c)(3), but it has been for several decades.

The Charter Members were the first members of St. Louis Writers Guild. A mix of the people who attended the first meeting on October 28, 1920, and those writers of the city who were already acquaintances. It was said that crowd numbered about thirty, plus the earliest information say there were about 20 members. The numbers appear to be more than a coincidence, but the thing that made me wonder the most was how did they know how many people would attend the first meeting? Two days before the event, the newspaper mentioned there would be about thirty people. However, there was no number to call or address to register.

Pure conjecture, but I assume the Charter Members consisted of people who pledged to be the first members, were present at the September meeting to recap the Missouri Writers Guild retreat, or authors already connected with their fellow scribes in the city—the St. Louis Literary Colony as they were known.

No matter their number, the Charter Members, early members, and every member since shared a kinship, commiserated on the written word, and formed the backbone of this organization.

The History of St. Louis Writers Guild

Known Charter Members (*because they announced it proudly in their biographies*)
Pearl Curran
May Wilson Todd
Louis Dodge

Probable Charter Members (*Those connected to SLWG in the beginning and before*)
Temple Bailey
Elinor Maxwell McCord
Grace Reeve Fennell
Margaretta Scott Lawler
Capt. Donald Wright
Susan Boogher
Robertus Love

St. Louis Writers Guild is for Poets too!
Though the early meetings were focused on novelists and short stories, the poets of St. Louis soon rose up and made their mark on the newly formed organization. On Sunday, October 30, 1921, an article in the *St. Louis Star* titled "Poets at the Writers' Guild" started off with this line: "Poets, both lyric and free verse, are numerous in St. Louis if one judges by the "poetical program" of the St. Louis Writers Guild."

One-week prior, during the second anniversary, St. Louis Writers Guild met at the home of Mrs. Margaretta Scott Lawler, on the 5000 block of Delmar Boulevard. Instead of reading from a novel or short story manuscript, the program was handed over to the poets of St. Louis. Poems were submitted unsigned, about thirty at the first meeting. They were read aloud by Miss Shirley Seifert, the chairman presiding over the event, and then the members voted on which poems were most popular. The three favorite poems of the nights were one free verse, "Miniatures" by Mrs. Lawler, and two in a lyrical style, Mrs. May Wilson Todd's "Last Leaf" and "I Wait for the Morning" by Mrs. Elizabeth Allen Satterthwait.

The evening featured guest poet, Miss Catherine Crammer, a

resident of Ottersville, Missouri, who contributed poems to leading magazines and was a member of Missouri Writers' Guild. She was also a recent applicant for membership to St. Louis Writers Guild, and was initiated at the meeting.

A Night of Ghost Stories

On Tuesday, December 6, 1921, a story appeared in the *St. Louis Star and Times* about an event the week before. On the previous Tuesday, November 29, members of St. Louis Writers Guild gathered at the home of Dean Hefferman, on the 5000 block of Clemens Avenue to tell ghost stories. Tales of ghostly-natured personal experiences were read by members around a roaring log fire which provided the appropriate atmosphere. The group of storytellers included Mr. Corrine Harris Markey, Mrs. Cecil G. Fennell, Ralph Mooney, Harold Shumate, and Miss Shirley Seifert, president at the time, who presided over the event.

St. Louis Writers Guild in the Headlines

During the early years of St. Louis Writers Guild, the city's newspapers often reported on the events, members, and other happenings within the organization, given that Sam Hellman was the editor of one of the biggest newspapers and Ralph Mooney worked for them as well; in fact, many of the early Guild members worked for the newspapers. Meetings were often announced in the newspapers, and an event recap might be reported as well. Some small-town papers announced each new member as if they had received an acceptance to a university. The St. Louis Writers Guild Contest winners were often announced, and later the newspapers ran ads for the contests. Every January, the newspapers announced the elections of officers, and who had been chosen as the new president.

Often, news about St. Louis Writers Guild or the writers of the city were listed in the society section of the newspaper. They were the literary elite and many were part of the city's wealthier families. Because so many women were an important part of the organization, the newspapers often put St. Louis Writers Guild news into the society section or the women's section. This would prove to be a boon for research into St. Louis Writers Guild's history. Often, when a man headed the organization, no news would be recorded, but when a woman was president, each event was listed. Plus, with editors and reporters in the organization, important events and elections were covered. However, because they worked for different papers, there was bias in some coverage. One paper would cover the event in detail, while the other provided only a summary, depending on who was involved.

For many years, especially in the 1920s and 1930s, the newspaper was more like social media of today. Events in people's lives were announced, from vacations or which relative was visiting, to each new accomplishment or club joined. Any new tidbit from people's lives were reported. One could keep up with everyone in town just by skimming the paper. Much of the information in this book was collected from newspapers.

The Missouri Writers Guild

Founded in 1915, and incorporated in 1926, the Missouri Writers' Guild held two meetings a year, one in Columbia, during Journalism Week at the University of Missouri, and the second, which had to be somewhere more picturesque. They even wrote this requirement into their by-laws. The autumn meeting was often at the Lake of the Ozarks, the Tennessee River Valley, or other such beautiful place.

At one MWG conference, a speaker had to cancel and could not make the trip. So, the assembled writers sent a Night Letter, a telegram tapped-out at night at reduced rates, which would be delivered the following morning. Night Letters were usually funny or clandestine. The attendees of the MWG Conference apparently voted on whether to send the Night Letter, and what should be contained. Although the content wasn't recorded, it became the thing everyone talked about after the conference.

In 1925, St. Louis Writers Guild was one of the literary organizations presenting at Journalism Week and the Missouri Writers' Guild Conference immediately following. The event, held every spring at the University of Missouri in Columbia, MO, had spawned the Missouri Writers Guild a decade earlier. Because many of St. Louis Writers Guild's members worked for, or were published through the leading papers of the day, they were the featured speakers at Journalism Week.

In 1926, MWG became incorporated, and everyone from the leading newspapers like the *St. Louis Globe-Democrat, The St. Louis Star Times*, the *St. Louis Post-Dispatch*, and many of the smaller regional newspapers, along with St. Louis Writers Guild and the other chapters, celebrated MWG's eleventh anniversary. Former MWG President Hugh Fox Grinstead described the organization, "The Missouri Writers' Guild is not a mutual admiration society nor is it a clan of literary highbrows, but rather a little band of earnest workers ever striving toward success."

A Co-operative Story Written by SLWG Members

In March 1923, the *St. Louis Globe-Democrat* featured an article, "Writers Unite in Co-operative Story: Best Features by Members of Guild to Be Incorporated."

At the St. Louis Writers Guild monthly meeting, they began the construction of a cooperative story. The story represented the efforts of all members and the hope was to publish it under The St. Louis Writers Guild name.

The first meeting for this story was hosted by Mrs. Corinne Harris Markey, at her sister's home, Mrs. Thomas R. Harris, on Yale avenue, in University City.

One "plot situation" was suggested by Miss Shirley Seifert, president of the Guild, and a second by Sam Hellman, the vice president. The members decided to develop the situation presented by Sam Hellman. Suggestions for plot development were made by members, who then left the meeting to write drafts of the story. During the meeting the following month, in April, at the home of Mr. and Mrs. Sam Hellman, the stories were read. By selection and elimination, the best features of the various drafts submitted were selected and incorporated into a final story.

Sadly, if the story was published, which I think it was, it has remained unfound. No title or any other information was mentioned. However, this co-operative writing, which the newspaper said was unique for the time, was quite popular with members and a fixture of St. Louis Writers Guild throughout the 1920s.

Three Celebrations of St. Louis Writers Guild

In 1921, St. Louis Writers Guild celebrated its formation with three publications. Each was to focus on the Guild's members, and two of them were able to be tracked down for this publication. The first was an article written by Louis Dodge about the formation of the Guild (below). The second was a poetry anthology that featured Sara Teasdale, one of the most distinctive of modern poets, and many other "lesser lights." Several of the charter members were featured in this collection. Third was a piece called "Frolicking With Guilders," composed by charter member and board member, May Wilson Todd.

An Anthology of Poems by St. Louis Writers
The anthology featured these poems by "Guilders."

The Chimney Pots of London by Margaretta Scott
Blackened, rakish, leaning against the sky
Like drunken old men
Puffing their winter pipes
And blowing the smoke
Into the dainty faces of the stars.

Baby of Mine by Elinor Maxwell
Just a wee thing with a dainty air,
And a shining mop of golden hair,
With eyes so soft and wistful, too,
That they bruise and hurt the heart of you.
Warm little hands that seek and cling,
And make you love this baby thing,
Dear little head against your breast,
Cuddling there like a bird in its nest,
Fragrant lips as cool and sweet
As a budding rose in the summer sweet –
But I open my eyes – and smile – and sign –

Baby of mine – the dream's gone by!

The Garden Tragedy by Patience Worth
There is a pale rose
In the garden pressing her wan cheek
To asken eve. She is loth,
Drooped, denying the winds;
She is weary of the ardorous sun.
She is crushed with the dinning day.
Phantom-like, she sways an instant
And with a tremorous quiver, falls.

There is a pale rose in the garden.
No longer nodding, no longer
Denying the winds. She hath surrendered
Willingly, becoming a foot cloth for Night.
Who shall weep upon her, leaving Morn
But her withering and the tears.

Passing by Elizabeth Satterthwait
The day crept slowly by –
I scarce can tell
Whether the bright sun shone
Or raindrops fell:
For hope and fear were one,
And love was strong –
And now I only know
The day was long.

And when the evening came,
I cannot say
Whether the stars came out
At close of day:
For though each thought was prayer,
We dumbly knelt.
Too stricken e'en to know
The grief we felt.

And when the midnight came,
I never knew
Whether the night was still
Or chill wind blew;
For then the veil grew thin –
I could not see –
And this poor heart of mine
Went up with thee.

My Quest by May Wilson Todd
I sought for love o'er the ocean wide,
In a distant place by the sea.
For his smile with a passionate voice I cried,
But only the waves moaned back to me.

I sought for love on the mountain high.
Where the clouds blew white on misty air;
Brave and sweet and long was my cry.
But echo returned my unanswered prayer.

I sought for love on the desert drear.
With yearning lips and heart aflame.
Calling "Come to me, my sweet, my dear."
But alas! and alas! Love never came.

I went back weary and worn and spent.
With broken spirit and wounded pride;
And my soul was filled with glad content.
For love waited there at my own fireside.

An Article about the Founding of St. Louis Writers Guild

On Wednesday, February 9, 1921 the *St. Louis Star-Times* featured an article written by Louis Dodge, one of the Charter Members and third president of St. Louis Writers Guild, about the founding of the organization after its first anniversary.

Brad R. Cook

"Writes of Formation of the St. Louis Guild, Members of Which Contribute to Many Magazines."

Louis Dodge, Novelist, Tells of Contributions St. Louisans are Making to Literature

When you see the bewildering display on the newsstands you may sometimes wonder where all the stories and articles come from.

St. Louisans are doing a very generous share of the work.

Within the past few years writers living in this city have had much to do with filling the pages of the Saturday Evening Post, the Ladies Home Journal, the Delineator, the Modern Priscilla, Harper's Magazine, Scribner's Magazine, the Smart Set, the American the Youth's Companion, the Argosy, the Cosmopolitan, Reedy's Mirror – these and many other periodicals or exacting standards.

So numerous indeed, are St. Louis craftsmen in this field that they began, some six months ago, to touch elbows; and out of this contact has arisen an interesting organization called the St. Louis Writers' Guild.

The guild now numbers about twenty members, and it is extending a welcome to others who are eligible to membership.

The organization came into being in a pleasantly casual fashion.

In September of last year Mrs. Cecil T. Fennell of Julian Avenue invited a dozen or so guests to her house, these included several leaders in the St. Louis Literary "colony." The Character of this somewhat informal function was distinctly literary. Mrs. Fennell has been for years a members and officer in a state organization, the Missouri Writers' Guild, which meets every spring in Columbia, MO, and is given the first day of Journalism Week, on which occasions it convenes in his historic Switzer Hall and listens to talks and addresses, included among which are always a few by editors or writers of national reputation.

The meeting at Mrs. Fennell's was so pleasantly successful that other meetings were obviously suggested.

A month later the same group, with additions, were invited by Miss Shirley I. Seifert to a meeting at her house. A month later, again, Mr. and Mrs. Terrell Croft of University City were host and hostess to the writers. The next meeting was at the home of Mr. and Mrs. Ralph E. Mooney; the next at Mr. and Mrs. Sam Hellman's home.

Miss Seifert President

The History of St. Louis Writers Guild

By this time the casual company had become a clearly defined organization, with Miss Shirley I. Seifert as President. The next meeting will be at the home of Mr. and Mrs. John H. Curran, which is also the home of Patience Worth – when she is not roaming among the stars.

The guild members are men and women who are actually doing something in a literary way. In order to become members they must have published a book, or produced a play, or have had several articles or stories or poems accepted by publications of a national type.

The members are in no instances disgruntled persons. Their creed is this; that editors are human beings who sometimes make mistakes, but who are eagerly seeking to welcome new writers who have something to say and who knew how to say it. Mere posers would find the meetings not to their liking at all. Several of the members make their livelihood by writing; others succeed in dividing their time between commercial and literary work.

At the meetings there are candid discussions, exchanges of confidences, a general comparing of notes. There's enough to eat and drink to make for good cheer. At the last meeting it was agreed that hereafter mutual criticisms would be in order. Will the guild break up in a row when this begins? It will not.

Here is a little something about the members:

Miss Shirley Seifert, the president is a graduate of Central High School and Washington University. She was born in St. Peters, St. Charles County, MO., but has resided nearly all her life in St. Louis. Less than two years ago she published her first story, "The Girl Who Was Too Good Looking." In the American Magazine. Since the she has had manuscripts accepted by the editors of Saturday Evening Post. Ladies Home Journal, The Metropolitan, Delineator, People's Home Journal, Scribner's and Everybody's. Her latest published story was, "Bittersweet," in the January Ladies Home Journal. She had the excellent faculty of discerning what the editors want, and the ability to write it. She "studies the market," as painstakingly and skillfully as she writes. Her ambition is to win wider fame as a writer of short stories: the longer forms of fiction have not as yet attracted her. She is a young woman of a highly effective personality.

Ralph E. Mooney's Work.

Ralph E. Mooney, secretary of the organization, still under thirty, has published twenty-nine stories, including two novels. "Currents of Fate," and "The Master Law" – the latter now being a serial feature in Detective Stories. The Saturday Evening Post has published his "The Improbable." "Tire

*Jockey" and "Miss Kent Understands." A story called "Like a Million" is
soon to appear in the American. He has also contributed to Popular, Smart
Set, Munsey's, Blue Book and Ladies Home Journal. Without infringing
upon anybody's patent, Mr. Mooney explains that he and Mrs. Mooney "have
evolved a system of their own for keeping the dew on the butterfly and the moss
on the rose. The secret is this: they see each other only once a day- that is except
when it is necessary for Mooney to go downtown or leave the house for some
reason." (Mooney formerly was a reporter for The Star.)*

*Miss Margretta Scott supplies no autobiographical information, but
her record as a writer is distinctive and impressive. She is a poet who won
the recognition of the later Willam Marlon Reedy, in whose Mirror her
poems have appeared. She has also contributed to Harriet Monroe's Poetry
Magazine, and to the Touchstone. Her play, "Three Kisses," won a prize in
a drama competition in 1919. Several of her poetic plays have been published
in The Drama (Chicago), in which her children's play. "The Bag o' Dreams,"
appeared last month. She possesses an exquisite gift of symbolism and lovely
fantasy.*

*Sam Hellman began his work in fiction by contributing more than
one hundred short stories to a local newspaper within the space of a year.
Many of these stories revealed extraordinary ingenuity as well as marked
adaptability. They had to be kept writing one thousand words, or thereabouts,
yet he managed to end them all with a period. As managing editor of the late
Republic, and as a political writer on the Globe-Democrat during the recent
campaigns, he turned to the sort of fiction which deals with more or less libing
persons, but of late he has been a first air to H. C. Meneken of the Sunart
Set, to which he contributes worldly epigrams, when he is not writing lay
sermons for a syndicate. He is also editor of Motor Vogue (St. Louis), and an
editorial writer on The Star.*

*Mr. Hellman is an affable chap, but not at all deficient in subtlety, and
possesses a somewhat enigmatic and "intriguing" personality – as the St. Louis
Art League would put it.*

Manteel Howe Farnham

*Manteel Howe Farnham (Mrs. Dwight T.) is a native of Atchison,
Kansas, but has resided in St. Louis about four years. She is a daughter of
the Kansas editor and novelist, E. W. Howe, whose "The Story of a County
Town," published some twenty-five years ago, was pronounced by the late
William Dean Howells to be one of the most distinctive of American Novels.*

The History of St. Louis Writers Guild

Mrs. Farnham's name, Mantell, was taken from her father's unique book. She early inherited – or acquired – skill as a writer, and at the age of 20 had won a prize of $500 in a literary contest, had sold an article to the New York Independent and a short story to the Ladies Home Journal. Other interests intervened for a period. Now she is resuming her literary activities, and is to publish a novel this summer, while she is at work on a new manuscript.

Dwight T. Farnham is a consulting industrial engineer, who writes books and articles having such titles as "Executive Control" "Scientific Industrial Efficiency," etc. He is a member of the faculty of St. Louis University Graduate School of Commerce and Finance, and is a lecturer at Illinois, Washington, and Iowa Universities. He is a graduate of Yale and Phillips Andover Academy, and among the many honors he has won is that of vice presidency of the Society of Industrial Engineers. He recently completed a five months survey of European industrial conditions; was a guest for a time of the Italian Government; was given special privileges as a visitor to a number of great industrial plants in France, and made a careful survey of the industrial districts of Great Britain. Rather a "far cry" from all this to a story in the All-Story Weekly – but the Guild is that sort of organization.

Grace Reeve Fennell (Mrs. Cecil T.) possesses one of the piquant personalities of the Guild. She writes for a greater variety of publications perhaps, than any other member; form first-class literary magazines to trade journals rarely seen outside their own field. She is interested in everything, and she has the rare happy knack of writing interestingly about it. She can make an artistic lamp-shade out of a bushel basket – figuratively speaking. Her "Bill Billheimer" in the American Magazine was a classic of its kind, and editors of such periodicals as the Mutual Life Quarterly, the Sample Case and The Motor Car look to her regularly for contributions. She has contributed a number of articles to The Missouri Woman. She is an unobtrusive, helpful power in the Guild.

H.C. Schweickert a Teacher

H. C. Schweickert is a teacher and editor who has the enviable capacity to temper pedagogic thoroughness with genuinely human and kindly qualities. He is a teacher of English in Central High School and is a member of the University Club. Originally a Pennsylvanian, he spent considerable periods at different times in Europe, and he has resided in St. Louis long enough to be entirely at home in this city. He is a collector of books; his apartments on Westminster place are half-filled with an extraordinary variety of volumes

— *books representing boyhoods tastes as well as various phases and fashion in literature. His collection of George Gissing is the completest I know of anywhere — and his liking for this fine, all-but-forgotten. English master is, I think, evidence of his genuineness and discernment. He has edited two textbooks: "French Short Stories" and "Russian Short Stories" — both excellent in selection and in their editorial aids. He has in preparation a volume of Spanish stories.*

Miss Elinor Maxwell has written and sold a number of dramatic pieces which have been used or are to be used in the world of vaudeville; she is co-author with Mrs. Lelia Chopin Hattersley of St. Louis of a play, "Pirates" which is soon to be staged by a New York Producer and she is the author of many short stories. Notwithstanding this excellent showing, she is one of the youngest members of the guild. She is also a poet, as readers of the Smart Set know. She is very much in touch with present-day manners and methods in writing. She deals in ideas rather than ideals. She has no ambition to reform anything or anybody. Her slogan is "Let's go." But for the decided smartness of her personality she might be regarded as a Bohemian. She knows that she is going to write a lot of "good stuff" before she quits. Her friends know this too.

Terrell Croft is the author of a text-book on electricity which is regarded as standard in high places. He is a directing engineer of the Terrell Croft Engineering Company, and in addition to directing his consulting engineering practice he devotes much of his time to semi-technical literary work. He is widely known for his happy faculty of presenting involved technical information in a straightforward, simple way, without sacrificing accuracy. He has worked all along the line in his profession — as lineman, wireman, stationary fireman and engineer. He is a graduate of Pratt Institute of Brooklyn, New York. He has an attractive home in University City where his professional desk is also located. His publishers are authority for the statement that he is the most widely read electrical author of today. In addition to the text-book to which I have referred, he is the author of six other volumes, all prepared for practical men who desire a better knowledge of electricity and its application and devices. During the world war he was connected with the Committee of Education and Special Training of the War Department, where he taught intensive courses for converting in minimum time, untrained men into electricians. The Croft books were used extensively, both in the United States and overseas, for the schooling of soldier electricians.

The History of St. Louis Writers Guild

Mrs. John H. Curran

Mrs. John H. Curran is the author of a story which was published in the Saturday Evening Post and which was made into a screen play – a real success. However, when I requested Mrs. Curran to send me something about her literary activities, she sent me – seventeen poems and a number of "sayings" signed by Patience Worth. Of course, you know about Patience Worth. She is still the great mystery of American letters, after several years of publicity, scientific investigation, and no end of discussion. She lived some hundreds of years ago, as near as we can guess. The catalogues of old time do not contain the name of Patience, among the authors of the day, and so we may assume that she did not learn to write as long as she lived – no uncommon case – and that she is now making up, in eternity, for lost time. The seventeen poems sent to me were said to represent one evening's work. She was expected to dictate – is that the word? – a few pages of a new novel, but Mrs. Curran was cleaning house, and so the poems came instead. There were in all about 300 lines. If Patience can equal this record for the remainder of eternity, it can be seen easily that within the next thousand years she will require all the paper that's manufactured to get herself printed. It is really an interesting problem. The extraordinary thing about it all I that critics of great ability have pronounced the Patience Worth writings distinctive, powerful, beautiful, profoundly significant. The late William Marion Reedy, generous champion of Patience acclaimed "The Sorry Tale" as equal to "Ben Hur." Henry Ho[w], published several Patience Worth books. There is now to be a sort of Patience Worth corporation which will publish the books in future, with a view to getting the [ripe] quality of the writings before a wider public, without thought of financial profit from the Patience Worth volumes. Mrs. Curran, by the way, is a highly effective personality, keenly intelligent, though she claims little book-learning, and emphatically shrewd. She is however, what you would call a nice person. There's none of the fustian about her person or mind which is usually associated with professional seerism.

Mrs. Elizabeth Allen Satterthwait is a Quakeress and a poet. She is the wife of Alfred F. Satterthwait, who is engaged in scientific work for the government, and who is at present in charge of the United States Entomological Laboratory in Webster Groves. She has published a volume of poetry, "A Gentle Heart" and her contributions to periodicals have been numerous. In her personality she reflects very happily the serenity, and a kind of beneficent aloofness, of the Religious Society of Friends. She is very much interested in good work, of all kinds, and despite a fine quietude of manner, she is very much a part of the spirit of the guild.

Mrs. May Wilson Todd is also of Webster Groves and is also a poet. She was formerly a fellow-townswoman of Mary McLean in Boise City, Idaho and later she resided in Texas and Mexico. She began her literary career by writing verses for Gulf Messenger of Texas, and recently she has attracted the attention of the editor of Judge (New York), and of other editors. A number of her poems have been set to music. "You Are The Radiant Morn to Me" with a setting by M. Rosini, was sung recently at a Kirkwood Choral Club concert.

A Versatile Entertainer

T. Elemore Lucey is a poet and lecturer: also an actor, an impersonator, an editor, a traveler. He is known from Cape Horn to Nome as a versatile entertainer. He has published several books of verse, which have had a wide circulation.

Dean L. Hefferman was to have been a lawyer, for which profession he made careful preparation; but along came the Muses, and his now writing very successfully for a group of editors who want what they want when they want it. Three of his stories have recently appeared in the All-Story Magazine. He will soon publish a novelette, "The Eye of Tasa-Maku." He is a contributor to the Writers' Monthly.

There are other members of the guild, all of whom have made notable beginnings, and some of whom have won enviable reputations; and the membership is still increasing. The aim of the guild is eventually to embrace in its membership all the writers in St. Louis who are more for writing than for other things, and who wish to hail their own comrades occasionally as they continue their efforts to make the grade.

The Presidents
1920 – Sam Hellman
1921 – Shirley Seifert
*1922 – Louis Dodge
*1923 – Shirley Seifert
*1924 – Ralph Mooney
1925 – No record
*1926 – Irving Mattick
1927 – No record

*1928 – Elizabeth Allen Satterthwait
1929 – Dr. Alfred F. Satterthwait

* Information discovered through research; **bold** means it has been confirmed

Board Members at this Time
1922
Louis Dodge, president
Temple Bailey, vice president
Dean Heffernan and May Wilson Todd, secretary

1923
Shirley Seifert, president
Sam Hellman, vice president

1926
Irving Mattick, president
May Wilson Todd, vice president

1928
A. F. Satterthwait, president
Mrs. G.N. Seidlitz, vice president
Donald Wright, secretary and treasurer

The Program Committee: Mrs. G. N. Seidlitz, Mrs. Margaretta Scott Lawler and Dean Heffernan.

Membership Committee: Mrs. Jay Gelzer, Miss Shirley Seifert, and Robertus Love.

Publicity Committee: Ralph E. Mooney, Mrs. J. Lindsay and Mrs. Mabel H. Malone.

Members of the 1920s
Irving (Irvin) Mattick, President, 1926

Mr. Irving Mattick gave a sketch of his talk on "The Attitude of Minds of a Writer" at the September 1928 Missouri Writers Guild retreat and at the following SLWG meeting. A writer of poems and short stories, he read a number of poems at different events. He served a few years on the board, and one term as president. He presided over and was a member of the Tuesday Writers of St. Louis.

The *St. Louis Globe-Democrat* on Saturday, November 27, 1926, said of a dinner event at the Hotel Gatesworth for Naibro Bartley, "*Irvin Mattick is the President of the Writers Guild which is always ready to entertain any well-known writer. During the Publishers' Convention last May the Writers' Guild gave a dinner for Homer Croy, to which other well-known writers in St. Louis at the time were invited.*"

Corinne Harris Markey

Mrs. Corinne Harris Markey was a short story writer and hosted several SLWG meetings. By 1923, "The Combination that Couldn't be Beaten" had been published in the *American*, and the *Woman's Home Companion* published, "Now, If It Only Hadn't Rained." Her sister, Mrs. Thomas R. Harris lived on Yale Avenue in University City.

Workshops and Events

The St. Louis Writers' Guild Meetings were held on the last Tuesday of each month during the Season, from September to May, in the home of a member.

Tuesday, January 31, 1922

Mrs. Cecil Gordon Fennell, 5000 block of Julian Avenue, hosted the meeting, which featured a presentation of charades. Each participant represented the title of a popular novel.

Tuesday, April 25, 1922

"This was "Poets Evening" at the Guild and the poets had charge of the program.

"Mrs. Margaretta Scott Lawlor presided over the reading of published poems and a few drafts by their respective authors at the home of Mr. and Mrs. Harold Shumate on Vernon Avenue. "Some of the magazines representing the work of Guild poets were *Scribner's*, *Harper's*, *Century*, *Judge*, *Poetry Magazine*, *Pictorial*, *Smart Set*, *Reedy's Mirror*, *Midland Magazine* and *Contemporary Verse*. Some of Louis Dodge's free verse and an unpublished poem entitled 'The Prodigal Son,' were read.

"The Guild announced it would meet again in May after the School of Journalism Week at Columbia, MO, which included Missouri Writers' Guild Day, the first day of the conference." – *St. Louis Globe-Democrat*, Sunday, April 30, 1922.

September 29, 1923

The meeting was held at the home of Mrs. G. N. Seidlitz of the 5000 block of Clemens Avenue. The guest for the evening was Joseph Hamilton, who made the motion picture, *The Spirit of St. Louis*. They also told stories about John M. Siddall, a member and magazine editor who had recently passed away.

In March or April of 1925

St. Louis Writers Guild held a special dinner for Mr. Norman C. Schlichter, poet and lecturer, who was on tour throughout the region. According to the *Lebanon Semi-Weekly News*, he was cordially received.

Tuesday, September 30, 1924

The fourth Season opened at the home of Dr. and Mrs. George N. Seidlitz in the 5000 block of Clemens avenue. Members shared their experience selling stories over the summer.

SLWG President, Ralph Mooney, read the fifth installment of the Guild's collaborative story. The other four installments had been completed in the spring, with each member contributing to the piece of fiction.

The poetry contest was announced with a deadline of November 1, 1924. The contest was open to all SLWG members.

Tuesday, October 27, 1925

Dr. and Mrs. George N. Seldlitz, on Clemens Avenue hosted the guest of honor, Miss Virginia Moore of St. Louis and New York. Her poems appeared in the October *Atlantic Monthly*.

Tuesday, January 26, 1926

Miss Shirley Seifert on DeGiverville Avenue hosted the meeting where Mrs. May Wilson Todd of Swan Avenue was elected vice-president and Irving Mattick was elected president.

Wednesday, May 12, 1926

St. Louis Writers' Guild hosted Homer Croy, author of *West of the Water Tower*, at the Town Club as part of the American Booksellers' Association convention. Homer Croy had spoken at the University of Missouri Journalism Week in Columbia.

For that day, St. Louis was named the "Literary Center of the Middle West" by all the newspapers because so many top authors were in the city for the convention.

The Guild's meeting was rescheduled to a noon luncheon and featured Temple Bailey, J Gelzer, Shirley Seifert, and a number of authors who spoke at the Washington University Field House later that night.

Sunday, May 16, 1926 (Date reported)

Irvin Mattick, president, writer of poems and short stories, spoke and read a number of poems. Richard Halliburton, lecturer, traveler, and author, was the guest speaker.

Saturday, November 27, 1926

St. Louis Writers Guild held a dinner at the Hotel Gatesworth for Naibro Bartley, novelist and author of *Her Mother's Daughter*. She was the guest of Mrs. John E. Stoker of Savoy Court, whom she stayed with while in town.

Tuesday, December 28, 1926

Holiday Frolic

The Holiday Frolic was held at the home of Miss Shirley L Seifert, in the 5000 block of De Giverville Avenue. Members, the novelists, short story writers, and magazine contributors were asked to appear in costumes representing the titles of books.

Sadly, there is no record of who showed up as which book.

June 18, 1927

The *St. Louis Globe-Democrat* ran an ad for the novel *David Rudd* by Ralph Mooney.

Tuesday, February 28, 1928

SLWG met at the home of Mrs. Grace Reeve Fennell, on the 5000 block of Julian Avenue. Roll was called and everyone spoke about the literary work they'd done in the last month. The speaker for the evening was author Thomas Hardy, which included a book review and study of his novel, *Tess of the d'Ubervilles*.

Tuesday, September 25, 1928

The first meeting of the eighth Season was held at the home of Mrs. George Malone, in the 2000 block of Bellevue Avenue. Mrs. Elizabeth Satterthwait, president, called the meeting to order, and led a discussion on changing the entry requirements for members to requiring three short stories or three poems published in national magazines; and either a novel or play accepted.

Mrs. Grace Fennell presented **Why and How I wrote the Last Story I Sold**. Each member was then given five minutes to discuss the subject. Mr. Irving Mattick presented **The Attitude of Mind of a Writer**, and Mr. Ralph Mooney spoke about, **Correcting the Manuscript**. Both speeches had been given at the annual meeting of the Missouri Writers' Guild in Columbia.

After the social hour, the next meeting was set for October 30 at the home of Mr. Dean Heffernan, at Clayton Road and McKnight Road.

Tuesday, November 26, 1929

Members met at the home of Robertus Love, in the 3000 block of West Pine Boulevard. SLWG president, A. F. Satterthwait, read letters from the editors of *Collier's*, *Life*, and *Liberty* magazines, who were the judges in the Short Story Contest, which closed on January 28, 1930.

Mr. Casper Yost opened the program hour with an invitation to join the Society of St. Louis Authors, and then Professor Lawrence Conrad read his article on Eugene O'Neil, published in *The Landmark*, a London magazine. Captain Don Wright spoke of his trip from Pittsburgh to Cairo by boat, as he attended the dedication of the Ohio River canals. Then Mrs. Florence Seidlitz gave a brief sketch of her European experience.

Mrs. Grace Grant Baker of Kansas City, the guest for the evening, talked about what was going on with the Kansas City Quill Club.

SLWG extended its appreciation to Mr. Love, Mr. Yost, and Mr. Thornton for the writeup in recent issue of the *Sunday Magazine* of the *Globe-Democrat*.

Elenor Maxwell McCord, President
1929 *St. Louis Globe-Democrat*

9 |
Motor Vogue

Several interesting oddities popped up when researching St. Louis Writers Guild's history, and one of them was *Motor Vogue*, a magazine produced for automobile enthusiasts. Several of the founders and first members worked together to write and produce this publication. Though we were unable to find an issue, articles about the magazine and ads for issues in the newspaper allowed this story to be told.

As names like Ford, Cadillac, and Chrysler joined brands like Winton, Packard, Oldsmobile, and Studebaker, the automobile transformed from unreliable horseless-carriages to the getaway vehicles of gangsters. Auto enthusiasts formed clubs around the country, but here in St. Louis they took it one step further.

Motor Vogue was a monthly magazine established by the Automobile Club of St. Louis and edited by Sam Hellman, St. Louis Writers Guild's first president. The first issue was 96 pages and was released in February 1921. Titled "Auto Show Number One," it featured an introductory editorial and an article, "The New Automobile Club of St. Louis," both written by Sam Hellman, and a one act play by Elinor Maxwell. Also included in the first issue were an article "The 1921 Cars by the Connoisseur" and two short stories, one by Stewart Holmes, as well as "My Car and I" by Ralph Mooney.

Other features in *Motor Vogue* included the page, "Bolts and Bits," which brought humor and smartness to the issue. Sections were devoted to the theater, fashion, and home decorations. Many pages held illustrations, ranging from new automobile models to classic dancers.

Counsel for the club, Roy F. Britton, wrote about the latest proposed motor vehicle law, and Harry B. Hawes discussed the $60,000,000 road bond.

Sam Hellman mentioned that "This magazine is not an organization organ in the accepted sense, though it will undertake to keep 'en rapport' with all matters affecting automobile owners, yet even in our serious moments we will see to it that you are not bored."

Motor Vogue was a fashion magazine for automobile enthusiasts, the cutting edge of car culture, and a voice of the automobile industry. The members of St. Louis Writers Guild led that charge.

Brad R. Cook

The History of St. Louis Writers Guild

1929 *St. Louis Globe-Democrat* Article

10 |
The Globe-Democrat Article in 1929

By 1929, the Fox Theater opened, and St. Louis Writers Guild became the preeminent literary organization of the city. Its accomplishments were recognized by the leading newspaper of the day. On November 10, 1929, the *St. Louis Globe-Democrat* ran an article about the Guild written by legendary St. Louis newspaperman, Hamilton Thornton.

The article's incredible title, "Many Names of Present and Former Members of the St. Louis Writers Guild are Preeminent in Current Publications" might be a mouthful, and more convoluted than current headlines. However, the piece covered two full pages with black-and-white photos and colored borders, an impressive feat for the day. Having just suffered Black Monday and the crash of the economy, the country needed something more pleasant to focus on, and it was undeniable that several great writers of the day had gathered together to create a grand organization, St. Louis Writers Guild.

Hamilton Thornton began the article by saying, "Out at the St. Louis Writers Guild they talk shop whenever they meet. That, in the main, is the *raison d'etre* for the club's existence."

The article showcased famous members of the day, starting with Sam Hellman, SLWG's first president. As a former St. Louis newspaperman, he was well-respected in the city, but by this time he was in either Hollywood, California, or Long Island, New York. Also featured in the article, were novelist Temple Bailey; reporter and author, Louis Dodge; playwright and poet, Margaretta Scott Lawler; and founder, Ralph Mooney.

Hamilton Thornton interviewed Elinor Maxwell McCord and Elizabeth Satterthwait, granting us insight into the personalities of these early members. Of Sam Hellman, Hamilton Thornton wrote, "Then there is Sam Hellman. His humorous yarns are known from coast to coast and from the Gulf to the Lakes." And Elizabeth Satterthwait said, "Hellman was a member of the Guild for years. And he was not a watcher and listener at their meetings; he was a talker and—well, a talker. As I remember him, Sam would sit rumpled in his chair, a brooding look upon his face. Then suddenly he would let go with some observation that was pithy and sometimes extremely acrid. He was given to writing epigrams in these days, and he was quite good at it. He was full of comment. A person always to hear from."

When mentioning Louis Dodge, the third president of St. Louis Writers Guild, Mrs. Elizabeth Satterthwait said, "He was a shy man, but a stimulating member of the guild. He was courteous to a degree and quiet. Only when his opinion was asked did he ever volunteer an observation, but when he did it was meaty and to the point. I've always considered him and Miss Bailey, who was a most considerate counselor to literary aspirants, two of the most inspiring of our members."

One of the gems within the article was a list of qualifications to join St. Louis Writers Guild. At the time, people petitioned to join, and were voted on by the membership. A perspective member must have one of the following four things:

- Have had a book accepted and published on a royalty basis
- Must have sold three articles to magazines
- Must have three poems bought and published
- Have had one play published and professionally staged

For everyone else, Hamilton Thornton added this… "Would-be writers must discuss their muses and rejections slips elsewhere."

When speaking of SLWG, the article said, "The Writers Guild came into existence eleven years ago, when a group of writers in the city decided they could gain some advantage in a communion of tastes, hates, and grievances. More than that there was the pleasure in discussing matters in which they were each vitally interested, in the exchange of ideas about writing and especially their experiences with editors. So they set about an organization."

Three cartoons of iconic writer woes fill the gaps between pictures. Two depict writers working feverishly at their desks, while the third showed a writer working in a pile of discarded papers. Hamilton brings a slightly-smug familiarity to the piece, giving the reader a glimpse of the days when "real" writers—journalists—held contention with those who pursued literary aspirations. There was no real tension. Hamilton Thornton was a friend of St. Louis Writers Guild, maybe even a member. Several announcements in SLWG's archives list him speaking at events over the years.

Hamilton Thornton said of the monthly meetings, "The members bring their manuscripts to the Guild meetings and read them. The assembled scribes then proceed in no quibbling terms to tell the authors what is wrong with their stuff. If we are to take the word of some members, the manuscripts which are pronounced by these writer folk the most unsuitable for publication, illogical, improbable, silly, and simply hopeless, are often the stories snapped up first by editors. And, provokingly enough, the bits which merit the most praise from these craftsmen so frequently whirl back and forth through the mails with disconcerting constancy. Which is one reason why these writers are not editors."

It wasn't all jabs; he also wrote, "Be this all as it may, certainly the Guild has produced a starry array of writing talent. Many of its members can be seen every day in the pages of the national periodicals – fiction magazines, scientific discussionistic, poetry, drama."

The article set the tone for the St. Louis Writers Guild, honoring both commitment of the organization to advancing this city's contribution to literature, and showcasing the members of St. Louis Writers Guild.

Discovered by David Motherwell

President David Motherwell, (2000-2005) discovered the

The History of St. Louis Writers Guild

St. Louis Globe-Democrat article and made the first copy. Two large, photocopied pages were loosely seamed together and mounted on poster board. Photos and other memorabilia were added to create a display of St. Louis Writers Guild's history. This became a fixture at SLWG events for several years in the mid-2000s. The article was faded and hard to read, the text curled, and the edges of the photocopy had torn, but it had the power to inspire.

One of the things I did when I became historian was to track down the article in the *Globe-Democrat* and make a clearer and bigger photocopy. I scanned sections of the article using the copier in the library, and then my wife stitched them together as best she could and we laminated the whole piece. This became a display for several presentations I gave during the 90th Anniversary celebrations, and it may have popped up at a few more events over the years. Now, it is mounted on my wall, and I give it a nod every once in a while.

The Mystery of Page Fourteen

When President David Motherwell acquired the article, he only copied the front page. The back page was not photocopied. The mystery began with the intriguing line at the end of the article, "Continued on Page Fourteen." Innocuous words, they fanned the flames of curiosity in all who read them. David Motherwell mentioned once that he had wanted to go back and get the page. Then it pulled at Robin Moore Theiss, who mentioned Page Fourteen when interviewing me for the historian's role. Finally, the mystery tore at my mind, and I had to know what it said. When I made a new copy of the article, I made certain to include Page Fourteen.

The mystery was worth the wait.

St. Louis Has A Number of Prominent Writers
(pg 14)
Continued from Page Nine

Not only did the rest of the article contain a complete list of members and officers in 1929, but also an explanation of why they had created writers' contests.

For the contest, the article mentioned, "To stimulate interest in their own club and as a means of exercising their pens for very love of the work, they hold an annual contest. The prize is nominal, $25. One year it is a short story the members of the Guild write, the next a one-act play, another year it may be a poem or essay or short-short story. The manuscripts submitted are shipped off to several judges of acknowledged rank in letters, and the winner selected. Many of these manuscripts later have been sent to editors and accepted. And, on the other hand, any which were considered good enough even to rank in the $25 contest have been sold for five or six times that amount."

Best of all, Hamilton Thornton listed every member of the Guild:
Florence Atkinson
Temple Bailey
Hazel Blair
Susan Boogher
Irving Brandt
Mrs. Irving Brandt
William Carson
Ida B. Cole
Catherine Cranmer
Lawrence H. Conrad
Terrell Croft
Mrs. Dr. H.H. Rodgers (Patience Worth)
Louis Dodge
Margery Doud
Louis B. Ely
Dwight T. Farnham
Mateel Howe Farnham
Grace Reeve Fennell
Ruby Freudenberger
Martha Griffith
Daisy V. Harris
Dean L. Hefferman
Sam Hellman

Claire Kenamore
Mrs. Claire Kenamore
Margaretta Scott Lawler
Mary E. Lee
Miriam Drane Lindsey
Robertus Love
Thomas Elinore
Lucy Ann Rice Ludlow
Mabel Malone
Corinne Harris Markey
Irvin Mattick
Elinor Maxwell McCord
Genevieve McConnell
Ralph E. Mooney
Alice Curtice Moyer-Wing
Ira D. Mullinax
Helen Diehl Olds
Harlan Eugene Read
Alfred F. Satterthwait,
Elizabeth Allen Satterthwait
H.C. Schwelkert
H. M. Shumate
May Wilson Todd
Rachel Louise Travous
J. Lillian Vandevere
Harry Williams
Donald T. Wright

Officers of St. Louis Writers Guild in 1929
Alfred F. Satterthwait, president
Mrs. Miriam Drane Lindsey, secretary
Donald T. Wright, treasurer

Members of St. Louis Writers Guild
(Some biographies are direct quotes from Hamilton Thornton's *Globe-Democrat* article [in quotation marks], others have had information added or were entirely rewritten for this book.)

Temple Bailey – Irene Temple Bailey (1885 – July 6, 1953)

Temple Bailey was a novelist, short story writer, and charter member of St. Louis Writers Guild. She was an integral part of the organization who helped forge the foundation of the organization and lent her clout to ensure its success.

Hamilton Thornton wrote, "Temple Bailey is a spinner of romantic tales. Those ever have had tremendous appeal, and she knows well how to tell them. She has written at least twelve novels and had the fortune to find most of them turn into best sellers. As a child she was not strong, so her regular school life was intermittent. But her father had her constantly writing themes, which he blue pencil. And evidently, he taught her not only her syntax, but the habit of looking for and finding romance wherever she goes. There was a time in her life when she had a season of stress and sorrow. Then she scribbled a story or two and found editors liked them. A prize came to her from a love-story contest in the Ladies Home Journal. She was encouraged and has been writing ever since."

Temple Bailey was the highest paid female author of her time. Beginning around 1902, she contributed to national magazines such as the *Saturday Evening Post, Cavalier Magazine, Cosmopolitan, The American Magazine, McClure's, Woman's Home Companion, Good Housekeeping, McCall's*, and others. In 1914, she wrote the screenplay for the film *Auntie*, and later, two of her books were also made into movies. *Publishers Weekly* listed three of her books among the bestselling novels in the United States in 1918, 1922, and 1926. In 1922 she was elected Vice President of St. Louis Writers Guild and probably served more years, before moving from St. Louis in 1926.

Her novel, *The Dim Lantern* sold 75,000+ copies upon its release, and she was the author of the leading serial in 1930. *Good Housekeeping* said, "Temple Bailey is known to hundreds of thousands who have read and loved *The Tin Soldier* and *The Dim Lantern*."

Hamilton Thornton's article continued, "She was an active member of the guild, and her success in the field of the novel needs no recounting. She is a most encouraging friend to young and aspiring writers."

Louis Cochran

Louis Cochran, a St. Louis Writers Guild vice president, was one of Hoover's G-Men who worked for the Federal Bureau of Investigations in St. Louis and several other cities. While living in Mississippi during the Depression, he wrote political articles about Theodore Bilbo, Huey Long, and Pat Harrison. During World War II, he served in the intelligence section of the Army Air Corps and later the Air Force. He produced a number of novels, including his 1966 memoir, *FBI Man: A Personal History*. Some of his other novels dealt with the plight of sharecroppers. He extensively researched William Faulkner and donated his works to the University of Mississippi to create the Louis Cochran Collection.

Louis Dodge

"Louis Dodge, author of ten novels, was a newspaper reporter in St. Louis. His first book was published in 1916, and the last one so far in 1921."

"And there is Louis Dodge, poet and novelist, who was a resident of the city for years and one of the best-liked members of the Guild. He now lives in California. Not many years ago he also worked in the editorial rooms of a local newspaper from which he sent out one manuscript after another with disheartening success. But finally landed and his name became widely known."

Louis Dodge was president in 1922 and was a guiding force in SLWG for years. While sitting in the newspaper's editorial room, he sent out numerous manuscripts before finding fame and moving to California in the late 1920s. His poem, "The Prison" was in the May 1929 issue of *Scribner's*. Dodge was the author of over a dozen books, some of them children's books. *The Sandman's Forest: A Story for Large Persons to Read to Small Persons*, published in 1918, is the story of how a little boy put himself to bed for the first time and how Superstork carried him off to a wonderful forest where all the animals lived peacefully together. Other titles included *Everychild, Children of the Desert, Bonnie May, Whispers, The Sandman's Mountain, A Runaway Woman, Rosy,* and *The American*. According to Miss Catha Wells, well-known writer of children's stories, *The Sandman's*

Mountain "is one of the really fine books for children."

On May 10, 1919, the Best Sellers of the Week in the *St. Louis Globe-Democrat* listed *Rosey* by Louis Dodge, #1 at Famous-Barr, #4 at Stix, Baer & Fuller, and #5 at Scruggs-Vandervoort-Barney.

Margery Doud

"Margery Doud accounts her accomplishments modest, but she has been published articles and verse in *House Beautiful, Life, and Pan*. Her 'To a Norwegian Mackerel' was included in Braithwaite's Anthology several years ago."

An author and poet, she was part of the KMOX Book Club, and was Chief of Readers' Advisory Service for the St. Louis Public Library. She also worked at the Buder and Carondelet branches and taught book selection in the library summer school of Iowa State University.

Margaretta Scott Lawler

"Margaretta Scott Lawler is the author of 'Her Children Shall Rise Up,' presented not long ago at the Artists' Guild. She has had several one-act plays staged by the guild and the players here, and has had plays published in drama."

Margaretta Scott Lawler became an early member of St. Louis Writers Guild. She wrote numerous one-act plays and several three-act dramas. Margaretta was also credited with bringing poetry to the regular schedule of St. Louis Writers Guild. Apparently, at her insistence, the first meeting dedicated to poetry was held in 1921, and the first poetry contest was held that same year.

Miriam Drane Lindsey

"Mrs. Lindsey has published in the *Psychology Magazine*, in John Martin's *Children's Stories*, and has won a $600 prize with a yarn in the *True Stories Magazine*."

Robertus Love

"Robertus Love has done a great deal of verse and published a book, *The Rise and Fall of Jesse James*." Robertus Love was a staff writer for the *St. Louis Globe-Democrat* and wrote many of their feature articles. He was a member of the Membership Committee and presided over and hosted meetings at his house on West Pine Boulevard.

Ann Rice Ludlow

"Ann Rice Ludlow has appeared in *Better Homes and Gardens, The Independent Woman* and *Psychology*."

Mable H. Malone (Mrs. George Malone, Mrs. M. M. H. Malone), president 1934 and 1935

"Mable H. Malone, writer of short stories and articles, has appeared in the *American Magazine, Everybody's Action Stories, Sports and Vanities* and *Game and Gossip*."

Mable H. Malone hosted many Guild meetings at her house on Bellevue Avenue.

Elinor Maxwell McCord – SLWG President in 1930, 1935, & 1936

"One of the most prolific of the St. Louis writers is Mrs. Elinor Maxwell McCord. Often her work is signed Elinor Maxwell. She has been writing since she was 15 and has at least 200 short stories, playlets and articles published in magazines of national standing. She also has a book of poems, and has contributed to *Plain Talk, The New Yorker* and *McClure's* in recent months."

Elinor Maxwell began her writing career at the age of fifteen and by 1929 had penned over 200 stories, articles, and playlets. She wrote for magazines like *Plain Talk, the New Yorker,* and *McClure's* and she had a column in the *St. Louis Globe-Democrat* every Sunday. (Read her complete biography in Chapter 12.)

Alice Curtice Moyer-Wing

"Alice Curtice Moyer-Wing has published a series of political articles in *Scribner's Magazine* during the last three years."

Harlan Eugene Read

"Harlan Eugene Read, a distinguished writer and resident of

St. Louis. He is the author of *Thurman Lucas* and published eight textbooks."

Mrs. Pearl Rodgers (Pearl Curran, Mrs. Dr. H. H. Rodgers, Mrs. John H. Curran)

"Mrs. Dr. H. H. Rodgers, who is known to an extensive public as Patience Worth. She writes poetry and verse through the medium of a ouiji board."

Pearl Lenore Curran began life in a simple and unassuming way, on February 15, 1883 in Mound City, Illinois. She soon moved with her family to Texas. Pearl attended school until she dropped out in high school, after experiencing a nervous breakdown from the strenuous academics. She briefly returned to St. Ignatius Catholic School in Marthasville, Missouri but this lack of education would be an important factor later in her life.

Pearl and her family moved to St. Louis when she was 14, and her interest turned to music. When the family moved to Palmer, Missouri, they sent Pearl for voice training in Kankakee, Illinois. She showed talent as a singer and pianist. Pearl then moved to Chicago, where she was trained by the renowned J.C. Cooper. She started working for the McKinley Music Company, addressing envelopes for six dollars a week, before switching and selling music for the Thompson Music Company. Until the age of twenty-four, Pearl worked in Chicago through the winter and spent her summers in Missouri giving music lessons. Pearl married John Howard Curran in 1907, and the two lived a modest but comfortable life

John Curran died June 1, 1922 and Pearl married two more times, though both would be short-lived. Her second marriage was to Dr. H. H. Rodgers, and they lived in St. Louis. During this time, she helped bring the St. Louis Writer Guild into fruition as a Charter Member, one of the original thirty members of the organization. In 1930, she moved to Los Angeles, California and lived the rest of her life with her friend, Dotsie Smith. Pearl passed away in 1937.

In 1913, during the height of the spiritualist's movement, Pearl underwent a remarkable experience. Using a Ouija board, she channeled a medieval noble woman named Patience Worth, and together they wrote a series of novels. Pearl claimed to have transcribed the novels during psychic experiences with Patience. A widely read and beloved writer, she grew famous not only as a literary sensation, but also from the many scholars who sought out her and her novels for the intimate details of medieval life she provided, details which were thought at the time to be impossible for a high school drop out to have known.

A thorough investigation was conducted by Dr. Walter Franklin Price who published his findings in *The Case of Patience Worth*, in 1927. It contained 509 pages of eyewitness reports, opinions, reviews, poetry, and an autobiographical sketch of Pearl. The book covers the years 1913 – 1927. In an article for the July 1926 *Scientific American*, titled "The Riddle of Patience Worth," Dr. Price requested anyone who could debunk Pearl come forward. No one ever could.

If you would like to read her poems, please visit www.patienceworth.org

Read more by checking out her novel, *The Sorry Tale* by Patience Worth.

Find her writings at the Missouri History Museum, http://www.travelchannel.com/video/writings-of-a-spirit

Dr. Alfred F. Satterthwait, President 1929

"Alfred F. Satterthwait, president of the Guild. He has written numerous pamphlets, issued by the government, on scientific research. His subject is insects."

Dr. Satterthwait was an entomologist and an esteemed member of the U.S. Bureau of Entomology. A collection of his writings was stored at the Smithsonian Institution Archives. He penned several books, but mostly wrote about the subject that drove his life's ambition, the world of insects.

No stranger to community leadership, in 1920 Satterthwait founded the Webster Groves Nature Study Society, or the "WGNSS" as it became known. In 1930, he helped start the *Nature Notes Journal*, for which he contributed many articles on various insect topics. Both the Journal and the Nature Study Society still thrive to this day. He was later elected President of the American Nature Study Society in 1931, and became the chairman of the St. Louis Academy of Science that same year. Satterthwait was born in 1897, and lived much of his life in Webster Groves, Missouri before finally moving to Urbana, Illinois in 1936. The University of Illinois at Champagne-Urbana still maintains his collection in their library.

Elizabeth Allen Satterthwait

"Mrs. Satterthwait, wife of the Guild president, has written poetry and scientific articles, a strange combination; she has published a volume of her verse, "A Gentle Heart."

She was president of St. Louis Writers Guild in 1928, and a poet who had a passion for ornithology. She and her husband, Dr. A.F. Satterthwait, were both distinguished members of the Wilson Ornithology Club and she wrote many articles on birds for the *Nature Notes Journal*, and other publications.

A Gentle Heart, 1936

Harold Shumate

The January 1929 issue of *Story World* had a two-column story about Harold Shumate, author of several photoplays. A St. Louis bond salesman, his first photoplay was "Unguarded Gates." He sold screenplays, and adapted novels for the screen, as well as writing photoplays which were plays filmed and shown as movies, or movies using still photos to tell the story.

May Wilson Todd – Mrs. J. W. L. Todd

May Wilson Todd, a charter member of SLWG, wrote for over twenty different magazines, including *Judge, Youth's Companion*, and others. She found success with the popularity of an early poem, "After Death." Published originally around 1896 or 1897 in the *Houston Post*, it was rerun in many major newspapers throughout the country including *The Buffalo Times*. She credited "My Quest," published in the 1920s, as her most successful poem. She lived in Webster Groves with her husband J.W.L. Todd, and their two children Wilson Todd and Kathleen Sheldon. She was secretary and vice-president of St. Louis Writers Guild.

She and her son Wilson Todd went to Lake Winona, Indiana in July of 1922. When not mentioned in society section, May Wilson Todd could often be found expressing her opinion in a letter to the newspapers or in one of her columns.

May Wilson Todd died on July 31, 1936 of heat prostration; she was 66 years old. She had been ill for six years, but suffered a heat spell two and a half weeks before. She passed away at her home on West Swon avenue in Webster Groves, and was laid to rest in Oak Hill Cemetery.

J. Lillian Vandevere

J. Lillian Vandevere was one of the youngest members of the St. Louis Writers Guild and remained a part of the organization through much of her career. J. Lillian Vandevere was published in the *Saturday Evening Post, Delineator, Munsey's, The Etude, Designer, Photoplay Magazine, John Martin's Book, Shadowland, Sunset* and many other national publications.

Brad R. Cook

Margaretta Scott Lawler
1929 *St. Louis Globe-Democrat*

Harlan Eugene Read
1929 *St. Louis Globe-Democrat*

11 |
Tis the Season for Writers

St. Louis Writers Guild had a Season, a time of the year when it held events. The monthly meetings started in September, right after the annual trip to the second Missouri Writers' Guild meeting of the year, usually at the Lake of the Ozarks, and continued until May when they broke for the summer. The start of the Season was also when the writing contests opened for submission.

Though it started in 1920 with a single monthly meeting, within a year, St. Louis Writers Guild met twice a month. The main meeting was held on the fourth Tuesday of the month, or the last Tuesday of the month (it's not entirely clear). These Tuesday evening meetings continued until the 1960s or 1970s when it moved to Wednesday evenings, before eventually moving to Saturday mornings in the mid-2000s. A second meeting was held some months in the 1920s and 1930s. It was a business meeting and was held on an earlier Tuesday in the month. It's unclear how long this second meeting lasted or if it was equivalent to the board meeting of later years. Officers were elected in January, at a meeting that for many years was held at Shirley Seifert's house, though only a short program would be held due to time needed to vote.

These monthly meetings were held in different members' homes until the 1950s when tearooms, the cafés of their day, became the setting for these events. SLWG found a home in several of the restaurants around town, then a glorious time in bookstores, before eventually having to rent out the community centers around town.

In the early days, dinner was provided, often as a picnic in the garden, and then members' work would be critiqued by the members and guests in attendance. Eventually food was provided by the tearoom or restaurants. Today, members will often have lunch together as friends after the workshops.

A variety of topics were discussed by a guest speaker. In fact, many of the workshop titles were the same or at least similar, regardless of the era. What writers needed to hear and what members talked about were universal to all writers. From panels of authors talking about their experiences to workshops on writing or how to promote their work, the topics were so similar that no matter the era, any writer could find assistance with St. Louis Writers Guild. Through at least the 1940s, and perhaps much longer, those who wanted to join St. Louis Writers Guild contacted the organization and submitted a request. Prospects listed their publications and then St. Louis Writers Guild members voted on who would be accepted into the organization. Then at the next meeting, the new members were welcomed and inducted into the organization. In fact, acceptance into St. Louis Writers Guild was usually listed in the newspaper. At one meeting in the 1930s, twelve new members were initiated into the Guild.

They used terms like "initiated" and "inducted," but no ceremony was listed or ever referred to in any publication. From descriptions of these events, part of a regular meeting was set aside for new members to introduce themselves and describe their work. This followed or was followed by regular members sharing their latest accomplishments.

The Season lasted until the mid-2000s when St. Louis Writers Guild went to a full-year schedule. The tradition of the Season continues to this day. Though St. Louis Writers Guild holds events all year long, the membership year begins on June 1 and ends on May 31, the last day of the traditional Season.

I discovered the Season when researching the members of the 1920's and 1930s. The opening or closing of the Season was often announced in the paper. As with today, there was a rhythm to the events of the year.

In the beginning, St. Louis Writers Guild held a single writing contest. This changed every year, starting with a short story contest, and then switching from year to year. In 1921, they held a poetry contest. In 1922, it was a character sketch, and in 1927, the contest sought one-act plays. The contest was announced at the first meeting of the Season in September, and had a November deadline. SLWG's current short story contest remains at the same time of year and has this same window of seeking submissions.

St. Louis Writers Guild used to hold elections at the end of January. The announcement of officers ran in the newspaper the following week. The three newspapers of the day announced the new president, though it was the person, not the office that was worth reporting on. With many of the members working in the newspaper business, or being the top authors of their day, there was a definite bias in coverage. I was able to fill in the gaps for several unknown presidents, leaving only two years unknown.

As is still true today, dedicated volunteers formed the backbone of the organization. Many remained board members and served the Guild for decades. This was epitomized by several members over the years, like Ralph Mooney who was president in both the 1920s and the 1940s, Norah Morgan, who coordinated the contests for decades, and served as president in 1947, and specifically, Charles Guenther, a writer, poet, and translator, who held the office of president multiple times over three decades. It continues today with members like Susie Meyer and Donna Springer who have remained active for several decades.

December or January was also when the "open meeting" was held, where anyone could come and be a guest of St. Louis Writers Guild. Guests were afforded guest privileges, which perhaps meant they could participate in SLWG activities like the monthly review. The event was held at the Glen Echo Country Club for a couple of years in 1930s, and perhaps in other venues a well. It was the precursor for the galas and holiday parties that were held in the following decades. The open meeting was often used to honor contest winners. In modern times, this tradition of an "open meeting" continued with a least one workshop a year, usually my

Pitching and Conference workshop held in the Spring, which was free to attend, and the Holiday Party held every December, which featured the winners of the Young Writers Awards. These truly carried on the tradition of the original open meetings.

The end of the Season was often celebrated with a party. In the beginning, it was simply a meeting, but soon it became an event, first held in late May at the Glen Echo Country Club, and then as the decades passed, it moved to the Chase, the Flaming Pit Restaurant, Orlando Gardens, and Llywelyn's Pub in Webster Groves. Eventually, this became the annual picnic held in June during the 2000s, and even the Gateway to Publishing Conference & Convention held at the St. Louis Renaissance Airport Hotel in the late 2010s.

Traditions of Yesterday that SLWG Carried through to Today

One of the joys of researching this book and the history of the St. Louis Writers Guild was finding out what had been done in the past that was still done today, or the echo of which remained, from Gateway Con (see Chapter 23 for Gateway Con Highlights) not being the first major conference, to more simple things like the 5+5 Critique Workshops.

5+5 Critique Workshops

The early meetings had a speaker, but then part of the time was dedicated to reading a portion of a short story, one-act play, character sketch, or novel, and then those in attendance commented on the work. This would be mirrored in the 5+5 Critique Workshop, a popular event, usually held to fill a vacant programming slot, when someone had to cancel. The event had a board member read the work for five minutes, and then everyone commented for five minutes. Hearing someone else read your words and then having constructive criticism made the event popular with members.

Critique Groups and the SLWG
Cycle Critique Groups

From its first meeting, St. Louis Writers Guild attempted to help writers write better through a group critique. In the beginning, they held a review at every meeting. This involved the chairman or president reading a section of a manuscript and then the members in attendance gave their opinions. It was not a sugar-coating session either. It was described as not being for the faint of heart. It was also said that there wasn't an editor in the lot, so I imagine much like current critique groups, everyone had an opinion, it just might not be a good one.

In the 2000s, St. Louis Writers Guild created the Cycle Critique Groups. Once each quarter, they would make a call for those interested in a critique group. People signed up, and then those who were in similar genres were paired together in groups that usually were of 5 people or fewer. It worked well for several years, but eventually it became an ongoing service, and members could sign up at any time.

Often these groups imploded after a few meetings, not from something St. Louis Writers Guild had done, but often personalities clashed, and it could take writers a while to find a group they could work with. Lifelong friendships and writing partners were formed from these groups. I went through a couple of critique groups before one I was in that had nine people broke up, and my current group formed out of that.

There was an attempt to have a critique group forum, where people could post their work and have members comment on it. This was a throwback to the forums that had been started in the 2000s, but in the end, not enough people used the service. Today, St. Louis Writers Guild holds networking events like Genre Talk, and out of each of those events, writing partners and small critique groups form. These groups tend to stay together better as members gravitate toward others with whom they have things in common.

The Monthly Meetings—Workshops for Writers

The biggest tradition that continued until modern day was the monthly meeting, St. Louis Writers Guild's main event. It was surprising to discover how much of the meetings remained the same no matter what era was researched. The venue may change, but the reason writers gathered every month, and what they discussed was similar. In the beginning, a roll call was taken and members could discuss their latest accolades. Today that continues at the start of every meeting where members are called upon to share their latest accolades. A topic about novel writing or the business of writing has been held every month of the Season for a century. The topics' titles don't even change that much over the years. In fact, some of the workshops held in eras past sound fascinating, and a similar topic may be held the at today's Workshops for Writers. The president or one of the board members still preside over every meeting. In the end, I think Shirley, Sam, Ralph, or any other member from 1920 could walk into the room today and see the similarities.

What do these Terms mean...

Founder – According to the records, there were six founders. It was due to their efforts that St. Louis Writers Guild was formed.

Charter Members – These people were the first members of St. Louis Writers Guild. They possibly had signed up before the first meeting or represented people who were interested in the Guild, and pledged to be a part of this literary endeavor. Many of them were instrumental in the early days, hosting meetings and events.

President – The head of the organization, the president sets the way forward and has the final say on the direction of the organization. Historically, they set the tone for the Guild, and each one brought something unique. Whether through their experiences, their demeanor, or their ambitions, the president is the one who holds St. Louis Writers Guild's members in their hands.

Host/Hostess – In the early days, St. Louis Writers Guild's monthly meeting was held in the houses of board members or general members. Some were even the parents' or sibling's houses of members. Dinner was served in a picnic style, which eventually became a potluck dinner. Hosts ensured all of this ran smoothly, and that the guests of St. Louis Writers Guild had a wonderful workshop.

Chairman – The chairman presided over the workshops or events. Usually this person was the president, but when they could not perform the duty, a chairman ran the meeting. This included announcements and introduction of the speaker. For many meetings, the host ran the house, and the chairman ensured the meeting went smoothly. The chairman addressed the members and guests in attendance at the beginning of the meeting. They directed dinner, called upon the president to make announcements, introduced the speaker for the evening, and then introduced the president again to read the selected stories for review.

Vice President – One of the original board of director positions, over time, the vice president job has been divided up to represent different aspects of the organization, like VP of Operations, or VP of Programs and Publicity. It has always been held by someone deeply involved in the writers guild, though, historically, it did not always mean that they were a president in waiting. Many Vice Presidents served several years and never held the office of president.

Secretary – One of the original board of director positions, the secretary records every meeting, keeps the organization on track, and holds board members accountable for their actions. They also created and held important documents like the bylaws, contest rules, and more.

Treasurer – One of the original board of director positions, the treasurer has always held the bank accounts of St. Louis Writers Guild. They take care of the taxes every year, and ensure that every bill is paid on time. A good treasurer also challenges the board's spending habits to ensure as little waste as possible and that Guild's funds were spent appropriately.

Vice President of Programs and Publicity – The oldest of the additional board positions, vice president of Programs and Publicity was created decades ago because of the amount of work needed to plan events. The VPoP&P invited every speaker, and ensured all promotional material was collected and disseminated. They not only ensured a variety of topics, but also made certain that speakers did not repeat too quickly. They arranged that popular topics were explored in multiple ways and that all aspects of writing were touched upon.

Historian – The first official historian position was created around the 50th Anniversary, and was added again to the board in 2005, when it was required by state bylaws. However, it has been an unofficial job, held by several members throughout the years, starting with Louis Dodge in 1921.

Director of Communications – Created in 2017, this role combined many roles into a single office. As the name implied, they were in charge of all communication from emails to the newsletters, and even social media.

Editor – As long as St. Louis Writers Guild published a newsletter or journal, it needed an editor. Currently the editor publishes each issue of Here's News! and reviews SLWG's publications.

Contest Coordinator – Since 1920, it has been someone's duty to collect the entries, process the entries, vet them to ensure the writers followed all submission guidelines, and then send the entries to the judge. Currently, this also involves contacting schools and other organizations across the region for the Young Writers Awards, which will often get whole classrooms submitting at once. At their height, St. Louis Writers Guild's contests received nearly 1,000 entries a year.

Membership Chairman – This unsung hero entered all members into the member database and kept the records up to date. Once a year in May and June, their world was turned upside down as membership renewals were processed. Other than that one time of year, the job mostly entailed adding a couple of new members a week.

Auditor – A board level position that mostly existed in the 1960s. There was a treasurer at the same time, and the exact duties were not listed. An assumption can be made that they took stock over the Season. Perhaps they were a second set of eyes for the treasurer; perhaps they made certain contests ran smoothly.

(A quick note: SLWG's name in the following chapter titles often depicts how the organization was referred to during that time. The question of where the apostrophe went can be found in Chapter 25.)

Mable H. Malone, President
1929 *St. Louis Globe-Democrat*

Alice Curtis Moyer-Wing
1929 *St. Louis Globe-Democrat*

12 |
The St. Louis Writers' Guild in the 1930s

With the 1929 article in the *St. Louis Globe-Democrat*, St. Louis Writers Guild was set to be a driving force of the Midwest literary community. As the Great Depression overtook the county, and here in St. Louis, the Lambert-Municipal Airport was dedicated and the Anheuser-Busch Budweiser Clydesdales made their debut, St. Louis Writers Guild continued the traditions begun the decade before. SLWG had found a home among the city's social elite and highly educated, which kept the worst of the Great Depression as the intense subject matter to be tackled or the entertainment with which to escape. Guided by a core group of members, like Elinor Maxwell McCord, Anita Knight, Mabel Malone, Rebeka Deitz, and Robert Hereford, meetings continued to be held at the homes of members, with different members hosting each event. The format of these events remained as it did in the beginning with the President reading a couple of scenes, short stories, essays, one act plays, or poems. Then members commented on the pieces and a social hour followed. Some of the greatest authors of the day were guest speakers at these events.

One addition was the regularity with which St. Louis Writers Guild had a speaker or speakers who would talk about writing or their writing. Each event mentions someone would be present, but it doesn't always say who the person was, and rarely reveals what topic was presented.

The Season schedule continued as the meetings were held

between September and May. The May 1935 announcement in the *St. Louis Post-Dispatch* mentioned it was the last meeting of the Season. There was an end of the year event in December, and officer elections were still held in January, which often made the end of the year dinner a sendoff for the departing president.

The decade ended with an event to honor Mrs. J.J. Gasporotti and her sisters, Miss Shirley Seifert (Second SLWG President, 1921), and Miss Adele Seifert. On April 24, 1939, near the end of the season, they gathered for an evening at the Park Plaza Hotel. They were once referred to as the Brontë sisters of the Midwest, as all were successful authors. Mrs. Gasporotti was visiting from her home in Moberly, Missouri. Her sisters lived with their parents in Kirkwood, Missouri. By this time, Shirley Seifert was no longer involved with SLWG operations. This special event appears to be a way for the organization to honor the contributions of all three noted authors.

Writing Contests

In the 1930s St. Louis Writers Guild expanded from members-only writing contests to ones that were open to all writers in the St. Louis area. It started with an unnamed writing contest for unpublished writers in 1932, but that was short lived.

St. Louis Writers Guild created a new way of holding contests. Members/Authors sponsored the first prize or half the prizes; both ways were mentioned. This became not only an advertising opportunity for the authors, but allowed the Guild to hold several contests a year. The poetry contest at this time was known as the Florence Seidlitz Poetry Contest, and then there was the Winifred Irwin Short Story Contest for unpublished writers. (How the contests got their names is detailed later in Chapter 30, Writing Contests, A Long History of Supporting Writers.) The members-only contest was still held and continued to rotate formats throughout much of the decade.

In 1935, Tennessee Williams won the short story contest with his story "Stella for Star." He was attending Washington University in St. Louis, at the time and still went by Thomas Lanier Williams. Robin Moore Theiss, SLWG President from 2006-

2009, discovered the letter St. Louis Writers Guild sent informing Thomas of his win, and which contained his winning check for $10. I found the story in a Texas library archive. More on all of these contests in the Writing Contest Chapter.

The Glen Echo Open Meeting

St. Louis Writers Guild has always held an open event, aside from the usual workshops. Today, this continues with the SLWG Holiday Party with readings by the Young Writers Award winners. In the 1930s, a similar event was held every year at the Glen Echo Country Club.

The *St. Louis Globe-Democrat* described it this way –
January 7, 1930
Writers' Guild to Hold Annual Session at Glen Echo Tuesday – Wednesday Club to Hold Meeting.

This week will see a general reopening of the activities of woman's clubs and organizations after the holiday recess, inaugurating the season of 1930.

Tuesday evening, January 7, 1930, the St. Louis Writers' Guild held its annual open meeting at the Glen Echo Country Club. The dinner meeting at 7 o'clock, was hosted by Mrs. Don Chylo McCord (Elinor Maxwell McCord).

The "open meeting" allowed members to have guest privileges. This referred to fact that guests could come to the event and participate, which was something guests at regular meetings could not do. At this time, not all meetings were open to the public. St. Louis Writers Guild events were for members only. In the coming decades, guests were able to pay a small fee to attend workshops.

At the close of dinner, everyone adjourned to the lounge where Caspar S. Yost, editor of the editorial page of the *Globe-Democrat*, introduced the speaker. Mrs. H. H. Rogers, gave a Patience Worth recital, not only reading the poetry which Patience Worth had given during the past years, but also producing a new piece at the event. She gave a glimpse into her early history, her introduction to the mysterious Patience Worth, and her experiences at the hands of skeptical critics. Her honesty and integrity stamped her work genuine. She read several poems of Patience Worth published in *Vanity Fair* and other magazines, and some not yet published.

The greeting to the Guild from Patience Worth was written in the form of a sixteenth century English poem. Mrs. Rodgers then asked for suggestions or favorite poems from the audience. Some of the poems read that day, "which Patience Worth's voice gave to Mrs. Rogers," were: "Modern Hero," "Jade Dream Child," "Firesides," "My Two Dons," "Shoestrings," "A Blue Stone," and about twenty others.

One hundred guests attended the dinner, and letters and telegrams from absent members like Sam Hellman, Temple Bailey, and others were read. Twelve new members were welcomed into the Guild: Harlan Eugene Read, Harry Bristol Williams, Casper S. Yost, Jasmine Stone Van Dresser, Prof Lawrence Conrad, Roy Turnbull, Prof Wm Bruce Carson, Alice Peck, Anita Gaebler Knight, Hazel Chaney Pentland, Marguerite Ely McDonald, and Anne Rice Ludlow.

A Short, Short Story contest was announced by Guild President, A.F. Satterthwait. The judges for this contest were the editor of *Collier's*, the editor of *Liberty*, and the editor of *Life*. Mrs. McCord had seen these editors a few weeks prior and obtained their consent to act as judges. There were two cash prizes and two honorable mentions.

Joseph T. David of the Safety Council extended an invitation to Guild members to submit radio stories for the Careful Children's Club.

The Presidents
1930 – Elinor Maxwell McCord
*1931 – Elinor Maxwell McCord
*1932 – Rebeka A.P. Deitz
*1933 – Rebeka A.P. Deitz
*1934 – Mable H. Malone
*1935 – Mable H. Malone
*1936 – Elinor Maxwell McCord
1937 – Dr. Harvey J Howard
1938 – Anita Knight

1939 – Robert Hereford
* information discovered through research; **bold** means it has been confirmed.

Board Members or the Executive Committee of St. Louis Writers Guild
1931
Mrs. Elinor Maxwell McCord, President
Mr. Casper Yost appointed Vice President, after the resignation of Mr. William F. Saunders.

1932
Mrs. Rebeka A. P. Deitz, President
Prof. Raymond Howes, Vice President
Miss Alice Peek, Secretary.

1933 (incomplete)
Rebeka Deitz, president
Rebeka Deitz, chairman of the contest committee

1934
Mable Malone, President
Donald Wright, Vice President
Elizabeth Satterthwait, Secretary-Treasurer
Winifred Irwin, Chairman of the Membership Committee

1935 (incomplete)
Mable H. Malone, president
Alfred F. Satterthwait, Chairman of the Contest Judges

Members from the 1930s
Frederick Hazlitt Brennan

Frederick Hazlitt Brennan was a successful author and playwright, best known for his work on *The Life* and *Legend of Wyatt Earp* television show. Officially listed as a writer and movie scenarist, he was a former movie critic and reporter for the *St. Louis Post-Dispatch*, after having spent several years at the *St. Louis Globe-*

Democrat. Two years after "The Guardian Angel" won first place in the 1928 *O'Brien Collection*, he left the paper and became a freelance writer, contributing short stories to *Collier's, Red Book, Cosmopolitan, American*, and other magazines. In February 1931, he was initiated as a member of St. Louis Writers Guild, and a few years later in 1935, his play, *Battleship Gertie*, debuted at the Lyceum Theater on Broadway. The play was a comedic satire with the US Navy as the background, and received a lot of praise. He followed it up a few years later with *The Wookey*, which he worked on with legendary Broadway producer Edgar Selwyn. The play was a hit during its run in 1941 at the Plymouth Theater and led to receiving honors at a White House dinner. *The Wookey* portrayed obscure folks from war-time London. The principal character, Horace Wookey, was a tugboat captain, World War Veteran, a sturdy champion of the rights of plain Englishmen, and a hard-headed opponent of the government's policy in the new world war.

Brennan graduated from the University of Missouri. For many years he lived with his wife Celeste Plank Brennan, two sons, and a daughter on Hillvale Drive in Clayton, Missouri. Brennan eventually moved to Hidden Valley, California. On June 30, 1962, Frederick Hazlitt Brennan was found in bed at his estate with a self-inflicted gunshot from a .45 caliber pistol. No note was left, and no motive was obtained. He was 60 years old.

His books included:
God Got One Vote, 1927
Pie in the Sky
We Sail Tomorrow, 1934
Battleship Gertie, adapted as a play for Broadway, 1935
Stick-in-the-Mud
The Wicker Book of Brother Barnabas
Memo to a Firing Squad
Smith's Life of Jones
One of Our H-Bombs is Missing

Fannie Cook

Fannie Cook was born in St. Charles. She received her B.A. from the University of Missouri in 1914 and her M.A. from

Washington University in 1916. Though published widely and a painter of some distinction, she is largely remembered for her novel, *Mrs. Palmer's Honey* (1946), which is considered an important literary contribution for the advancement of African Americans. Cook was a dedicated member of the Mayor's Committee on Race Relations, an adviser to the NAACP, and the 1940 chairperson of the Missouri Committee for Rehabilitation of Sharecroppers. Cook resigned her position as instructor of English at Washington University and began to write articles, short stories, and novels. Her first success came in 1935 when she won first prize in a *Reader's Digest* contest. Cook's short works, published between 1940 and 1946, reflect her conviction that unions are the only solution for the ailments of struggling people. In "A Killer's Knife Ain't Holy," Ambor, the preacher-protagonist, is asked to choose between the church and the union. The themes of all her novels revolve around the coming of age of the individual and, often by extension, of the group to which he or she belongs.

Rebeka A. P. Deitz (Rebka Dietz, Mrs. Paul C. Deitz) – President 1932 & 1933

Mrs. Rebeka A. P. Deitz was a powerhouse in the organization. She hosted events, led meetings as the chairman, ran the contests, and other aspects of SLWG operations. She wrote character sketches that appeared in the *American, the Delineator, the Woman's Journal, the Forecast* and other magazines. She apparently had done ghost writing for politicians in Washington and New York, and collected material for speeches by President Hoover and Secretary of the Interior Wilbur. In 1947, she was chosen as area chairman for a $2,000,000 development campaign for Mount Holyoke College. Her husband, Mr. Paul C. Deitz, was a beloved mathematics teacher at Principia College. (*The Paul Dietz who published a book on railroad firemen was unrelated.*)

Robert Hereford – President 1939

Author, lecturer, and a teacher at Washington University, Robert Hereford was the manager of the St. Louis Bureau of International News Service, and for many years was a staff writer at the *St. Louis Globe-Democrat*. He wrote detective novels and continued the work of Louis Dodge in researching the history of St. Louis Writers Guild. His writings corroborated much of the information discovered. A lifelong resident of Ferguson, he spent many years on Tunstall Place. In June 1950, he talked to the Lions Club about the Animal Protective Association of Missouri and what the association was doing to take care of unwanted dogs, including holding roundups in Washington, Missouri and taking them to St. Louis to find homes.

In May of 1952, Robert Hereford was one of the speakers to open the 43rd University of Missouri Journalism Week. Missouri Writers' Guild was featured, and Mrs. Adelaide Jones of Springfield, Missouri was elected president of the state organization. Elston J. Melton of Boonville, and Robert Hereford were elected Vice Presidents. Robert Hereford served as Vice President of MWG again in 1953.

Mrs. Birdie Hoffman – Member in 1938
Mrs. Birdie Hoffman, formerly Miss Birdie Holmsly, was a funny and successful author from Sedalia, Missouri.

Dr. Harvey J. Howard, President in 1937
Dr. Harvey J. Howard was the ophthalmologist and physician for the last Chinese Emperor Pu Yi (1921-25). Born in Churchville, New York on January 30, 1880, Harvey went on to earn his A.B. from the University of Michigan, his M.D. from the University of Pennsylvania, his A.M. from Harvard University, and his Oph.D. from the University of Colorado. The author of 100 clinical and scientific contributions to ophthalmology, he also devised the critical depth perception test for the selection of flying personnel in the Army, Navy, and the Department of Commerce before it was adapted worldwide. His novel, *Ten Weeks With Chinese Bandits*, published in 1926, recalled his capture, ransom and near death at the hands of Chinese bandits. It went into eight printings and was translated into seven languages. The Howard family is directly descended from the Duke of Norfolk line, and the Howard family of England can trace its lineage to the 9th century, further back

than any other family in Europe. Awarded Tiger Fifth Class by the Chinese Government in 1926, he was also one of the founding fathers of the Acacia Fraternity.

Dr. Howard married Maude Irene Strobel on June 25, 1910 and they had three children. After his wife passed away, Harvey married Alice Tilson Eastes. He passed away at his home in Clearwater Florida on November 6, 1956.

Mrs. Anita Knight – President in 1938

Mrs. Anita Knight authored two pageants, one of which was titled, *St. Louis on Parade* and was presented by the Convention Committee of the Chamber of Commerce. Pageants were like plays, or several small skits performed on a stage with a single set piece. Anita Knight also penned several plays and a considerable amount of poetry. A prominent member of St. Louis society, she brought a great deal of attention to the organization with numerous stories and articles about her and the Guild in the newspapers of the day. Her husband, Walter J. Knight, developed property and housing on the riverfront. Her daughter, Miss Adhen Knight, was the Maid of Honor for the Veiled Prophet Ball in 1936.

Elinor Maxwell McCord (Elinor Maxwell, Mrs. Don Chylo McCord) – President in 1930, 1931, & 1936

Born in 1892, Elinor Maxwell began her writing career at the age of fifteen, and by 1929 had penned over 200 stories, articles, and playlets. She wrote for magazines like *Plain Talk, the New Yorker,* and *McClure's* and had a column in the *St. Louis Globe-Democrat* every Sunday. She married Don C. McCord and they had a son who became a noted author in his own right.

One of the first members of the St, Louis Writers Guild, Elinor Maxwell McCord often played bridge with Sam Hellman and his wife. She was even their neighbor in Great Neck, Long Island, New York. She always spoke highly of the SLWG's first president. In the November 10, 1929 *St. Louis Globe-Democrat* article about the Guild, she says of him, "It was better listening to him than reading one of his stories. He keeps a running chatter of conversation, couched in the most marvelous slang imaginable, and some unimaginable." Elinor and her husband often hosted meetings at their home, a common practice in the early days of the Guild. A vibrant force in the organization, she remained heavily involved in St. Louis Writers Guild for at least two decades.

In 1933, Elinor Maxwell McCord and her family moved to Chicago, Illinois. She went on to be the correspondent at the Chicago World's Fair for the *St. Louis Globe-Democrat*. Each week she wrote another installment in her series, "Vignettes of the Chicago World's Fair." Her descriptions took the reader right through the main gate, told them of the ample parking lots, and all the hotel facilities. She depicted what they looked like, where they were, what it cost, and what it's all about. She described each place to eat, but spent a large section focused on the Old Heidelberg, a popular restaurant at the fair. Of the fair she said, "It seems you can't take your dog in, but you can have your appendix out on the grounds. You may see a live two-headed baby, or prefer to watch a movie being made in the Hollywood Village; if you're in the right spot at the right time, you will be able to see George Rector do a bit of cooking, after which you dash someplace else and observe a 10 foot robot, with a transparent digestive tract, digest." She reported that this feature was interesting, but not pretty.

She reported on Miss Eleanor Frost of Syracuse, NY, the millionth visitor to the fair. As the woman passed through the turnstile, she was presented with a gold medal.

Of Tony Sarg, a noted artist, the article said, ...she caught him "painting enchanting ducks and cows and milkmaids on the walls of one of the booths." She even verified the boasts of Mr. Gordon about his Greyhound buses. For fifty cents they took people on an hour and twenty-minute trip through the entire grounds hearing the latest fair news.

One of the latest tidbits came from the Century of Progress – Waffles and Sausages, where a sausage was wrapped in a waffle and eaten enroute.

A dynamic force during her time with St. Louis Writers Guild, Elinor Maxwell McCord brought in the most interesting and far-afield speakers to the Guild. One could even venture to say that she was the greatest events planner for the organization. Not only did she get leading publishers of the day to judge all the contests, but beyond university professors, the top authors of their day, and even the writings of presidents and secretary of state, she also invited international guests like the physician to Mahatma Gandhi, who spoke about Hindu literature.

She appeared to have met many of these people through her everyday life as a fabulous author and then arranged for them to speak to the Guild.

Continuing St. Louis Writers Guild's outreach, she partnered with the St. Louis Safety Council to produce radio plays for the Careful Children's Club in 1930. Those plays were written by members of St. Louis Writers Guild as contest entries.

Elinor Maxwell McCord passed away in 1970.

Workshops and Events
Tuesday, January 7, 1930

The Guild held its annual open meeting at the Glen Echo Country Club. The seven o'clock dinner meeting hosted by Elinor Maxwell McCord featured Caspar S. Yost, editorial page editor of the *Globe-Democrat*, who introduced the speakers, including Mrs. H. H. Rogers, who gave a Patience Worth recital.

February 16, 1930 - from the *St. Louis Globe-Democrat*
"Writers' Guild to Aid Careful Children's Club

"The Careful Children's Club of the St. Louis Safety Council set a new record in radio broadcasting, E. K. Easthan, chairman of the Careful Children's Club Radio Committee, announced today. Since the inauguration of this club in the fall of 1926, Safety Sam and the Careful Twins have broadcast every night, with the exception of Sunday, continuously for 179 weeks and now have a membership in the club of more than 470,000 boys and girls under 15 years of age.

"Beginning Monday evening, February 17, at 4:30 o'clock, a progressive safety story will be put on the air over KMOX. This is made possible through the co-operation of sixteen well-known writers of St. Louis, most of whom were members of the St. Louis Writers' Guild.

"Mrs. Don C. McCord of the Writers' Guild organized this committee several weeks ago and Mrs. Genevieve Knapp McConnell served as chairman. A definite schedule has been prepared whereby every member of this committee will write six short stories for a week's broadcast. Through the various members of the Brown family and their friends, the characters of this story, the children will learn about safety through stories, playlets, dialogues, poems, etc. The characters of the story will all be active, healthy children who are all living the life of an average boy and girl going to school, taking vacation trips and journeys, having their various celebrations and doing many other things."

February 25, 1930

At the February meeting of the St. Louis Writers Guild, a report on members activity was read. A partial list of the activities and successes of Guild members was published in the March 8, 1930 issue of the *St. Louis Globe-Democrat*:

Shirley Seifert – two plays accepted for production by the Art League; novel published in London by John Lang entitled "Oriflamme"; serial story, "The House-Party Murder" in Smart Set.

Jasmine Stone Van Dresser – Two plays accepted for production by the Art League.

Ann Rice Ludlow – Article on barbecuing in Country Gentleman.

Genevieve Knapp McConnell – Plays accepted for production by the Art League and the Little Theater: six short stories broadcast by KMOX for the Careful Children's Club.

Mrs. Ralph Mooney – Six stories for the Careful Children's Club.

Elinor Maxwell McCord, new president of the Writers' Guild – Story "At Sea" in St. Louis Town Topics.

Grace Baker – Article entitled "Price Cutting Under Fire" in Radio Record.

William Carson – Three articles in American Institute of Biography.

Lawrence Conrad – Article on Theodore Dreiser in The Landmark London.

Jay Gelzer – "Redhot Blues" story in Collier's.

Anita Gaebler Knight – Six short stories for broadcasting by Careful Children's Club.
Marian Smth Lindsey – Story sold to John Martin's Book.

Tuesday, April 29, 1930
Winners of the SLWG short story contest were announced at a meeting at the home of Mrs. Marian Smith Lindsey, in the 900 block of Newport Avenue in Webster Groves. Mrs. M. H. Malone read an original short story. Mrs. Margaretta Scott Lawlor read her one-act play, "The Randals of Virginia," and Mrs. Genevieve Knapp McConnell read her play, "The Grape Vine."

Tuesday, May 27, 1930
The winners of the SLWG Short Story Contest read their stories at the home of Mrs. Margaret Ely McDonnell, of the 100 block of South Gore Avenue in Webster Groves.

August 30, 1930
On Saturday, the *St. Louis Globe-Democrat* ran "Toll Bridge" by Sam Hellman (Harper & Bros, New York):

"Sam Hellman wise-cracks about the perils of contract bridge in this brief twenty-five-page story of a married couple who educate a bachelor uncle into the intricacies of the game, and incidentally precipitate him into matrimony with a contract partner."

Tuesday, December 30, 1930
The Guild met at the home of Mrs. Don C. McCord on Davis Drive. Mrs. McCord presided over the event. Casper S. Yost read one of his short stories; Mrs. Ann Rice Ludlow read her article "After Twenty Years on Crutches," which was published in *Psychology Magazine,* and Mrs. Jay Gelzer spoke about her experiences with editors and motion picture producers.

Tuesday, January 27, 1931
The annual business meeting was held at the home of Mrs. Gutherie McConnell on the 4000 block of Argyle Place. Mrs. Don C. McCord presided. The election of officers replaced the evening's program.

February 24, 1931

Meeting was held at the College Club, 5428 Delmar Boulevard. Jay Gelzer and Alice Peck hosted the evening. The program featured Casper Yost reading one of his own short stories. Margery Doud read a group of poems by Harry Williams. Frederick Hazlitt Brennan, who was a recent member of the Guild, gave an analytical study of his story, "The Guardian Angel," which held first place in the *O'Brien Collection*, 1928.

Tuesday, March 31, 1931

Anne Rice Ludlow and Lenora McPheeters hosted the evening meeting at the home of Mrs. Percy Ludlow on Jefferson Road in Webster Groves. Elinor Maxwell McCord introduced Dr. B. M. Sharma, professor of anatomy at Tibbi Medical School, Delhi, India, and the former physician to Mahatma Gandhi. He was in the United States under the auspices of the World Institute of Current Affairs and spoke on **The Literature of India.** Mrs. M.M.H. Malone analyzed one of her published stories, and A.F. Satterthwait announced the awards in the SLWG radio series contest.

May 26, 1931

A dinner meeting started at 6:30 p.m. in Mr. and Mrs. A.F. Satterthwait's garden on Waverly place in Webster Groves. They announced that the 1932 contest would focus on radio plays.

Mrs. Chester McPheeters gave a constructive analysis of her recently published short story. The guest speaker was Charles Dillon, author of the play "Zombie," which had been produced by the Little Theater at Artists' Guild.

Tuesday, September 29, 1931, 8 p.m.

The first meeting of the Season was held at the home of Mrs. Walter J. Knight, on the 6000 block of Pershing Avenue. Harlan Eugene Read, author of *Thurman Lucas*, and writer and producer of humorous radio sketches presented "Radio Markets for Writers." Mrs. Samuel P. Goddard, chairman of the committee for the Wednesday Club Verse, spoke on the "Hazards of Private Printing," and Thomas W. Parry Jr. read one of his own character sketches and discussed this type of writing.

Character Sketches was chosen as the subject of the Guild's annual contest for 1931, for which the first prize was $25 and second prize $15. The Guild's annual contest closed on Dec. 1. Then the manuscripts were read and judged over the holidays by three American editors – Seward Collins, editor of the Bookman, Harry Hansen, literary editor of the *New-York World Telegram*, and Perry Waxman, managing editor of *Pictorial Review*.

Tuesday, October 22, 1931

The second meeting of the Season was held at the home of Mrs. Carl Hoffman, of the 5000 block of Devonshire Avenue.

Programs focused on Character Sketches, which was the SLWG contest that year. Louis La Coss spoke. Then Raymond R. Howes, assistant professor of English at Washington University and editor of the *Alumni Bulletin*, gave a critical analysis of this own character sketch, "A Poet in a Cathedral," a study of Chancellor John A. Bowman of the University of Pittsburgh, which appeared in the *American Mercury*. **Personalities in the Making** was presented by Mrs. Rebeka Deitz, whose personality sketches had appeared in the *American*, the *Delineator*, the *Woman's Journal*, the *Forecast* and other magazines.

Mrs. Elinor Maxwell McCord, president of the Guild, announced that the Executive Committee appointed Mr. Casper Yost vice president, to fill the vacancy caused by the resignation of Mr. William Flewellyn Saunders, who was spending the winter in the East.

Tuesday, November 24, 1931

The meeting was held in the apartment of Mr. and Mrs. Casper S. Yost in the Forest Park Hotel.

January 5, 1932

The annual open meeting and dinner was held in the French room of the Coronado Hotel. The speakers were Frederick Hazlett

Brennan, novelist, who discussed, **The Literary Racket**; Harlan Eugene Read, author of *Thurman Lucas*, presented, **Literary Purpose**, and Edgar Curtis Taylor, spoke about, **Literary Feeling**. Mr. Taylor of Washington University was also head of the Taylor School for Boys in Clayton. He and Mr. Read had both graduated from Oxford.

The meeting marked Elinor Maxwell McCord's last appearance as Writers' Guild president before moving to Chicago. Mrs. M.M.H. Malone was in charge of the entertainment.

Tuesday, February 25, 1932

Members met at the home of Mrs. Rebeka Deitz in the 5000 block of Maple Avenue. The new SLWG officers were announced.

The program included an analysis of the personality sketch market by Mabel Malone. David Flourney Jr. presented **Continuity Writing for the Radio**, and a personality sketch of Charles Nagel was read by its author, Professor Howes.

A. F. Satterthwait announced the winners of the Guild's annual contest. The topic that year was personality sketches.

Tuesday, March 31, 1932

Members met at the apartment of Mrs. Joseph E. Irvin of the Park Plaza. SLWG President Mrs. Rebeka Deitz presided.

Miss Margery Doud read her prize-winning personality sketch written about the artist, Gisella Loeffer. Miss Doud tied for first place with Mrs. A. F. Satterthwaite, who had submitted "George Washington Carver, an Appreciation."

Bennett C. Clark was interviewed about his literary ambitions and his political aspirations. He had written a biography of John Quincy Adams.

April 26, 1932

The April meeting was held at the home of Mrs. Frank Schaberg, of the 4000 block of Flora Boulevard. Professor William Glasgow Bruce Carson presented **How to Write the One-Act Play**. Mrs. M. M. H. Malone and her committee reported on the play market.

October 25, 1932

The winners of the Florence Seidlitz Lyric Poetry Contest were announced at the home of Mrs. Thomas F. McDonald of the 100 block of South Gore Avenue in Webster Groves. Mrs. McDonald and Mrs. Percy M. Ludlow hosted the meeting. Mrs. Edwa Robert Moer, program chairman, presented Miss Elizabeth C. Robert of St. Louis, a former staff member of *Time Magazine* in New York, whose poems appeared in the *Saturday Review of Literature*. Miss Robert discussed editing "The Forecast" section of the St. Louis Review. Mrs. Rebeka Deitz, SLWG president, presided over the meeting, and Mrs. Elinor Maxwell McCord was the guest speaker.

The judges were Mrs. George C. Gephart; Dr. William Roy MacKenzie of the Washington University English Department; and Edgar Curtis Taylor, head of the Taylor School for Boys.

Monday, November 14, 1932

The prize-winning poems in the recent Florence Hess Seidlitz Lyric Poetry Contest by St. Louis Writers Guild were read at a meeting of the Women's Auxiliary of Grace Episcopal Church in Kirkwood. Each judge selected a different poem submitted by Mrs. Otis E. Turner, and so she was awarded first place for all three poems. Their titles were "The Pathway to the Moon," "To a Sun Dial," and "Reincarnation."

November 30, 1932

Members met at the home of Mrs. Edwa Robert Mooser of the 7000 block of Northmoor Drive. Mrs. Mooser and Miss Josephine Johnson jointly hosted the event, which was postponed from the previous night as a courtesy to Mrs. Walter J Knight. Her play, "More Latitude," was produced at the Wednesday Club. The play had won first prize in a contest from the Drama Study Section of the Wednesday Club.

Mrs. Moer and Mrs. Percy M. Ludlow presented the techniques of writing a short story using the Gallshaw books as a background.

The Florence Seidlitz Lyric Poetry Contest winners were announced. It was then announced the contest would be held the following year.

Tuesday, January 17, 1933

Mrs. Rebeka Deitz, SLWG President, presided over the annual dinner and open meeting at the Winston Churchill Apartments. A photo of her appeared alongside the article in the *St. Louis Post-Dispatch*.

Dr. Roland Usher of Washington University presented **The Pursuit of the Autor,** and Dr. Arthur E. Bostwick, St. Louis Librarian, spoke on **China-Its Present Day.**

Dr. Bostwick had visited China, at the invitation of the Chinese, representing the American Library Commission, to confer with the Chinese on libraries and library methods.

Mrs. Edwa Robert Moser was program chairman, and Mrs. Carl Hoffman was in charge of arrangements and reservations. An informal reception followed the dinner.

November 21, 1933

The November meeting was held a week early due to the Thanksgiving holiday. Mrs. Rebeka Deitz hosted the event at her home on Chamberlain Avenue. Mrs. Walter Knight served as chairman of the program. Mrs. W. K. Freudenberger presented her experiences collecting data for a genealogy book. Mrs. F. Schoenfeld read the prize-winning poem of the Baltimore League of American Pen Women, and Mrs. May Wilson Todd read two original poems. Mrs. Winifred Irwin read an original short story, and Dr. Cyrill Clemens presented an article on play writing.

No December meeting was held.

January 30, 1934

The winners of the SLWG Short Story Contest were awarded and the newly elected officers were announced.

February 27, 1934

Mr. and Mrs. Donald Wright hosted the Guild in their home

on the 600 block of Sherwood Drive in Webster Groves. Frederick Hazlett Brennan read and analyzed one of his stories, and Mrs. Margaretta Scott Lawlor reviewed her one-act play, "Three Kisses"

Mrs. George Malone, SLWG president, talked about current writing news and the four short story contest winners, H.R. Buerman, M. L. Hurni, Edward Orr, and Miss Ruth Josephine Baggot.

Mr. and Mrs. A. F. Satterthwait reported on the national meeting of the American Nature Study Society and the Association for the Advancement of Science in Boston.

Mrs. Genevieve Knapp McConnell spoke about the Safety Council playlets.

Mrs. Gustave Lippmann, discussed the Writers' Club's latest meeting.

Miss Margery Doud reported on the Library Group.
Mrs. Walter Knight invited members to the Creative Class.
Mrs. Rebeka Deitz talked about the Principia Articles Class.
Mrs. W.K. Freudenberger updated everyone on Missouri Writers.

Tuesday, March 27, 1934

The meeting was held at the home of Mr. and Mrs. George Seidlitz, of the 6000 block of Clemens Avenue. Donald Wright presented, **What has Helped me Most in my Writing Career**. Mrs. Thomas MacDonald reviewed her prize-winning story published in *Cosmopolitan Magazine*. Anonymous stories written by members were read by Mrs. Walter Knight, and critiques were given by Mrs. Rebeka Deitz, Mrs. Seidlitz, Mrs. Genevieve McConnell, Mrs. W.K. Freudenberger, A.F. Satterthwait, Mrs. Winifred Irwin, Mrs. MacDonald, and Mrs. Otis Turner. Two new members, Mrs. Franklin Miller and Dr. Harvey Howard, were welcomed into the Guild.

Tuesday, April 24, 1934

Members met at the home of Mrs. Winifred Irwin in the Park Plaza Hotel. Mrs. Rebeka Deitz discussed literary groups. Mrs. Otis Turner read her poem, "Imprisonment," and Mrs. Gustave

Lippman read her poem, "God in Man," which had received third and fourth honorable mentions in the Wednesday Club poetry contest.

Charles Compton reviewed his article published in American Mercury. Mrs. George Malone read her article, "Bridge Brings 'Em Out," published in *Household Magazine*.

Donald Wright presented **Your Most Difficult Point in Writing and How You Have Mastered It**.

Lastly, letters from out-of-town members were read.

Tuesday, May 29, 1934

Members met at the home of Mr. and Mrs. A.F. Satterthwait on Waverly Place in Webster Groves, where a buffet supper was served in the garden at 6:30 p.m.

Mrs. W.K. Freudenberger reviewed the talks made during Journalism Week at Columbia, MO, including Thomas H. Uzzell and Sumner Blossom, editor of *American Magazine*.

The history of the Guild was the second feature on the program. The President, Mrs. George Malone, presented **Play Days and Good Old Times Since 1920**.

Mr. Donald Wright oversaw the – Three Guild Histories – "Formation of the Guild," written by Louis Dodge, was read by Mrs. G. K. Seidlitz. "Frolicking with Guilders," written by Mrs. May Wilson Todd, was read by Mrs. Thomas MacDonald. An anthology of poems of Guild members, which was published in a St. Louis newspaper in 1925, was read by Mrs. Winfred Irwin.

The program chairman, Mrs. Carl Hoffman, read "Ancient Announcements and Cards." "Fashion Notes by a Scientist" was read by Mr. A. F. Satterthwait. Old members talked about interesting incidents and stories from SLWG's history.

Tuesday, October 30, 1934

The meeting was hosted by Mr. and Mrs. Paul Deitz at The Cottage on the corner of Chamberlain and Belt Avenues. The Winifred Irwin Short Story Contest, sponsored by the Guild was announced, and all manuscripts were to be sent to president, Mrs. George Malone, Bellevue Avenue. The Florence Seidlitz Poetry

Contest closed on October 30.

"Now in November" was reviewed by the author, Miss Josephine Johnson. **I Meet Earl Stanley Gardner and Roger Torrey,** was given by Mrs. Carl Hoffman. Casper S. Yost, editor of the editorial page of the Globe-Democrat, spoke on editorial writing. Donald Wright read "How Famous Writers Write," and gave a talk about, **How I Write. Mrs**. Clara Alger of Webster Groves was welcomed as a new member.

January 6, 1935

The Winifred Irwin short story contest, sponsored by the St. Louis Writers' Guild, closed on Thursday, January 10, at midnight.

The contest was open to any writer in the metropolitan area of St. Louis. About 100 manuscripts were entered, Mrs. Malone reported.

January 29, 1935

Members met at the home of Mrs. Walter J. Knight in the 6000 block of Pershing Avenue to elect officers for 1935 and the winners of the Guild's tenth annual contest were announced. Thirty manuscripts were submitted. The subject was any historical sketch. (*I'm not certain why the newspaper claimed this was the tenth annual contest. From all records, this was the 15th contest held by SLWG. However, this does relate to an old myth that SLWG wasn't officially incorporated until 1925, but there was no evidence of this in the records.*)

January 31, 1935

Prizes were awarded in the Winifred Irwin Short Story Contest at 8 p.m. Thursday at the Cabanne Branch Library, 1106 Union Boulevard. The meeting was attended by contest officials, participants, and their friends. Contestants submitted one story on any subject, ranging in length from 1000 to 5000 words. First prize was $10, and second prize was $5. Two honorable mentions were awarded.

Included on the program were Mrs. M. M. H. Malone, president of the St. Louis Writers Guild; Mrs. Bertram Hoffman, Mrs. Winifred Irwin, Miss Josephine Johnson, Casper S. Yost, Mrs.

Walter J. Knight, A.F. Satterthwait, chairman of the judges, and Miss Margery Doud, who read the prize stories.

Thomas L. Williams of Enright Avenue, University City, a 23-year-old clerk at the International Shoe Co., received the first prize of $10. Second prize was awarded to Joseph D. Nolan Jr., 24-year-old salesman. Honorable Mentions was given to Mrs. H. B. Tinker of McCausland Avenue, and Miss Dorothy Angove of Mexico, MO.

Tuesday, May 28, 1935

The final meeting of the Season was held at the home of Mrs. F. Schaberg on Flora Boulevard. An informal talk was given by Miss Josephine Johnson, winner of the Pulitzer Prize for her book, *Now in November*, and Miss Marle Cooper, winner of the Artists' League of America national radio contest for her song, "Love Girl." The response was given by Casper Yost.

R. Jennings, principal of Clayton High School, spoke about the Scribblers' Club of Clayton High School. Miss Ruth Duhme discussed her Ann Arbor prize poem, "Music as a Therapy."

There was a round table discussion on **What You Are Writing?**

November 26, 1935

Mrs. Alice Lipman won the Florence Seidlitz Lyric Poetry Contest

Tuesday, January 28, 1936

Prof. Richard F. Jones of Washington University lectured on poetry at the home of Captain and Mrs. Donald T. Wright on Sherwood Drive in Webster Groves.

Winners of the annual essay contest were announced by Mrs. Guthrie McConnell, chairman of the contest. They also elected officers.

Saturday, February 1, 1936

The second annual Winifred Irwin Short Story Contest for young non-professional writers was announced by Mrs. Gutherie

McConnell, contest chairman. It continued until midnight on March 4. The contest was open to nonprofessional writers between the ages of 18 and 25, who resided in the St. Louis metropolitan district. Stories were limited to 3000 words, and had to be typed on one side of the paper only and accompanied by an addressed and stamped return envelope. Entries were sent to Mrs. Guthrie McConnell on North Newstead Avenue.

March 18, 1936, 7:30 p.m.
John G. Cole won the second Winifred Irwin Short Story Contest, in a ceremony at the Cabanne Branch Library, 1106 Union Boulevard.

November 24, 1936
The last meeting of the year was held at the home of Mrs. Gustave Lippmann on Alexander Drive in Clayton.

Miss Inez Stekman, head of the English department of the City College of Law and Finance, read "Strawberry Pickings," which was published in the *Atlantic Monthly*, and Saunders Cumming of Webster Groves read his mystery story, "The Veiled Prophet Murder."

Tuesday, February 21, 1937
Members met at the Winston Churchill Apartments. Mrs. Anita Knight spoke about her trip to Hollywood.

December 4, 1939
The *St. Louis Post-Dispatch* ran a photo of a Guild Meeting, captioned, "Members of the St. Louis Writers Guild, made up of authors of published books or articles, chatting after a recent meeting. From left, Robert Hereford, Mrs. Fannie Cook, Louis Cochran and Mrs. Walter J Knight." (*Photo could not be shown due to copyright issues.*)

The History of St. Louis Writers Guild

FIRST ANNUAL
WRITERS' CONFERENCE

BROWN HALL,
WASHINGTON UNIVERSITY
ST. LOUIS, MISSOURI

SEPTEMBER 27, 28, 1946

Sponsored by University College and
St. Louis Writers' Guild

Conference Program from 1946

13 |
The St. Louis Writers' Guild in the 1940s

After the highs of the 1920s and 1930s, St. Louis Writers Guild stepped into the 1940s, the war years, with renewed vigor. As the world departed and returned from the Second Great War, the writers of this city banded together and encouraged one another. Even as this city faced off against itself in the 1944 World Series as the St. Louis Cardinals defeated the St. Louis Browns, the Guild continued to thrive. One dramatic shift occurred: the organization became dominated by playwrights and journalists, moving away from novelists and short story writers, a change brought on, perhaps, by events in the world. St. Louis Writers Guild was founded by a couple of journalists, and many journalists had been members in the 1920s. That shifted toward novelists and short story writers in the thirties, but in the 1940s, everyone appeared to be connected to the newspapers in one way or another.

The number of one-act plays, scenarios, monologues, and full musical or multi-act productions was one reason the playwright dominated the forties and fifties.

St. Louis Writers Guild still held meetings in members' living rooms, with dinner often laid out in a member's garden, or even the common rooms of places like the Chase Park Plaza Hotel, or the Winston Churchill Apartments, named for the author and not the British Statesman. Some public places, like the tearooms or clubhouses of the day, were used for special events.

The History of St. Louis Writers Guild

As journalists dominated St. Louis Writers Guild, they increasingly became the featured speakers at the University of Missouri's Journalism Week. In 1949, James A. Worsham, president of St. Louis Writers Guild, was one of the featured speakers at Journalism Week. St. Louis Writers Guild members had long been featured speakers at the Missouri Writers' Guild's annual meeting held either at the beginning or the end of Journalism Week, but with more prestigious journalists, both Journalism Week and the Missouri Writers' Guild featured more and more presentations by St. Louis Writers Guild members.

St. Louis Writers Guild's First Writers' Conference

The biggest and most standout events of the 1940s were the writers' conferences. Starting in 1946, St. Louis Writers Guild conducted its first conference, a grand event held at Washington University. SLWG had been part of other conferences and conventions since the 1920s, but this was the first one planned and produced by the SLWG itself. A program from this event still exists in the archive and was photocopied by David Motherwell. Every year, the Mayor of St. Louis opened the event with a keynote speech. The descriptions conveyed the impression this was one of the preeminent writers' conferences in the Midwest.

The First Annual Writers' Conference was held in Brown Hall at Washington University on September 27 and 28, 1946. The event was sponsored by the University College and St. Louis Writers Guild.

It cost $5 ($70 in 2019) to attend all the lectures, conference groups, and reception; or $2 ($28) to attend a single workshop.

The conference administrative board consisted of:

From the University College: Willis Howard Reals, Ph.D. and Eugene R. Page, Ph.D.

From St. Louis Writers Guild: Ruth Rodgers Johnson, President; Rose L. Brown, Conference Chairman; and James A. Worsham, Vice Chairman.

Members of the SLWG conference committee: Bert Hoffman, Frank E. Poindexter, Norah Berford Morgan, Ruth Grosby, Emily Berry Pope, Robert Hereford, and Margaret Powers

Greenbury.

St. Louis Writers Guild brought the community together with this event. Known as Cooperating Groups, they represented much of the literary community within the city. The Cooperating Groups were the St. Louis Board of Education, Radio Council of St. Louis, Brown Pen Club, Pen Women of America, College Club, Wednesday Club of St. Louis, St. Louis Newspapers, and St. Louis Radio Stations.

People registered by mailing a check payable to: Registrar – Norah Berford Morgan, 122 E. Adams Avenue, Kirkwood 22, Mo.

Below are the speakers for the conference:

Who's Who on the Conference Platform (Their title, not mine)

O.K. Armstrong – Contributor to *Reader's Digest* and other well-known magazines

Jack Bennett – In Charge of Special Events Broadcasts, Radio Station KWK

Dorothy Blackwell – Assistant, Division of Audio-Visual Education, St. Louis Schools

Alexander Buchan – Dept. of English, Washington University

Peggy Cave – Director of Women's Activities, Radio Station KSD

Ruth Collins – Well known Writer for "pulp" magazines.

Fannie Cook – Author of *The Hill Grows Steeper*, *Boot Heel Doctor*, *Mrs. Palmer's Honey*, also short stories

Elaine Debus – Audio-Visual Education, St. Louis Public Schools.

Teresa Fitzpatrick – *Atlantic Monthly*

Ruth Grosby – author of *Barbara Ann* series

June Geraghty – *St. Louis Star-Times*

Loyd Haberly – Dept of English, Washington University

Dr. Bertram Hughes – News Analyst, Radio Station KXOK

Robert Hereford – Author of *Old Man River*, Special Articles, *St. Louis Globe-Democrat*

Fannie Hurst – Author of *Stardust, Back Street, Humoresque,*

Gaslight Sonatas
>   Lt. Roger Johnson – Editor *Saipan Target*
>   Reverend Elmer Knoernschild – production manager Radio station KFOU
>   Don Lochner – Programs Director Radio Station WEW
>   Edwa Moser – Author of *The Mexican Touch, Wedding Day*
>   Mildred Planthold – *St. Louis Globe-Democrat*
>   Fay Profilet – *St. Louis Post-Dispatch*
>   Shirley Seifert – Author of *Waters of the Wilderness, River out of Eden, Captain Grant.*
>   Edgar Taylor – Director of Taylor School for Boys
>   Ben Wilson – Director of Continuity, Radio Station KMOX
>   James A. Worsham – author of *The Art of Persuading People, Winning Your Way, Low Pressure Selling*
>   Sewell Peaslee Wright – Contributor to S*aturday Evening Post, Good Housekeeping* magazines and other well-known publications.

The conference featured publishers taking pitches. Quoting from the brochure, "Publishers' representatives hope to attend and meet the authors. The following publishers are especially interested in receiving your manuscripts – D. Appleton, Dodd, Mead and Company, Bobbs-Merrill, Duell, Sloan and Pearce, Henry Holt and Company, L. B. Fischer, Alfred A. Knopf, Little Brown and Company, Farrar and Rinehart, Reynal and Hitchcock Inc. Bring your manuscripts."

There was also a place within the conference to display books by Missouri authors.

The conference schedule was packed with lectures from prominent writers and discussion groups on pertinent topics. A reception took place on the second floor of Brown Hall after the Saturday evening program. All members of the conference were invited to meet the authors and guests in attendance.

The conference began at 10 a.m. on Friday with an opening speech from Dr. Eugene R. Page and Ruth Rodgers Johnson. This was followed by "Tribulations of an Army Editor" with Lt. Roger L. Johnson, "Feature Writing" with Robert Hereford, "Accent on Living" with Teresa Fitzpatrick, and "The Historical Novel" with Shirley Seifert. The morning was presided over by James A. Worsham and ended at noon for lunch.

The conference resumed at 2 p.m. for small group discussions on Feature Writing, Short Story, Poetry, and a whole track of Radio Writing, from Basic Rules, Commercial Radio Writing, Preparing the News, and a Demonstration of FM Broadcasting.

The event continued on Saturday, from 2 p.m. to 4 p.m. with small group discussions on "Write About Things You Know," "Poetry," and "Writing for the Juvenile." Then the conference took a break until 8 p.m. when it continued with "Grass Roots in Literature," "The Novel," and "Auld Lang Syne."

The Second Annual Writers' Conference

On Sunday, September 14, 1947, an article ran in the *St. Louis Globe-Democrat* titled "Editors Held Human in Error of Judgment."

"'There is no editor whose taste is not bad at times,' Nelson Antrim Crawford, editor of Household Magazine, confessed last night in the closing address of the two-day second annual writers conference at Washington University.

"'Maybe he got up with a bad taste in his mouth,' Crawford explained. 'Maybe he had a quarrel with the foreman of his composing room. Such factors warp the judgement of an editor, just as they warp the judgement of anyone else, for incredible as it may sometimes seem, editors are human beings.'"

The second conference, held on Friday and Saturday, was once again sponsored by SLWG and University College. Speakers included Robert A. Hereford and Beulah Schacht, feature writers for the *St. Louis Globe-Democrat*. The conference closed with a reception in Brown Hall.

The Third Writers' Conference

The third annual St. Louis Writers' Conference at Washington University was held on September 17 and 18, 1948.

Speakers included well-known writers from Missouri and Illinois, including Fannie Cook, author of the best seller, *Boot Heel Doctor*; Shirley Seifert, author of *Captain Grant, The Proud Way*, and other books; and Sewell Peaslee Wright, contributor to *This Week*, *The Saturday Evening Post*, and other national magazines.

On the two-day program were classes in fiction, nonfiction, playwriting, poetry, and radio writing conducted by authorities in each field.

The conference ended with a Round Table discussion on modern writing, presided over by Sterling Harkins, radio and television producer for KSD and KSD-TV. Also serving on the panel besides Mrs. Cook, Miss Seifert, and Mr. Wright, were Leonard Hall, *St. Louis Post-Dispatch* columnist; Robert Hereford, *St. Louis Globe-Democrat* feature writer and author of *Old Man River*; and Kensinger Jones, author of the radio program *The Land We Live In*.

St. Louis Writers Guild and University College of Washington University sponsored the conference. Once again, information or conference registration was handled by Norah Berford Morgan, registrar.

The History of SLWG as told by Robert Hereford

For St. Louis Writers Guild's 25th Anniversary, Robert Hereford wrote a history for the *St. Louis Globe-Democrat*. It ran on Sunday, September 22, 1946.

Many Writers Now Famous Got Start Here
by Robert A. Hereford
Globe-Democrat Staff Writer

"I see in the newspapers," remarked a friend the other day, "where Fannie Hurst may come to St. Louis next weekend for a Writers' Conference to be sponsored jointly by Washington University and the St. Louis Writers Guild. I naturally, have heard of Fannie Hurst, who went to fame from St. Louis, as a short story writer and novelist; I am familiar with Washington University, but what is the St. Louis Writers' Guild?

To one familiar with the activities of the Writers' Guild and brilliant array of authors associated with it during its quarter of a century of existence, many of whom have become nationally known, the question bordered on sacrilege. It seemed unbelievable that an organization which had brought so much publicity to the city through the reflected glory of its literary sons and daughters should not itself be better known locally.

Some research, however, revealed hoe little had been written about the Guild, whose members had written so much and so capably about a variety of other things. An appeal for data was made to Mrs. Ruth Johnson, 4024 Hartford st. short story writer, who is the current present of the St. Louis Writers Organization.

Group First Met 26 Years Ago

Twenty-six years ago, it seems a handful of St. Louisans, having the common interest of creative writing met at the home of Miss Shirley Seifert on De Giverville avenue. Several had been approached, Miss Seifert recalls, to join a state writers' group of literary St. Louisans found one another's company so congenial and stimulating that they decide to form an organization of their own.

Thus was born the St. Louis Writers' Guild.

So far as can be determined, no formal minutes were kept at that pioneer meeting, but among those present to the best of Miss Seiferts's knowledge, were Sam Hellman, Temple Bailey, Louis Dodge, Elinor Maxwell, Ralph Mooney, Margaretta Lawlor, Capt. Donald Wright, Susan Boogher, Robertus Love and Miss Seifert herself.

The list reads as though it might have been lifted from a directory of successful American writers. Hellman, who was installed as the president of the Guild, is a former managing editor of the old St. Louis Republic, later became nationally known for his slangy classics in the Saturday Evening Post, and now is one of the giants among the Hollywood screen writers.

Temple Bailey's books, such as "The Green Lantern" are classics in their field, and her reputation as a novelist speaks for itself. Elinor Maxwell, whose column runs each Sunday in the Globe-Democrat, also is a nationally known novelist. Robertus Love, who wrote the "Rise and Fall of Jesse James" was a St. Louis Newspaper man as was Louis Dodge, who later became a successful short story writer and playwright. Ralph Mooney, Margaretta Lawler and Capt. Donald Wright are familiar to St. Louisans, the first for his noels, Miss Lawler for her plays, and articles and Capt. Wright as publisher of the Waterways Journal which helps keep alive St. Louis' rich river traditions.

Miss Seifert herself, who was to become the second president of the Guild, has established a reputation as one of the country's foremost writers of historical fiction with such books as "Waters of the Wilderness, and "Captain Grant."

There are many human-interest stories to challenge the typewriters of its members tucked away in the roster of unusual personalities who have joined the Guild. There was Louis Cochran, a vice president of the Guild, who regular vocation was that of a G-man, but who spent his spare time writing novels about share-croppers. The studios-looking federal agent found real life drama in his work. He was one of the band of G-men who rounded up and shot to death a noted bandit on a St. Louis street.

A former president of the Guild is Dr. Harvey J. Howard, noted eye specialist, and father of Col. James Howard, army flyer and one of the heroes of World War II, who is now aviation expert for the city. Dr. Howard a captive for "Ten Weeks With Chinese Bandits," made a best seller book of his experience. Frederick Hazlett Brennan, former Globe-Democrat reporter, now one of the country's leading short story writers, a playwright and a Hollywood screenist, was a Guild member.

A regular attendant at Guild meetings is Franklin Miller, former Circuit Attorney, whose wife, Mrs. Maude Miller, is the author of poetry which has been published in the Saturday Evening Post, among other magazines.

The career of the three Seifert Sisters, Shirley, Adele, who writes detective novels, and Mrs. John Gasparotti, whose book to that of the three famous Bronte Sisters.

Among the novelist Guild members who have won national prizes are Josephine Johnson, whose "Now in November" was a Pulitzer Prize Winner, and Mrs. Fannie Cook, who won a national competition with her "Mrs. Palmers' Honey."

Well Known St. Louisans Members

The Later Casper Yost, editor of the editorial page of the St. Louis Globe-Democrat, author of numerous books, including a text on journalism, was a Guild member and a speaker at Guild functions.

Among former presidents of the organization are Mrs. Walter J. Knight, playwright and short story writer; Mrs. Carl Hoffman, short story writer; Mrs. Nelson Pope, playwright; Mrs. David Bruce Alger, short story writer; James A. Worsham, book author and article writers.

One of the Qualifications for membership in the Guild is that an applicant have published in a magazine of national circulation two short stories, articles or poems or that he have published at least one book.

The organization recently reached a high point in endeavor when in conjunction with Washington University it made plans to promote the writers' conference. Among notables scheduled to appear in addition to Fannie Hurst, who is tentively scheduled are Sewall Peasley Wright, short story writer, and O.K. Armstrong whose articles appear in national magazines. A number of publishers' representatives also are expected.

Helping with arrangements for the ambitious program have been Mrs. Rose Brown and Mrs. Francis Greenbury. The Guild appears determined to carry on in the traditions of these two great literary figures of an earlier St. Louis, Eugene Field and Marion Reedy.

St. Louis Writers Guild 25th Anniversary

On November 15, 1948, St. Louis Writers Guild celebrated twenty-five years with a silver anniversary dinner at the Missouri Athletic Club. The guest speaker, Harnett T. Kane of New Orleans, discussed his novel, *Bride of Fortune*, based on the life of Mrs.

Jefferson Davis. The *St. Louis Globe-Democrat* quoted him as saying, "The southern states are producing some of the best writers."

Other featured speakers were O.K. Armstrong, staff correspondent of Reader's Digest; Mrs. Walter J. Knight, who discussed poetry; Robert Hereford, author of Old Man River, who told river stories; and Williams H. Reals, who spoke about St. Louis Writers Guild's annual Writers' Conference in association with Washington University. Mrs. Rose L. Brown was the general chairman for the evening and introduced the speakers.

A number of St. Louis authors were honored, including Fannie Cook, Shirley Seifert, Fannie Hurst, Elinor Maxwell, Dr. Harvey J. Howard, Edwa Moser, Eugene R. Page, and Don Lechner.

Mrs. Nelson Pope, Mrs. David Alger, Mrs. Frank Morgan, Mrs. Carl Hoffman, and Mrs. Irl Johnson hosted the dinner, which had a cocktail party beforehand.

The answer to the riddle of why they held the 25th Anniversary in the Guild's 28th Season was difficult to ascertain. They didn't mention a reason, though it plays into a long-held rumor that St. Louis Writers Guild, though founded in 1920, didn't incorporate until a couple of years later. This may be the case, but there was no evidence, only a whisper spread through the decades.

The Presidents
1940 – Bert Hoffman
1941 – Ralph Mooney
*1942 – Emily Pope, (Mrs. Nelson Pope)
1943 – James A. Worsham
**1944 – Clare Fleeman Alger
*1945 – Clare Fleeman Alger
1946 – Ruth Rodgers Johnson
**1947 – Norah Morgan
**1948 – James A. Worsham
*1949 – Franklin E. Poindexter

** Name changed to correct the list. * Information discovered through research. **Bold** means it has been confirmed.

Board Members from this time:
1947
Norah Morgan, president
James A. Worsham, vice-president
Mrs. W. C. Collins, secretary
F. E. Poindexter, treasurer

1948
James A Worsham, president
Ruth Collins, vice president
Frank Poindexter, treasurer
Ruth Grosby, secretary

1949
Franklin E. Poindexter, president
Ruth Grosby, vice president
Mrs. Chester McPheeters, secretary
Mrs. Morgan, treasurer

Members from the 1940s
Clare Fleeman Alger (Mrs. D. Bruce Alger) - President 1944 and 1945

Clare Fleeman Alger, poet and writer, contributed to a variety of religious and literary publications throughout her life. She married David Bruce Alger on October 13, 1916. David Alger worked in the banking industry for much of his life. They had a son, Bruce Reynolds Alger, who was born in Dallas, Texas, on June 12, 1918. Then the family moved to Webster Groves.

Bruce, her son, enlisted in the Army Air Corps after the attack on Pearl Harbor. He was stationed with the Fifth Squadron at the Army Air Corps Advanced Flying School at Kerry Field, Texas, and eventually saw action in the Pacific theater in 1945. He later represented Texas' 5th District in the United States House of Representatives (1955-1965).

The Clare Fleeman Alger collection contained correspondence and documents which included several religious tracts, as well as drafts of poetry and essays. In a series of letters to her parents, friends, and family, Clare described her life as a newlywed and, later, as a new mother.

Also contained in the collection were Clare's manuscript submission records, an account of every submission she'd ever made. A series of index cards, grouped alphabetically by poem or essay title, held the name of the work, the publication she submitted to, and the date. The cards run from 1917 to 1943. Rejection letters and various drafts were also included.

Ruth Rodgers Johnson, President 1946

Ruth R. Johnson was a writer and musician. Not only a contributor to national magazines, Ruth was state music chairman of the Missouri Federated Clubs in the 1930s, a past president of the St. Louis Writers Guild and a past president of Mu Phi Epsilon, a music sorority. She hosted St. Louis Writers Guild meetings in her house in the 4000 block of Hartford Street near Tower Grove Park. She married Irl Johnson and they had a son, Rodger, and three grandchildren. Ruth passed away on October 26, 1970, two days before SLWG's 50th Anniversary at the age of 77.

Norah Berford Morgan (Mrs. Frank H. Morgan), President 1947

Norah Morgan was an important part of the St. Louis Writers Guild for decades. Though she only helmed the organization for a couple of years, she served many other duties such as vice-president and treasurer. However, she wins one of the longevity awards for her work as the contest coordinator. For decades, starting in the 1930s and lasting at least until the 1960s, her address at 121 East Adams in Kirkwood was the mailing address where everyone submitted their contest entries and other payments. Sometimes her address or the information address was listed as 122 East Adams, and currently no building exists at that address, but rumor was it may have been a duplex, or small apartment building that the Morgans owned.

Norah and Frank H. Morgan were longtime residents of Kirkwood, Missouri. They had five children; their youngest, Jean Young, went to Canada with several other debutantes shortly after graduating high school. In 1932, The Society Section of the *St. Louis Post-Dispatch* recounted the trip to meet her aunt and uncle and told the story of how she and her friends were presented to the Governor of Ottawa.

F. E. Poindexter, President, 1949

Franklin E. Poindexter was an Associate Professor of Physics at St. Louis University. He appeared in many scientific journals and industry-related publications like *Marine Electrochemistry*, and *An Introduction to Coal Technology*. He had a patent listed in 1959. He lived in the 1000 block South McKnight Road in Richmond Heights.

James A. Worsham, President, 1948

James Worsham was born in Long Beach, California, and beyond serving as president of St. Louis Writers Guild, he was also president of Missouri Writers' Guild in 1951. He was the author of *The Art of Persuading People*, *Winning Your Way*, and *Low Pressure Selling*.

Workshops and Events
Tuesday, October 24, 1948, 7 p.m.

Can Feature Articles Be Sold? was presented by Miss Mildred Weller. James A. Worsham, SLWG President, presided over the meeting at the Winston Churchill Apartments.

March 28, 1949

Franklin E. Poindexter of Richmond Heights, former associate professor of physics at St. Louis University, was elected president of the St. Louis Writers Guild at the monthly meeting held at the home of Mrs. Norah Morgan.

April 14, 1949

James A. Worsham was a featured speaker for Journalism Week at Missouri University, which included the Missouri Writers' Guild's annual meeting.

Brad R. Cook

Dr. Alfred F. Satterthwait, President 1929
1929 *St. Louis Globe Democrat*

14 |
The St. Louis Writers Guild in the 1950s

St. Louis Writers Guild stepped into American expansion with the same exuberance that had overtaken the country. As the St. Louis Browns left for Baltimore and the Red Scare enveloped the world, St. Louis Writers Guild was described as the centerpiece of the region's literary community. Its members consisted of the leading journalists of their day, numerous writers for the biggest magazines and publications of the day, and a few playwrights and novelists. St. Louis Writers Guild served as the main social group and professional network for the literary elite in the city and the surrounding region. Whereas the 1940s had been dominated by names like Ralph Mooney and Robert Hereford, now, members like Ruth and Dr. Jerome Grosby and Florence Armstrong guided the Guild. However, many names like Norah Morgan and James A. Worsham, remained with the organization and ensured the continuation of SLWG traditions.

The Monthly Meeting

In the 1950s, the monthly St. Louis Writers Guild meeting was held on the third Wednesday night of each month at Nelson's Café, Lindbergh Boulevard and U.S. Highway 66. Full SLWG membership was for professional writers, and applicants had to meet certain publication requirements. Aspiring authors could join as associate members, who had no voting powers and could not serve as officers but could attend and participate in SLWG events and contests.

Meetings were still held in members' houses, like Franklin E. Poindexter, Mrs. Fred Armstrong, or Mr. and Mrs. Grosby, but more and more, they were beginning to meet in the tearooms. Places like the Castlereagh Tea Room on Delmar Boulevard in the University City Loop, had small round tables covered in linen. They served hot tea, small sandwiches, and other fare.

St. Louis Writers Guild also held a yearly award dinner, usually in October. The winners of the contests were honored and other awards were handed out. The event was held for many years at Nelson's Café, Hwy. 66 and Lindbergh.

By 1957, St. Louis Writers Guild boasted 50 members, most of whom were professional writers and well published for their day. Most worked for the newspapers as columnists, reporters, or feature writers, but members wrote for all aspects of the publishing industry, like plays, short stories for magazines, novels, and poetry.

The Writers' Conferences continued into the 1950s

The 7th Annual Writers Conference, October 16-17, 1953

Pulitzer Prize Winner Hodding Carter, celebrated author Arthemise Goetz; several other authors, noted magazine editors, poets, and newspaper editors, spoke at the Seventh Annual Writers' Conference sponsored by St. Louis Writers Guild.

The two-day conference included a series of lectures and a dinner-discussions by noted professionals in the field of writing. The event was open to the public and was held in the SBF Founders' Hall. To attend, one registered and paid the fee at Stix, Baer, & Fuller's Street Floor Information Desk.

St. Louis Writers Guild held a banquet in the Missouri Room of Stix, Baer & Fuller Co. at 6:30 p.m. during the two-day conference to honor the members of Missouri Writers' Guild who attended as guests of St. Louis Writers Guild. The following day, on the 17th at 6:30 p.m., at the Mark Twain Hotel, Missouri Writers' Guild held its annual banquet. Charles C. Clayton, Globe-Democrat editorial writer, addressed the group on "Fact Gathering as a Basis of the Writer's Work."

St. Louis Writers Guild partnered with Missouri Writers'

Guild, the St. Louis branch of the National League of American Penwomen, and Stix Baer & Fuller Department Store.

Saga of the Meramec

In 1953, Mrs. Bess Gephart wrote the play *Saga of the Meramec*. As the play entered production, Mrs. Gephart passed away. Dorothy O. Moore, Secretary of St. Louis Writers Guild, who was involved with production, stepped forward to ensure they opened on time. *Saga of the Meramec* honored Bess Gephart, both at the performances and in the reviews, which mentioned it was quite a successful production.

The Presidents
1950 – Ruth Grosby – 20th President
1951 – Ruth Grosby
1952 – Florence Armstrong
1953 – Dr. Jerome S. Grosby, DDS.
1954 – Marion O'Brien
1955 – Marion O'Brien
1956 – Charles Norton
1957 – **Nicolette Stack** (Nicolete Stack)
1958 – **Caroline Ward** (Mrs. Thomas H. Ward)
1959 – Charles Guenther

* information discovered through research; **bold** means it has been confirmed.

Board Members from this time:
1951
Ruth S. Grosby, President
Florence Armstrong, Vice President
Dorothy O. Moore, Secretary
Norah Morgan, Treasurer

1952
Florence Armstrong, President
Dr Jerome Grosby, Vice President
Dorothy O. Moore, Secretary

The History of St. Louis Writers Guild

L.L. Armantrout, Treasurer

1958
Caroline Ward, President
Charles Guenther, Vice president
Mrs. Chester J. McPheeters, Secretary
Mrs. A. B. Squires, Treasurer.

Members from the 1950s
Bess Gephart

Bess Gephart was a member of St. Louis Writers Guild, and the playwright of *Saga of the Meramec* (1953).

Dr. Jerome S. Grosby, President 1953

Jerome and Ruth Grosby were one of several husband and wife duos to be involved in the Guild. Not only did they host many SLWG events at their home on Broadview Drive in Clayton, both served as president of St. Louis Writers Guild.

Dr. Jerome S. Grosby was a dentist, teacher, and columnist. An oral surgeon with offices in University City, he specialized in treating persons needing dental surgery who had heart problems. A member of the board of director of the St. Louis Heart Association, he was a professor of oral surgery at Washington University and at St. Louis University. He earned his doctorate at Washington University in 1929.

Dr. Grosby wrote a weekly column called "Your Dental Health" for the *St. Louis Globe-Democrat* for about 10 years.

He passed away in January 1985 at his home in Clayton at the age of 78.

Ruth Grosby, President 1950 and 1951

Ruth Grosby was the author of the *Barbara Ann* series. She not only led the organization for a couple of years, and served on board for many more, she also hosted events, served as chairman for others, and helped out with contests, the writers' conference and other St. Louis Writers Guild Events. Along with her husband,

Jerome, they influenced the Guild for many years. They lived on Broadview Drive in Clayton with their daughter, Jane, and son, James.

Dorothy O. Moore
Dorothy O. Moore was secretary of St. Louis Writers Guild in 1953. When Bess Gephart passed away, she helped ensure the production of *Saga of the Meramec* completed its run.

Workshops and Events
Wednesday, January 23, 1951
Elections were held at the monthly meeting at Nelson's Café, Lindbergh Boulevard and Hwy 66. Ruth Grosby was elected president, Mrs. Fred Armstrong, vice-president; Mrs. Dorothy O. Moore, secretary; and Mrs. Frank Morgan, treasurer. They also discussed the short story contest, which was open to the public.

January 30, 1952
Florence Armstrong, a member of the *St. Louis Globe-Democrat* editorial staff, was elected SLWG president at the monthly meeting.

Wednesday, October 15, 1952, 6:30 p.m.
St. Louis Writers Guild honored Fannie Hurst with a dinner in the Women's Building of Washington University. Miss Hurst was in town to celebrate the university's centennial. Plans for the SLWG Writers' Conference to be held at Washington University the following April were presented.

October 16-17, 1953
Pulitzer Prize Winner, Hodding Carter, and other celebrated authors, spoke at the Seventh Annual Writers' Conference sponsored by St. Louis' Writers' Guild, in the SBF Founders' Hall.

The two-day conference included a series of lectures and a dinner-discussions by noted writing professionals. The event was open to the public.

The History of St. Louis Writers Guild

Those interested needed to enroll and pay the registration fee at Stix, Baer, & Fuller's Street Floor Information Desk. St. Louis Writers Guild held a banquet in the Missouri Room of Stix, Baer & Fuller Co. at 6:30 p.m. during the two-day conference.

St. Louis Writers Guild held a banquet to honor the members of Missouri Writers' Guild on the 17th at 6:30 p.m., at the Mark Twain Hotel. Missouri Writers Guild held its annual banquet. Charles C. Clayton, *Globe-Democrat* editorial writer addressed the group on Fact Gathering as a Basis of the Writer's Work.

August 15, 1955

The short story contest for unpublished writers closed on August 15, 1955. Manuscripts were sent to Mrs. Edward A. Kruger on Parkside Drive, Clayton.

October 10, 1955

St. Louis Writers Guild celebrated Poetry Week and the formation of the St. Louis Poetry Center. Acting Mayor Donald Gunn signed the proclamation. Looking on were Mrs. Glenn Burroughs, Mrs. W.C. Collins, Charles Guenther, and Mrs. Nicholas J. Donnelly. A program began at noon and was held in the Young People's Room at the Public Library; poems were read by Tennessee Williams, Dylan Thomas, and T.S. Eliott. The event was sponsored by St. Louis Writers Guild, National League of American Pen Women, and the Poetry Center.

October 27, 1955

The annual awards dinner was held at Nelson's Café, Hwy 66 (Watson Road) and Lindbergh Boulevard.

April 11, 1957

Mrs. Allene Albrecht, an SLWG member who was featured in the April issue of *This Day*, delivered a lecture about her recent trip to the Holy Land. The article included color photos of Mrs. Albrecht in the Holy Land. She was a teacher at the Gethsemane School in St. Louis. Accompanying Mrs. Albrecht were 74 members of the Lutheran Missouri Synod.

Wednesday, November 17, 1957, 6:30 p.m.
Forest E. Wolverton, executive director of the St. Louis Suburban Teachers Association, discussed Missouri writers at the Castlereagh Tea Room, 6820 Delmar Boulevard, University City.

Wednesday, January 17, 1958
Caroline Ward was elected as president for 1958 at the Castlereagh Tea Room, 6820 Delmar Boulevard, University City. She succeeded Nicolette Stack as president of the 50-member guild.

Wednesday, April 16, 1958, 6:30 p.m.
The St. Louis Public Library and its Services, was presented by chief librarian Louis M. Nourse at the Castlereagh Tea Room, 6820 Delmar Boulevard, University City. The talk was illustrated with colored slides.

Castlereagh Apartments, University City
the Tearoom was on the ground floor

15 |
St. Louis Writers Guild in the 1960s

The last piece of the Arch's construction, the keystone, was set on October 28, 1965, St. Louis Writers Guild's 45th Anniversary. The sixties brought about the Planetarium in Forest Park, the first Busch Stadium, and the Poplar Street Bridge. As the modern façade of St. Louis rose up, SLWG saw a fundamental shift in its membership. Novels became more of the focus, and more of the presidents were novelists. There were still journalists and other writers in the Guild, but the shift was noticeable. New members like Charles Guenther, Marcella Thum, Bernice Roer, and more, guided St. Louis Writers Guild for the next decade and beyond. St. Louis Writers Guild's writers' conference ended in the 1950s, and the organization focused more on meetings and contests, but they continued to support writers by teaming up with other organizations to hold writers' conferences. St. Louis Writers Guild didn't get pulled in by the counterculture of the day, but the ideals of the that era did work their way inside. More socially aware novels appeared, and members definitely represented the intellectual renaissance of the 1960s. One might say this was the literary period of St. Louis Writers Guild.

Though much had changed, St. Louis Writers Guild and the writers of the city were still involved with Journalism Week at Missouri University. In May 1967, several St. Louis Writers Guild members were in attendance. The Missouri Writers' Guild annual meeting was still held immediately after Journalism Week. Several awards were handed out, including one from St. Louis Writers Guild, which sponsored the Best Feature Newspaper Article. The award in 1967 was presented to Janie Lowe Paschall of St. Louis, Missouri.

The Monthly SLWG Meeting

In the 1960s, in addition to the meetings now being held in tearooms or restaurants instead of members' homes, the meeting format changed slightly, moving the focus from critiquing members' work, to solely being about the presentation. Members met at the tearoom or restaurant, had dinner and then heard from the speaker. Special events included an end-of-year banquet dinner, usually held in November or December. The Season continued as well, with St. Louis Writers Guild only meeting from September to May.

The Presidents of the 1960s
*1960 – Bernice Roer
*1961 – Lois Rea (Mrs. Charles L Rea)
1962 – Devere Stephens – 30th
1963 – Merna Lazier
1964 – Janet Neavles
*1965 – Bessie Megee
*1966 – Bernice Peukert (Mrs. Norman L. Peukert)
1967 – Marcella Thum
1968 – Dorothy Sappington
1969 – Richard Lynch

*Information discovered through research; **bold** means it has been confirmed

Board members from the 1960s
1960
Mrs. Bernice Roer, President
Mrs. Louis Rea, Vice President
Mrs. Helen Kruger, Secretary
Mrs. Margaret Squires, Treasurer
Charles E. M. Norton, Auditor

1961
Mrs. Charles L. Rea, President
Mrs. W.K. Megee, Vice President
Mrs. N. L. Peukert, Secretary
Mrs. Arden Squires, Treasurer
Charles E.M. Norton, Auditor
Mrs. I.L. Johnson, Chairman of the nominating committee.
Retiring president, Bernice Roer, was in charge of the installation ceremony.

Members from the 1960s
Mrs. June Hartman

Mrs. June Hartman was a member of St. Louis Writers Guild. Employed by the Madison County Highway Department, she had two children and lived in on Prickett Avenue in Edwardsville. She was president of Vida Nueva Toastmistress Club in 1961 and also served as secretary, treasurer, and vice president of the organization.

Mrs. Bessie J. Megee—(Mrs. W.K. Megee), President, 1965

Bessie J. Megee was a freelance writer and contest writer, who loved playing bridge. She was a member and served as president of both St. Louis Writers Guild and the St. Louis branch of the American Pen Women. She lived on East Swan Circle in Brentwood and worked for a magazine. In 1961, she spoke at the annual chapter banquet at the Jefferson City Chapter of Missouri Writers' Guild. In March 1961, she spoke to St. Louis Writers Guild at the Colonial Tea Room, 201 Bolivar Street. Her topic was "Don't Wait for Inspiration." In 1965, she was presented the Joplin Chapter award for the best adult fiction story. Her story, "Aunt Myrt and the Turkey Money," was published in *Mother's Home Life Magazine* and *Household Guest*.

Bernice Roer – Bernice Neal (*Possible maiden name or married name*) President, 1960

Bernice Roer, author of *How to Write Articles*, worked on

the conference staff of the McKendree Writers Conference at McKendree Collage, Lebanon, Missouri. She lived in the 7000 block of Kenridge Lane in Shrewsbury. She wrote articles and stories for several national magazines. A member of the literature committee of the Metropolitan Church Federation of St. Louis, she taught creative writing for night school and at writers' conferences. Bernice Roer was on the board of directors for the Missouri Writers' Guild, and received the Springfield chapter award for best feature article for "St. Louis Bicentennial."

Mrs. Marcella Thum, President, 1967

Marcella Thum was an award-winning author and librarian. Not only a driving force within the organization through the 1960s, she also extensively researched the history of St. Louis Writers Guild. She wrote over twenty books on a wide variety of subjects, from children's fiction to military non-fiction.

Marcella Thum won several awards. Her first book, *Mystery at Crane's Landing*, published in 1964, was set in New Madrid, MO. She won Mystery Writers of America's "EDGAR" for best juvenile mystery for the book, even though her story didn't include a murder. She won the American Library Association's Children's Notable Book Award for *Exploring Black America* and for *Mystery at Crane's Landing* and the Missouri Writers' Guild Award for best book by a Missouri author for *Treasure of Crazy Quilt Farm*.

Her novel *Mistress of Paradise* was about the U.S. takeover of Hawaii.

Born in 1925 to Frank and Louise Thum, Marcella had two sisters, Sylvia and Gladys, and a brother, Arville. Marcella spent many years in Affton. In World War II, she served in the Air Transport Command for the Army Air Forces. She wanted to be a pilot, but at 5-foot-2 was two inches too short. In the 1960s, she lived on Smiley Avenue in St. Louis.

On April 1, 1990, John J. Archibald wrote an "Update on Marcella Thum" for the *St. Louis Post-Dispatch*. The column was a way to request updates on people who had been featured in the newspaper. He interviewed her about her latest book, which took place in Kenya during World War I, and wrote about her award-winning novels, her work as a librarian, and teaming up with her sister to write. He quoted Marcella, "I usually try to show the other side of history." In the photo that accompanied the article, Marcella had short white hair, bright eyes, and a big smile.

On July 11, 2002, Lynn Venhaus of the *Post-Dispatch* wrote the obituary article for Marcella Thum, titled "Award-winning Author." She passed away from lymphoma at St. Mary's Health Center at the age of 77.

Her sister, Gladys E. Thum, worked overseas as a writer for the Defense Department and was an editor at the newspaper *Stars and Stripes* in Okinawa She died of diabetes in October 2005. She was 84 years old.

Awards:

American Library Association's Children's Notable Book Award for *Exploring Black America*

Mystery Writers of America's, Edgar Award in 1965 for best juvenile mystery for *Mystery at Crane's Landing*

Missouri Writers Guild's plaque for the best creative writing published by a member in 1965.

Missouri Writers' Guild Award best book by a Missouri author for *Treasure of Crazy Quilt Farm*, May 4, 1966

Published Works:
BOOKS FOR YOUNG PEOPLE:
Mystery at Crane's Landing, Dodd Mead, 1964
Treasure of Crazy Quilt Farm, Franklin Watts, 1966
Anne of the Sandwich Islands, Dodd Mead, 1967
Librarian with Wings, Dodd Mead, 1967
Secret of the Sunken Treasure, Dodd Mead, 1969

NONFICTION FOR YOUNG ADULTS:
Exploring Black America, Atheneum, 1975
Exploring Literary America, Atheneum, 1979
Exploring Military America (with Gladys Thum), Atheneum, 1982

NONFICTION FOR ADULTS:
The Persuaders, Propaganda in War and Peace (with Gladys Thum), Atheneum, 1972
Airlift, Story of Military Airlift Command (with Gladys Thum), Dodd Mead, 1986
Hippocrene USA Guide to Black America, Hippocrene, 1992

GOTHIC/MYSTERY:
Fernwood, Doubleday, 1973
Abbey Court, Doubleday, 1976

HISTORICAL ROMANCES:
The White Rose, Fawcett/Ballantine, 1980
Blazing Star, Fawcett/Ballantine, 1983
Jasmine, Fawcett/Ballantine, 1984
Wild Laurel, Fawcett/Ballantine, 1985
Margarite, Fawcett/Ballantine, 1987
Mistress of Paradise, Fawcett/Ballantine, 1988
Thorn Trees, Fawcett/Ballantine, 1991

Louise Travous

On March 22, 1965, it was announced that SLWG member, Louise Travous, had passed away. Born in Edwardsville, Illinois on April 25, 1882, she was the great-granddaughter of John T. Lusk, a pioneer of Madison County. A recognized authority on local history, she traveled extensively through Illinois to lecture to schools, clubs, and civic organizations. Miss Travous was a former editor and feature writer and teacher in the Edwardsville school system. Her most notable accomplishment was the restoration of Woodlawn and Lusk Cemeteries.

Workshops and Events from the 1960s
Wednesday, March 16, 1960, 6:30 p.m.
Albert J. Montesi, professor of English at St. Louis University, spoke at the Castlereagh Apartments, 6820 Delmar Boulevard.

Wednesday, January 18, 1961

The forty-first year for SLWG began with a dinner meeting at the Castlereagh Tearoom, where officers were installed, including president Mrs. Charles L. Rea. A picture of her accompanied the article.

The meeting consisted of a round table discussion with Mrs. Fred Armstrong, Mrs. J.H. Bryan, Mrs. Merna C. Lazier, Mrs. Franklin Miller, Mrs. Nicolette Meredith Stack, and Mrs. Thomas H. Ward.

November 15, 1961, 6:30 p.m.

The dinner meeting was held at the Castlereagh Tea Room in University City.

Wednesday, April 18, 1962

The meeting featured Bertha Halpern at the Castlereagh Apartments Tearoom, 6820 Delmar Boulevard.

June 25-30, 1962

The annual McKendree College Writers' Conference was held June 25 to 30 at the campus in Lebanon.

Mrs. Bernice Roer, a member of St. Louis Writers Guild and a board of directors for the Missouri Writers Guild, led the workshop.

Cost of registration, membership and room and board at the conference was $41.50 for adults and $39.50 for students. Several scholarships were available for high school students interested in creative writing. One hour of college credit could be earned through the conference if college requirements were met. The program was open to anyone interested in writing.

January 16, 1963, 6:30 p.m.

It happened Only Once in History, presented by Max Dimont, author of *Jews, God and History* at a dinner meeting at the Salem House Restaurant, 9993 Manchester Road in Warson Woods. DeVere A. Stephens presided.

The History of St. Louis Writers Guild

Wednesday, May 15, 1963, 6:30 p.m.
Webb Bracy, a professor at St. Louis University, spoke at Salem House Restaurant, 9993 Manchester Road, Warson Woods.

June 21, 1964
St. Louis Writers Guild members were part of the McKendree Writers Conference at McKendree College, in Lebanon, MO. Bernice Roer, former SLWG president was serving her third year on the conference staff. Charles Guenther was also part of the faculty of the conference.

May 6, 1965
Three St. Louis area writers were presented awards at the annual spring meeting of the Missouri Writers Guild at the University of Missouri's Journalism Week.

Mrs. Bernice Roer of Shrewsbury, author of the book *How to Write Articles*, received the Springfield chapter award for the best feature article for "St. Louis Bicentennial." She is a former president of the St. Louis Writers Guild and taught creative writing in night school classes and at writers' conferences.

Mrs. Bessie J. Megee, of Brentwood, an employee of a magazine, received the Joplin Chapter award for best adult fiction story. Her story, "Aunt Myrt and the Turkey Money," was published in *Mother's Home Life Magazine*, and *Household Guest*. Mrs. Megee, president of the St. Louis Branch of the American Pen Women, also won that award last year.

Mrs. Estelle Finnegan won the Columbia chapter award for the best poem for "This New Year," which was published in the December issue of *War Cry magazine*. She was a former member of the Jefferson City Writers Guild.

Wednesday, January 18, 1967, 6:30 p.m.
Miss Marcella Thum, author of books for young persons, was elected the newest SLWG president at the Salem House Restaurant.

May 2, 1967

The new Missouri Writers' Guild President, Elwyn L Cady, Jr. of Independence, MO, was chosen at the annual MWG meeting at Missouri University's Journalism Week. The Walter Williams Award (founder of MWG and the MU School of Journalism) went to Ralph Richard of Columbia, MO, a senior at MU. MWG's most outstanding published work last year was won by Mrs. Cleo M. Stephens. The St. Louis Chapter award for the best newspaper feature article was presented to Janie Lowe Paschall, St. Louis.

The History of St. Louis Writers Guild

50th Anniversary

St. Louis WRITERS' Guild

1920 - 1970

50th Anniversary Member Booklet

16 |
St. Louis Writers Guild in the 1970s, Half a Century

In the 1970s, St. Louis Writers Guild found its focus once again on journalists. Longtime St. Louis reporters like King McElroy and Elizabeth Mulligan guided the Guild through its meetings, contests, and events. Charles Guenther remained a fixture of events, having first served on the SLWG board in the late 1950s. Others, like retired construction company owner, James Nash, inspired people enough with his words to warrant having a writing contest named after him. St. Louis Writers Guild in the 1970s was a close group, all professional writers, but they shared deep friendships, and many stayed together throughout the decade.

The Monthly Meetings in the 1970s

St. Louis Writer Guild's monthly meetings were held on the third Wednesday of every month during the Season. They left behind members' homes and the city's tearooms and moved into local restaurants. One establishment used more than any other location – the Flaming Pit Restaurant, 11715 Manchester Road in Des Peres, Missouri.

Reservations were required to attend a meeting, and those interested called the number listed. The phone number changed occasionally and was not always the president's. The numbers belonged to board members, and for a couple of years, a position on the board named Reservations took care of this duty. For much of the 1970s, the cost to attend the meeting, which went to the meal, was $5.25.

The meetings began at 6 p.m. with cocktails, but that was soon changed to 6:30 p.m. Dinner was served at 7 p.m. The program began at 8 p.m. and featured an author or industry professional giving a talk on a certain topic. Sometimes a poetry reading was hosted by a member.

The Flaming Pit Restaurant was most known for its hand-carved roast beef sandwiches. An ad for the Flaming Pit that ran on the same page in the *St. Louis Post-Dispatch* as an SLWG announcement advertised, "the Catch of the Week—Filet of Sole—Fried up crisp and golden outside, light and tender inside. We serve it with your choice of potato, our extraordinary salad bar, warm rolls, and butter. Adults $4.45, Kids 10 and under $2.25, Thursday and Fridays after 5 p.m."

The Fourth Annual Metro-St. Louis Writers' Conference

The Fourth Annual Metro-St. Louis Writers' Conference was held on November 10 and 11, 1978 in the Busch Memorial Center at St. Louis University's Metropolitan College. The conference attracted writers from St. Louis and the surrounding region for an event on Friday night from 7:30 p.m. to 9:30 p.m., and Saturday from 9 a.m. to 4 p.m.

The speakers included a historian, a poet, several authors, and an editor. The Rev. William B. Faherty, a history professor at St. Louis University and the author of books on St. Louis history presented, "The State of the Art in Missouri." He also conducted an afternoon workshop on style.

Gregory W. Franzwa, author of *The Story of Old Ste. Genevieve* presented a talk on self-publishing at the noon luncheon.

Marcella Thum spoke about Gothic novels, and Wayne E. Warner, president of Missouri Writers' Guild discussed writing for religious markets.

Poet Jean Fulkes discussed publishing poetry, and author Francis M. Nevins presented a lecture on mystery fiction.

The fee to attend the writer's conference was $20 ($76 in 2019) which included the luncheon.

Martha Carr's Column in the St. Louis Post-Dispatch

For several decades, Martha Carr's advice column was a fixture of the *St. Louis Post-Dispatch*. All kinds of questions were asked and occasionally St. Louis Writers Guild was mentioned.

On July 24, 1978, S.R. asked, "Dear Martha: Can you give me the names of some amateur writers' clubs? Thank you."

She replied, "Two in our area are The Silver Pens, in care of Lois Bishop, and The St. Louis Writers' Guild in care of Joyce Flaherty. Also, the Poetry Center of St. Louis is made up of a group of local poets who get together one Sunday Afternoon monthly to listen to a professional poet or teacher who critiques their poems. Call Christ Church Cathedral (where they meet) for further information."

On August 7, 1978, Martha Carr's column featured a write up of SLWG. "The St. Louis Writers Guild is a professional organization that requires its members to have published at least several times for pay. Associate members without voting privileges do not have to be published. The St. Louis Writers Guild is an affiliate of the Missouri Writers Guild."

She also said this of the St. Louis Poetry Center: "Members of the St. Louis Poetry Center, Inc. would not like your amateur appellation either, although an open-door policy is maintained and all poets are always welcome. A member of the Arts and Education Council of St. Louis and the American Academy of Poets, the St. Louis Poetry Center meets the third Sunday of each month, September through May in Webster Groves at the Farm and Home Building on West Lockwood. Anyone wanting further information about the Poetry Center can call the president, Leslie Konnyu, or the first vice president Lucy Hazelton, a member of both groups."

The Presidents of the 1970s
1970 – King McElroy
1971 – Elizabeth Mulligan
1972 – Antonio Betancourt

1973 – Art Hoglund
1974 – James H. Nash
1975 – Virginia McCarthy
1976 – Charles Guenther
1977 – Charles Guenther
1978 – Joyce Flaherty
1979 – Mary Gorman

* Information discovered through research; **bold** means it has been confirmed

Board members from the 1970s
1970
King McElroy, President
Elizabeth Mulligan, Vice President
Mrs. Edward V. McMahon, Secretary
Leslie Konnyu, Treasurer
Carolyn Wood, Historian

1973
Art Hoglund, President
James Nash, Vice President
Mary Gorman, Secretary
DeVere Stephens, Membership
Gene Stefacek, Treasurer
Eupha Richie, Reservations
Irene Kennedy, Public Relations

Members from the 1970s
Rev. William Barnaby Faherty—Father Faherty

Rev. William Barnaby Faherty was an author, and a local historian, and a fixture of St. Louis Writers Guild in the 1960s and 1970s, who would remain involved in the city's literary community until the 1990s. He published over 50 books, though possibly many more, as well as numerous articles. Much of his writing focused on history, and he chronicled many aspects of St. Louis' past. He wrote about Catholics and Jesuits within the city, as well as books on the Irish and German populations in St. Louis. He also wrote about Henry Shaw and the Missouri Botanical Garden. His interests didn't stop with religion or St. Louis; he wrote about space exploration, and the Apollo program.

Born in 1914 at the family's home on Arsenal Street in St. Louis, Rev. Faherty graduated from St. Louis University High School in 1931 and had already won his first writing contest. He was ordained in 1944 and received a doctorate in history at SLU in 1949. From 1948 to 1956, he taught at Regis College (now Regis University) in Denver. During this time, he wrote about women's rights from the Catholic perspective in his 1952 book, *The Destiny of Modern Woman in the Light of Papal Teaching*. From 1956 to 1963, he returned to St. Louis as a pamphlet editor for the *Queen's Work*. From 1963 to 1984, he served as a history professor at St. Louis University. He was the archivist for the Catholic order of Jesuits, the Society of Jesus, Missouri Province, and worked with the St. Charles Historical Society.

His first novel, *A Wall for San Sebastian* (1962) was a hit and became the movie, Guns of San Sebastian starring Anthony Quinn and Charles Bronson. From 1972 to 1973, he lived in Florida, researching and co-writing *Moonport: A History of Apollo Launch Facilities and Operations* for NASA.

In 2000, he told the *St. Louis Post-Dispatch* that his best book was probably, *American Catholic Heritage: Stories of Growth* (1991). In one chapter titled, "Roman Misjudgments," he explained, "Rome has never allowed the church in this country to develop in such a way that it would reflect the American genius while remaining totally Catholic."

In a 2000 *St. Louis Post-Dispatch* interview, Father Faherty said America should reduce its conspicuous consumption. "We need to return to pioneering American simplicity and away from excessive flaunting of wealth, excessive materialism. Teddy Roosevelt, where are you when we need you?"

Father Faherty's novel, *Daughter of Rising Moon* (2007), dealt with Native American issues.

Father Faherty loved the St. Louis Cardinals; even the access code to his residence at Jesuit Hall was derived from the chest and waist measurements of famous members of the Cardinals' 1934 Gas House Gang.

He passed away in 2011, at the age of 96, and was said to be working on a novel when he died.

Charles Guenther – President 1959, 1976, and 1977

"My purpose is to make a poem from a poem." – Charles Guenther (Wikipedia)

Charles Guenther, the Prince of Poets, was a translator, poet, critic, and novelist who served on the board of St. Louis Writers Guild for over three decades. His book, *Phrase/Paraphrase,* was nominated for the Pulitzer Prize in Poetry.

Born in Kirkwood, Missouri on April 29, 1920, Charles first started translating poetry at age 15 while attending Roosevelt High School in Kirkwood. In his essay, "On the Art of Translation," he said, "I spent hours in the library reading poetry, especially European poetry, in translation at first and later in the original language."

After graduating from high school, Charles worked as a copy boy for the *St. Louis Star-Times*. The newspaper influenced him and guided him to become a writer. Of the experience at the *St. Louis Star-Times*, he said, "Newspaper people—then, anyway—were a special and temperamental breed. It exposed you to the human comedy."

Charles Guenther attended Harris Teachers College and earned a master's degree at Webster College (now Webster University). He did his doctoral work in languages at St. Louis University but was never listed as Dr. Guenther.

Charles enlisted in the U.S. Army Air Corps during World War II and translated information, like the opening and closing of foreign runways. He served as a historian, librarian, and supervisory cartographer for the U.S. Air Force at the Aeronautical Chart and Information Center of St. Louis.

Charles was well-known for his encouragement of new and emerging writers. Aside from his three years as SLWG President, his name appears on the board of directors across three different decades, serving as Vice-President and Treasurer. It can't be determined exactly how long he volunteered for St. Louis Writers Guild, though it started in the 1950s and lasted until his last appearance in 1999, making him the longest-serving member of the century.

Charles died of cancer in 2008 at the age of 88, surrounded by his wife Esther, their three children, five grandchildren, and four great-grandchildren. His only son, Charles Guenther Jr., told the *St. Louis Post-Dispatch* that "Poetry and his family were his life."

The Author of 10 books
Moving the Seasons,
Phrase/Paraphrase, nominated for the Pulitzer Prize in Poetry,
The Hippopotamus: Selected Translations 1945-1985,
The Complete Love Sonnets of Garcilaso de la Vega,
Three Faces of Autumn: A Charles Guenther Retrospective.

The Book Critic
A literary critic for 50 years, Charles Guenther began writing reviews for the *St. Louis Post-Dispatch* in 1953. Starting in 1972, he also wrote for the *St. Louis Globe-Democrat*. That ended in 1982, shortly before the paper filed for bankruptcy. Before retiring as a book critic in 2003, he said he considered reviewing a "civic honor, and I still do." He reviewed the novels of hundreds of authors, like Seamus Heaney, Ted Hughes, William Stafford, Mona Van Duyn, and Anthony Hecht.

The Poet
Charles Guenther was a prolific writer of poetry. He favored a clipped, concise style of traditional rhyming verse but frequently used free verse as well, most often writing about nature and rural scenes, like the wintry landscape of "Snow Country," regional, "Missouri Woods," and nature, "Spring Catalog."

Other poems, like "Escalator" and "Arch" were more experimental and avant-garde. Charles Guenther also wrote elegies and poems commemorative of places, people, and events.

Charles also worked tirelessly to promote poetry and poets. He was a frequent correspondent and mentored many younger poets. For 15 years he served as Regional Midwest Vice-President for the Poetry Society of America.

"Three Faces of Autumn" (from the book *Phrase/Paraphrase*) by Charles Guenther

> Now sunfire stains
> the tupelos
> and the shadows
> in trapeziums
> off the haybarns
> straggle and gather
> by rocks and birches
> where the crickets'
> still-fast whirr
> cries against the closed
> season
> (from Part I, *Three Faces of Autumn*)

The Translator

Charles Guenther, who started in his teens, was prolific in translating poetry from roughly a dozen foreign languages. Many poets were translated into English for the first time by Charles.

In an essay entitled "Reflections," from the book *Three Faces of Autumn*, he credits Ezra Pound as an early influence on his work. The two met in 1951 when Charles visited Ezra Pound while he was at St. Elizabeth's Hospital in Washington, D.C. Charles said, "It was the start of a lively correspondence with this fascinating, obstinate poet who had put new vigor into American literature."

Charles Guenther was also versatile in his translation work. He translated into English from such varying poets as Edgar Degas, Paul Valéry, Pablo Neruda, Salvatore Quasimodo, and Dante Alighieri. He also extensively translated the works of Garcilaso de la Vega, Juan Ramón Jiménez, Jules Laforgue, and Jean Wahl.

Most of his translations and poetry were published in literary publications, including *The American Poetry Review*, *Black Mountain Review*, *The Formalist*, and *The Kenyon Review*.

In 1973, Italy decorated him with a knighthood with its

Commendatore Ordine al Merito della Repubblica (Order of Merit of the Italian Republic). Other nations also honored Charles for his work in translating their native poets into English, many for the first time. About the work of translation, he wrote, "In a great poem there is something magic, a haunting spirit. It's so rare that you keep looking for it."

In an essay on the craft of translation in *Guardian of Grief: Poems of Giacomo Leopardi,* Charles Guenther claimed most of his translations were "reformations, recasting, a foreign poem into its original form or free verse form." Guenther said "My own practice when translating early poets is to place them in their own time, with a hint of antiquity, avoiding the grossly archaic language of their contemporaries. My purpose is to make a poem from a poem."

He translated thousands of poems into English from languages such as French, Italian, Spanish, Eskimo, Greek, German, and Hungarian. He corresponded with scores of authors, including Ezra Pound; Kirkwood, Missouri native Marianne Moore; and E.E. Cummings.

Awards
The Order of Merit of the Italian Republic (1973)
James Joyce Award, Poetry Society of America (1974)
French-American Bicentennial Medal (1976)
Witter Bynner Translation Grant, Poetry Society of America (1979)
Missouri Arts Award (2001)
St. Louis Arts Award (2001)
Emmanuel Robles International Award in Poetry (2002)

Quotes
"It is the work, not the prize or the honor, that matters most. The work endures."

"In a great poem, there is something magic, a haunting spirit. It's so rare that you keep looking for it."

Ralph L. Maisak
Ralph L. (Larry) Maisak, a writer and aerospace engineer,

retired in 1974 from McDonnell Douglas Corp. Prior to that, he was an engineer at Emerson Electric Co. In 1966, he wrote a book *Survival on the Moon* and after his retirement, he wrote articles on energy and ecology.

Mr. Maisak was a member of the St. Louis Writers Guild, the British Interplanetary Society, the Midwest Programs Organization, and the past-president of the Missouri Writers Guild.

He lived in St. Charles with his wife, Lucille, a son and two daughters. He passed away in April 1975, at the age of 65.

King McElroy

King G. McElroy, besides having one of the coolest names of all the presidents, was a reporter for the *St. Louis Globe-Democrat*. He was the contributing editor to the *Washington University Record*, *(the Wash U Record)*, a weekly magazine produced during the school year.

King had a long, distinguished career as a journalist. In the 1990s, King McElroy covered school board meetings as a Special Correspondent for the *St. Louis Post-Dispatch*, writing about the new director of buildings and grounds for Webster Groves School District and their new medical insurance program, as well as covering stories like how the Clayton School Board endorsed Prop B on the ballot, or Eureka's efforts to get more crossing guards.

King G. McElroy attended SLUH, St. Louis University High School before moving on to St. Louis University, in pursuit of his journalism career. His obituary reported, "He delighted many with his wit and humor, inspired them with his courage and wisdom, and was truly a man for others."

He was a St. Louis Cardinals fan, and one of his favorite places was Busch Stadium. He loved golf, iced tea, ice cream, and his steaks well-done. He was married to Barbara McElroy for 57 years and they had six children and twelve grandchildren.

King G. McElroy lived in the Central West End and Webster Groves. He passed away on July 26, 2019, at the age of 83.

Elizabeth Mulligan

Elizabeth Mulligan was a freelance writer from Sunset

Hills. She attended the University of Indiana and Northwestern University. Regularly published in the *St. Louis Post-Dispatch*, she wrote featured articles about a wide variety of subjects from adoptions out of Vietnam, to the decline of the iron lung, and a piece about bonsai.

Workshops and Events
January 4, 1970

The 50th Anniversary began with the election of officers: King McElroy, president; Mrs. Elizabeth Mulligan, vice president; Mrs. Edward V. McMahon, secretary; Leslie Konnyu, treasurer; and Mrs. Carolyn Wood, historian.

January 22, 1970

St. Louis Writers Guild sponsored a creative writing course for adults entitled, **Two Dozen Ways to Make Money Writing**, at Kirkwood High School in cooperation with the Kirkwood Adult School. The class met on Tuesdays from 7:30 to 9:30pm for 10 weeks.

SLWG Members taught the course, which covered publicity, newspaper, article, short story, poetry, and television documentary writing. Manuscript criticism was provided. Information about the course was obtained by calling the number provided.

Wednesday, January 18, 1976, 6:30 p.m.

Monthly SLWG meeting at the Flaming Pit Restaurant, 11715 Manchester Road, Des Peres. The cost of the dinner was $5. Reservations could be made by calling the number provided until the Monday before the event.

Wednesday, March 17, 1976

The Rev. William B. Faherty, author of *Wide River, Wide Land*, spoke at the dinner program at the Flaming Pit Restaurant. Reservations were $5.05 and had to be made by 3 p.m. on March 15. Writers and other interested persons were invited to attend.

September 9, 1976, 6:30 p.m.

Confessions of a Book Critic was presented by June Darby Ellison, author of *Greater Futuristic Attitudes: What Social Changes do we Futurists Desire?* at the Flaming Pit Restaurant. Dinner was $5.25 and reservations could be made by calling the number provided.

Wednesday, November 17, 1976, 6:30pm
Harry N. D. Fisher, author of *29 Ways Not To Sell Your Book* at the Flaming Pit Restaurant. Reservations were $5.25 per person.

Wednesday, December 15, 6:30 p.m.
Blending Research with Writing was presented by Carl R. Baldwin, former writer for the *St. Louis Post-Dispatch*, at the Flaming Pit Restaurant, 11715 Manchester Road, Des Peres. The cost of dinner was $5.25. Reservations could be made by calling the number provided.

February 16, February 24, March 3, and March 16, 1977
A call was placed in the Crafts/Hobbies section of the *St. Louis Post-Dispatch* – "For professional and novices in all fields of writing" – it invited them to the dinner meeting held on the third Wednesday of each month, September through May, at 6:30 at the Flaming Pit, 11715 Manchester Road, Des Peres. For more information, interested persons could call Charles Guenther at the number provided.

Wednesday, September 15, 1977, 6:30 p.m.
Taking Up Residence in Another Person's Head was presented by Dick Richmond, music writer for the *St. Louis Post-Dispatch*, at the Flaming Pit Restaurant. Dinner $5.75.

Wednesday, October 19, 1977, 6:30 p.m.
The New Journalism: And What Happened To It, was presented by Harper Barnes, editor of the *Sunday Pictures Magazine* at the *St. Louis Post-Dispatch*, at the Flaming Pit Restaurant. Dinner reservations were $5.75.

Wednesday, December 21, 1977, 6:30 p.m.
Poetry Readings. Lucy Hazelton led a panel of poets at the Flaming Pit Restaurant.

January 18, 1978 or April 19, 1978, 6:30
The Idea is Gold, was presented by Walter Armbruster, executive vice-president of D'arcy, McManus, and Masius Advertising agency, at the Flaming Pit Restaurant. (*Event was probably rescheduled.*)

May 17, 1978, 6:30 p.m.
Writing for the Radio was presented by KMOX radio personality Anne Keefe, at the Flaming Pit Restaurant.

November 10 & 11, 1978
The Fourth Annual Metro-St. Louis Writers' Conference was held at the Busch Memorial Center at St. Louis University's Metropolitan College. SLWG and its members were involved.

Wednesday, November 15, 1978
St. Louis author, Anne Marie deMoret, addressed a joint meeting of Women in Communications Inc. and the St. Louis Writers' Guild, at the Flaming Pit, 11715 Manchester Road, Des Peres. Cocktails were served at 6:30 p.m., dinner was at 7 p.m., and the program at 8 p.m.

March 21, 1979
The Other Side of Tennessee Williams was presented by the playwright's brother Dakin Williams, at the Flaming Pit Restaurant on Manchester Road in Des Peres.

October 17, 1979
Anna Lee Waldo, author of *Sacajawea* was the guest speaker at the Flaming Pit Restaurant. Reservations required by the Monday of the week before the event.

An ad for the Flaming Pit ran on the same page in the *St. Louis Post-Dispatch* – "*the Catch of the Week – Filet of Sole – Fried up* *crisp and golden outside, light and tender inside. We serve it with your choice of potato, our extraordinary salad bar, warm rolls and butter. Adults $4.45, Kids 10 and under $2.25, Thursday and Fridays after 5 p.m."*

Logo and Header for *Here's News!* in 2013

17 |
The Writers' Guild of St. Louis in the 1980s

As St. Louis Blues legends like Bernie Federko, Al MacInnis, Brian Sutter, and Brett Hull skated around the ice, and the St. Louis Cardinals compiled one of the all-time classic teams with guys like Willie McGee, Tommy Herr, Jack Clark, Vince Coleman, Ozzie Smith, helmed by a character of a manager, Whitey Herzog, an eclectic crew of poets, novelists, journalists, and more, defined the members and officers of St. Louis Writer Guild in the 1980s.

Poets, short story writers, novelists, and freelance writers made up the members of St. Louis Writers Guild, a variety that remains to the current day. Genres ebbed and flowed in terms of how many members and probably followed trends in the greater publishing industry, but the journalists, the playwrights, and the charter sketch writers disappeared... though not completely.

SLWG still ran on the Season from September to May, but the term "Season" faded from use.

The Monthly Meeting of St. Louis Writers Guild

The monthly meetings were held on the third Wednesday of the month at different restaurants in Kirkwood or Webster Groves. One of those restaurants was Howard Johnson's Restaurant at 1130 South Lindbergh Boulevard, just north of I-44. A couple of the events were held at Garavelli's Restaurant, 9739 Manchester Road in Rock Hill or the Windsor Room, at the Cheshire Inn (or The

Cheshire as it's known today), at 6300 Clayton Road. The location was relayed to those who called and registered for the event. The format remained the same as the 1970s: cocktails and networking began at either 6 p.m. or 6:30 p.m., dinner was served at 7 p.m., and the program started at 8 p.m. The discussion lasted about an hour. Reservations were required by the Monday before the event. Several of the newspaper announcements even mention the times to call, between 8 a.m. and 5 p.m.

The fee, $6-$7, at the time, covered both the meal and the program. The 1980s brought the first tiered-pricing for event fees, something that continues to the modern day. The meetings were open to all guests, but the standard fee of $6, which was applied to members and guests alike, was first increased to $7. By September 1989, there were two prices, $11 for members and $14 for non-members. St. Louis Writers Guild continued having two tiers of members, full members (professional writers only), and associate members (those who didn't yet have enough publishing credits to qualify for full membership).

Martha Carr's Column in the 1980s

As referenced in the section on the 1970s, Martha Carr's column in the *St. Louis Post-Dispatch* ran for many years and she continued to talk about St. Louis Writers Guild.

In March 1985, a prospective writer (M.S. was the name used), asked Martha Carr a question about writing organizations in St. Louis.

Titled: "When Writers Get Together," the writer asked, "Dear Martha Carr: Are there writers' clubs, groups for struggling writers? I would like to know about any writers' groups you may know about having meetings in the St. Louis area. If yes, would you give me the names/addresses? M.S."

Martha Carr responded with, "The St. Louis Writers Guild meets every third Wednesday for a dinner program at the Howard Johnson's Restaurant at 1130 South Lindbergh Blvd., just north of I-44. Cocktails at 6 p.m., 7 p.m. for dinner meeting.

"Full members are those who have published; associate members are those who are still waiting for their first publication.

For more information, call Ron Lightle (His phone number was listed.)

"There are also more specific groups such as romance writers, children's book writers, etc., but you can learn more about the subgroups by attending one of the Writers Guild meetings and getting acquainted with the interesting people who belong."

On May 25, 1987 in a question about publishing, Martha Carr was asked by K.B., "Dear Martha: I have been writing for many years, mostly poetry, but also short stories. I believe that some of my work is worth publishing. Do you know of any organizations that I could contact about publishing my work?"

Martha responded, "You might be interested in joining the Writers Guild and its poetry subgroup to talk with other writers about publishing. For information about the organization write, to St. Louis Writers Guild." (a PO Box address was listed.)

On May 28, 1987, SLWG appeared again when D.H.M. asked, "Dear Martha: I have a fantastic story to tell, and I'm not a writer. How do I go about getting someone to write it for me? It would make great movie for TV or Cinema. I need to know right away, as I want the money from it to try to save my farm from foreclosure."

Martha responded, "No Matter who the author of your story might be, you won't get any money right away. In fact, depending upon how you work out your writing arrangement, you may have to pay the writer to write your story regardless of whether or not you can sell it. Not many writers are willing to go into a joint arrangement whereby the profits of your idea and his or her talent are split, subsequent to a potential sale.

"You may be able to find a writer through the Writers Guild, PO Box (address was listed).

"Write a letter to the guild office, describing what kind of story it is, (mystery, adventure, social commentary, fantasy, etc. – do not include your plot, however) and designate exactly how the writer will be paid for his or her part. Give some kind of schedule for beginning and finishing, and indicate whether you are planning to narrate a story that will then work through to presentation quality, or you are submitting only an idea that the writer must research and develop as he or she writes.

"Although your story project may, indeed, turn into a reality, I suggest that you would do well to look elsewhere for funds to save your farm."

Joe Pollack Called Out St. Louis Writers Guild and KWMU

On February 16, 1986, Joe Pollack wrote a column in *St. Louis Post-Dispatch* in which he took issue with certain changes made to St. Louis Writers Guild's and KWMU's writing contests.

In his column titled, "Show-Me, But Don't Wake Me Up," Pollack wrote, "Paging the Authors: The St. Louis Writers Guild is holding a contest for short stories of 500-3500 words, with an April 1 deadline and prizes of $100, $50, $25. Writers who live within a 50 miles of St. Louis are eligible. There is an entry fee, and full information can be obtained by sending a stamped, self-addressed envelope to contest at (the P.O. Box listed.)

"Oddly, contest rules state that manuscripts will not be returned, which is one of the most puzzling things I've ever read. As a matter of course, writers send self-addressed envelopes for return of material: typing and copying take time, and often money, and freelance writers usually want their rejected material so they can weep a little, and then submit it elsewhere.

"So, it seems very strange that a contest supervised by writers would keep—and probably discard—manuscripts."

"The same non-return policy is in effect at a KWMU radio drama contest, and it has brought complaints from several local writers, for the same reasons. The care and feeding of writers is a delicate matter (oh boy is it!) and they are an endangered species that needs all the help they can get.

"I can understand why the guild, or the station, does not want to absorb the mailing expense, but I think that if the writer sends return postage, the submission should come back.

"Rejection is bad enough; loss makes it worse."

Missouri Author Week

In 1989, Governor John Ashcroft proclaimed the last week of April Missouri Writers Week.

The Presidents of the 1980s
1980 – Dorothy Nash
1981 – Ron Lightle
1982 – Gwen Lowder
1983 – Marcella Holloway
1984 – Linda Madl – 50th President
1985 – N. Paul Dusseault
1986 – Carolyn May
1987 – Linda Sage
1988 – Cynthia Georges
1989 – Sandy Palmer

* Information discovered through research; **bold** means it has been confirmed

Members from the 1980s
Eleanor Marie Cooper

The *St. Louis Post-Dispatch* ran an obituary on Monday, July 15, 1985 for Eleanor Marie Cooper, author and composer. She had a book of lyrics and poems called *Language of Lovers*, published in 1980. She composed many songs from the 1930s to 1960s, including "Sweet to Be In Love (with Someone Like You)," "Wanting You," "Have a Heart" and "If You Love Me." A native of St. Louis, she was a member of the Veterans of Foreign Wars, Post 2101, the American Society of Composers, Authors and Publishers, and St. Louis Writers Guild, and was laid to rest at Valhalla Mausoleum.

She was 90 years old when she passed away.

John H. David

John H. "Jack" David, was a publishing executive and marketing manager for Doane Information Services where he worked in promotion and circulation for 20 years. He was a member of the St. Louis Writers Guild, the North County

Writers Group, the Direct Marketing Association, and Mensa. He graduated from Drake University in Des Moines, Iowa.

He had two sons, State Rep Michael P. David and Maj. William C. David; a daughter, Karen Headley of Cincinnati; and five grandchildren.

John H. David passed away in November 1987at his home in Ferguson after suffering a heart attack. He was 60 years old and was laid to rest in Bellefontaine Cemetery.

N. Paul Dusseault, President, 1985

Paul Dusseault was an author and drummer. He played in several local bands, and toured throughout the region. Bob Baker, another musician and former St. Louis Publishers Association (SLPA) President and longtime friend to SLWG, had played with Paul and spoke fondly of him:

http://www.riverfronttimes.com/stlouis/boardroom-blitz/Content?oid=2463370

Marcella Holloway, President, 1983

Sister Marcella Marie Holloway, author, poet, and English Professor, was born in St. Louis in 1914. She entered the convent of the Sisters of St. Joseph of Carondelet in 1932, professing her final vows in 1938. She started her teaching career in 1935 at Rosati-Kain High School and then at St. Louis Cathedral School. Sister Holloway graduated magna cum laude from Fontbonne College in 1938 with a bachelor's degree in English. She taught at two high schools in Georgia before returning to Missouri to pursue a master's degree from the University of Missouri at Columbia, which she obtained in 1945.

On April 26, 1993, the *St. Louis Post-Dispatch* ran an article on Sister Marcella Holloway titled, "Nun Has Seen Many Changes Over 60 Years of Work in Order."

She passed away November 19, 2003 at the Nazareth Living Center in St. Louis at the age of 89.

Ron Lightle, President, 1981

Ronald G. Lightle was born in 1939 and passed away on

December 14, 2008. He lived in Troy, Illinois after being a longtime resident of St. Louis, Missouri.

Gwen Lowder, President, 1982
Gwen Lowder was one of the board members who fielded phone calls and took reservation for SLWG events. Her phone number appeared in the newspaper for many Guild events.

Linda Madl, President, 1984
From Linda Madl's Amazon author page:
"Linda Madl's work includes historical romance novels, novellas, short stories, book reviews, and nonfiction articles. The settings of her books are as far ranging as her travels. She has visited England, the Isle of Sky, the Rocky Mountains, and the Ozarks, all settings for her stories.

"Her current releases, *Happy Holidays from the Gates of Hell* and *Serafina* fulfill a life-long desire to write what she loves to read, stories about ghosts and the paranormal.

"She loves chocolate, crisp October days, piano music, and a good ghost story.

"She is active in professional writing organizations including the St. Louis Writers Guild, Kansas Writers, Inc., and Novelists, Inc. She has presented readings, programs, and workshops at numerous meetings including RWA regional and national conferences, libraries, and adult learning centers. She has also served as a docent in local ghost tours.

"Currently, she and her husband split their time between Florida and the Kansas Flint Hills. She fills her non-writing hours with family, friends, and travel."
http://www.amazon.com/Linda-Madl/e/B000AQ1CA6

Dorothy Nash (Dorothy Conzelman) – President, 1980
Dorothy Jean Nash was born in Chicago in 1920. She traveled to Europe as a USO Singer during World War II. While touring, she met her husband, Garett, and moved with him to St. Louis when they returned to America in 1946. Long-time residents of Webster Groves, they moved there in 1962 and raised six

children.

Dorothy Nash worked for the Washington University Department of Otolaryngology for more than twenty years. She never stopped pursuing her singing career. She performed on *The Charlotte Peters Show* and the *St. Louis Variety Club Telethon*. She was also part of the Muny Opera. At age 72, Dorothy joined the Peace Corps and worked in Senegal, West Africa, for three years. While in Senegal, she was instrumental in building a clinic. Dorothy passed away on August 26, 2010 at the age of 89.

Dorothy had five children, Camille Nash, Duff Nash, Amy Wind (Daniel), Kevin Nash (Jacque) and Kristin Nash; daughter-in-law, Deanna Nash, and ten grandchildren.

Her second husband, author and poet, James H. Nash was SLWG president in 1974.

James H. Nash

James H. Nash, owner of the Nash Construction Co., didn't start writing poetry until he retired in 1962. His first wife, Edmee Baur Nash, helped him discover his interest in the written word. After her passing in 1966, he published a book of poems. He later married Dorothy Conzelman, who encouraged him to continue publishing his poetry.

James was an active member of the St. Louis literary community. Not only was he a past president of the St. Louis Writers Guild, but also chancellor of the St. Louis Poetry Center and former first vice president of the Missouri Writers Guild. After his passing, he was honored with an annual short story contest by SLWG and poetry contest by the St. Louis Poetry Center.

He passed away in December 1980, at the age of 78, in his home in Glendale, and was laid to rest at Valhalla Cemetery. He was survived by his daughter, Esmee Jeane Lovine, eight grandchildren and eight great-grandchildren.

Quick story—an SLWG myth, as it were: apparently, James spent his life as a serious man, the owner of a construction company. When he retired, his wife, Edmee, encouraged him to pursue his passion for poetry. She passed away soon after his retirement, and James was crushed. Dorothy, Edmee's childhood friend, had moved back to St. Louis in hopes of reconnecting, but Edmee passed away shortly after her return. James met Dorothy at the funeral, and they bonded over poetry. Dorothy also encouraged his writing and to seek publication. Dorothy and James married later that year and became important figures within St. Louis Writers Guild.

Linda Sage, President, 1987

Linda and Martin Sage were from Great Britain but resided in St. Louis for many decades. She was a science writer at the Washington University School of Medicine, he a longtime professor and administrator at the University of Missouri-St. Louis. In 1998, Linda and Martin applied for U.S. citizenship. Martin was quickly approved, but Linda's was held up because she didn't provide a religious exemption for why she wouldn't bear arms. The 59-year-old woman cited her personal dislike of war, her health, and her age as reasons. One of the questions was, "If the law requires it, are you willing to bear arms on behalf of the U.S.?" The only allowed exemption was for religious reasons and documentation had to be provided. She challenged the ruling with the help of American Civil Liberties Union of Eastern Missouri, citing her membership in the Ethical Society of Missouri and Supreme Court precedence. She became a citizen, and she and her husband retired to Oregon.

Workshops and Events
Wednesday, May 14, 1981, 6:30 p.m.

Writers' Workshop, SLWG hosted a mini-conference for writers at a restaurant in the Compton Heights area. The program began with dinner which cost $6.50, there was no charge for the conference.

October 15, 1981, 6:30 p.m.

Running A Small Newspaper, presented by Ray Hartman, publisher of three local newspapers. The monthly meeting was open to the public and was held at a Webster Groves Restaurant which was announced at registration. The event was $6 which included the meal and the program.

May 13, 1982
Writers at Work, a panel discussion. The meeting was open to the general public, the price was $6, and it took place in a Kirkwood restaurant which was given when the reservation was made. For information, call G. Lowder or C. Rancillio (call between 8 and 5).

Wednesday, Feb 10, 1983
How to Write and Sell Magazine Articles, presented by Judie Blattner, editor of *Where Magazine* and a freelance writer; Carolyn Callison, editor of *AAA's Midwest Motorist* magazine and freelance writer; and James Jackson, writer/photographer and author of *Pulse of the Forest* and numerous magazine articles. For location and reservation call G. Lowder or C. Rancilio (between 8 and 5 weekdays)

March 10, 1983, 6:30 p.m.
Taxes and the Freelance Writer was discussed at a dinner meeting of the Writers' Guild of St. Louis. $6 fee for dinner. Location was provided at registration.

April 14, 1983, 6:30 p.m.
How to Write and Sell Romances, a discussion on paperback romance novels was presented by Marcella Thum, author of Blazing Star, and Joyce Flaherty, a literary writer. Dinner meeting in a Kirkwood restaurant, $7.

May 12, 1983, 6:30 p.m.
Being a Writer with guest speakers Dean Wooten, feature writer; Noel Leicht, advertising copywriter; Shirley Schooner, ghost writer and editor; and Charlotte Rancillio, a freelance editor. Dinner was $7 at a restaurant in Kirkwood. Call G. Lowder for reservations and location.

November 10 1983, 6 p.m.
How to Write Plays and Screenplays at a Kirkwood Restaurant. Open to the public, reservations required, and the restaurant location was provided at the time of reservation. Cost was $7 which included dinner and the program.

Thursday, May 18, 1984, 6 p.m.
Humor Writing with guest speakers Elaine Viets of the *St. Louis Post-Dispatch*, and award-winning writer, Charles Guenther. Both speakers offered tips on what made good humor writing using examples from the Guild's humor writing contest winning entries. The meeting was held at a Kirkwood Restaurant, $7.

Thursday, September 3, 1987
Novelist Glenn Savan read from his book, White Palace, a love story set in St. Louis. The meeting opened with a get-acquainted cocktail hour at 6 p.m. followed by dinner at 7 p.m. and the program at 8 p.m. in the Windsor Room, of the Cheshire Inn, 6300 Clayton Road. Admission $11.

October 14, 1987
William H. Gass, award-winning author and Washington University professor, was the featured speaker at the dinner meeting in the Windsor Room, at the Cheshire Inn, 6300 Clayton Road. Cocktails served at 6 p.m. followed by dinner at 7 p.m. and the program at 8 p.m. Dinner: $11, program free. Daytime and evening phone numbers were provided for reservations.

Wednesday, January 18, 1989
Authors and Agents presented by author, Linda Madl, and her agent, Joyce Flaherty. The program began with a 6 p.m. social hour, followed by 7 p.m. dinner at Garavelli's Restaurant, 9739 Manchester Road. Admission: $11. Reservations required by January 15 by calling Harriet Marks.

Wednesday, September 20, 1989, 6 p.m.
The Agony and Ecstasy of Writing Garavelli's Restaurant,

9739 Manchester Rd. $14 non-members, and $11 members. Reservations handled by Harriet Marks.

Wednesday, October 16, 1989, 6 p.m.
Writing Opportunities in Public Relations presented by Paul Dusseault, senior account executive for Fleishman-Hillard Inc. at Garavelli's Restaurant.

November 2, 1989
In the *St. Louis Post-Dispatch*, *Letters from the People*, Charles Guenther wrote in to express his displeasure at their coverage of Edgar Award winning authors. They omitted a local winner and he corrected them.

Author, Author

Babette Morgan's Oct 22 Sunday Magazine cover story on Francis M. Nevins Jr. is a fine, warm portrait of an author of highly unusual talents and strong creative energy.

Like his fellow author John Lutz, mentioned as another Edgar Award winner, Nevins has been generous in sharing the secrets of his success with newer and younger writers. As a law professor, he also has counseled writers and artists on legal aspects of their work.

It may interest readers that another St. Louis author, Marcella Thum, won the coveted Edgar Award from the Mystery Writers of America in 1964 for her young adult novel, "The Mystery of Crane's Landing." Thum is the author of nearly 20 volumes of fiction and non-fiction on a wide range of setting and themes.

Charles Guenther, St. Louis

Brad R. Cook

SLWG Logo created in 1996

18 |
St. Louis Writer's Guild in the 1990s

As the MetroLink started to roll around St. Louis, the Trans World Dome became the home of the Rams, and the Cardinals fell under manager Joe Torre, St. Louis Writers Guild moved into a time of transition not only for the organization but for the publishing industry as a whole.

By the early 1990s, St. Louis Writers Guild moved away from journalism. The newspaper no longer dominated the organization. With the rise and prominence of the St. Louis Press Club, there was no longer a need for journalists to be part of the organization unless they were publishing books, in which case many slipped back into SLWG. A new dynamic formed between the old-school writers who believed solely in the traditional established ways of submitting to publishers and magazines, and the new-school of writers who sought more independent forms of publishing. This shift was caused by the dwindling resources for writers, magazines, journals, and other traditional ways of getting short stories and articles published that happened during the nineties. With many of the publishing houses consolidating or closing, there were fewer opportunities for novels, especially those not in popular genres. This rift grew until the e-publishing revolution a decade later. Now, many authors were hybrids, or both traditionally published by a publisher and independently publishing other projects. As novelists and academics became the driving force, genres took over. For a time, romance and mystery became the leading genres, but that shifted as organizations like MORWA (Missouri Romance Writers of America) and Greater St. Louis Chapter of Sisters in Crime became more popular.

The origins of the 1920s, the elegance of the 1930s, the prominence of the 1940s and 1950s, the literary stylings of the 1960s, the journalistic 1970s, and the popularity of the 1980s led to an interesting time for writers and St. Louis Writers Guild. The Writers Guild's membership always ebbed and flowed, as the economy changed, as the city changed, as the publishing industry changed. In the 1990s, a perfect storm of factors led SLWG to drop to its lowest membership since the 1930s, but it never wavered or teetered as an organization. A handful of members carried the organization to the millennium. This isn't a story of how the Guild was saved or how it almost died; that wasn't the case. This is the tale of how St. Louis Writers Guild returned to its roots as the millennium approached.

In the beginning, about 30 people gathered every month through the Season, and currently about 60 people meet monthly throughout the year for a two-hour workshop for writers. In the 1990s, St. Louis Writers Guild returned to those early days. It needed to. In returning to its origins, the organization set the foundation of what a literary organization should be, one that was focused on the writers. Each board since the 90s has looked back, not to some obscure beginning, but to a time not long ago, when a few dedicated writers banded together to help other writers. Writers need each other, to answer common problems, to encourage, and celebrate publications. Several members of this time are still part of St. Louis Writers Guild. Their continued inclusion meant that when St. Louis Writers Guild reached its largest membership ever, it still held on to its beginnings, to helping writers thrive.

The Monthly Meetings during the 1990s

At the beginning of the decade, St. Louis Writers Guild met monthly at Garavelli's Restaurant, 9739 Manchester Road, across from Hacienda Restaurant, or The Salad Bowl in the Central West End. This shifted in the middle of the decade to St. Louis Community College at Forest Park theater department, the Mildred

E. Bastian Center for the Performing Arts, Room T-007, 5600 Oakland Avenue. By the end of the decade, the monthly meeting was held at McNulty's Irish Pub and Grill at Westport Plaza. The yearly award ceremony was held at Schneithorst's Restaurant at Lindbergh Boulevard and Clayton Road.

The monthly meeting was held on the third Wednesday and retained the format of the 1970s and 1980s, with cocktails beginning at 6:30 p.m., dinner at 7 p.m., and the program following at 8 p.m. However, with the switch to St. Louis Community College, the meetings began with the program at 7 p.m., and the length of the program extended to the two-hour format that dominated the next several decades. This schedule continued when the organization moved to McNulty's Irish Pub and Grill. Dinner was now the responsibility of the guest, and the program began at 7 p.m. The format consisted of the president usually presiding over the meeting. Roll was called and members were allowed to share their latest accomplishments. Then the speaker was introduced and held a discussion on a variety of topics, though often it was an author discussing their process or their work.

The Season schedule continued with workshops being held from September to May, though this coincided with the class schedule for St. Louis Community College.

St. Louis Writers Guild's 75th Anniversary

Once again, St. Louis Writers Guild was featured in the newspaper. On Sunday, March 3, 1996, St. Louis Writers Guild was showcased in the *Webster-Kirkwood Journal* in an article titled, "The Write Stuff: Guild Attracts Local Wordsmiths" by Charles Mosley. He opened the article, "In an age of voice mail, fiber optics networks and satellite communications, it is reassuring to know there still are people who share a passion for the written word." The article highlighted St. Louis Writer's Guild's 75th Anniversary.

Mary Schirmer, SLWG president described the organization, "A main purpose of the Writers Guild is to allow writers to get to know each other. I think the most important thing the Guild has done for me is get me in touch with other writers and allow me to learn more about the art and craft of writing."

The History of St. Louis Writers Guild

Chris Wayland, the vice president said, "We have a real wide range. We have technical writers, journalists, scriptwriters, poets, novelists. We always welcome new members."

Ins + Outs

In the archives of St. Louis Writers Guild, there is an old issue of Ins + Outs, the Guild's newsletter in the 1990s. Much like The Scribe that followed, it was an 11x17 piece of paper that was folded in half, long ways, to create a newsletter that was 8.5x11. That was folded in half and sealed with sticker, leaving a 5.5 x 8.5 packet that could be stamped, addressed, and mailed.

Not only did it contain the news of the day about St. Louis Writers Guild and its events, it published the winners of the poetry and short story contests. Each year, the winning entries were given cash awards and had their work published in the newsletter.

Several members served as editor for Ins + Outs. One of them was Louis Lanier, who was editor in the early 1990s.

The Classic Logo

In 1996 as Terry Gibson became president, he decided the organization needed a proper logo. Branding had never really been needed before. Words had been SLWG's brand, in the newspapers, or through the accounts of those writing them. However, in the 1990s, as flyers, letterhead, nametags, and other promotional material required a singular identity, the need arose for a logo for websites and other official Guild documents. It was fortuitous that Terry Gibson sought a logo when he did.

St. Louis Writers Guild held a design contest. The logo contest was open to anyone, and announcements were made in the newspapers, which ran throughout the month of October, and called on marketers and advertising people to enter.

A cash prize of $50 was awarded to the winning designer, though they lost all rights to the image. Submissions had to be on 8.5 x 11 white paper in black ink and the design had to be versatile enough to be set on buttons, mugs, and stationery, and be appropriate to writers in all genres. Lastly, St. Louis Writers Guild had to be prominently displayed. Entries had to be submitted with a $3 entry fee to the P.O. Box listed by October 30, 1996.

The design that won featured a quill pen with St. Louis Writers Guild in a script font with oversized first letters. The Classic Logo, as it became known, went through several incarnations. First, it was only the quill pen and St. Louis Writers Guild written in script. Then, "founded in 1920" was set in italics below the writing. Next, the phrase, "A Chapter of Missouri Writers Guild" stretched across the whole bottom. Soon, an inkwell was added. It remained only filled with ink until the two-digit year was included and changed with new each Season from 2010 to 2015. Finally, a rounded corner border was added that encapsulated everything in a rectangular shape.

From 1996 onward, the quill became an iconic image for St. Louis Writers Guild. The Classic Logo appeared on all SLWG material from 1996 to 2015, including t-shirts, polo shirts, coffee mugs, journals, and more.

The Classic Logo was an icon of St. Louis Writers Guild and remained fondly in use, until the need for a square-shaped logo, for social media platforms, the new website, and more, took precedence. Another design contest was held. The Classic Logo was still available on merchandise at the time of printing this book, and could be found displayed on the current website's history page.

The identity of the person who designed the Classic Logo could not be ascertained. Many inquiries were made, but no one could remember the individual's name. Given the reactions, it was possible the person was not a part of the SLWG. No matter who the person was, the icon they helped create defined an era of St. Louis Writers Guild.

The Memorial Writing Contests:
Deane Wagner Poetry Contest and the James H. Nash Short Story Contest

In 1994, St. Louis Writers Guild honored two deceased members who had greatly impacted the organization and the city's literary community. With the annual poetry and short story contests now memorializing Deane Wagner and James H. Nash, the contests became known as St. Louis Writers Guild Memorial Writing

Contests. Both contests were popular. They had been before, and after being named for these members, their popularity only grew. The James H. Nash Memorial Short Story Contest had started out as the Winifred Irwin Short Story Contest for Unpublished Writers, so it wasn't odd to have it named. Plus, because the name when not memorializing was the St. Louis Writers Guild Annual Short Story Contest, many presidents and contest coordinators over the years had tried to rename it.

Deane Wagner was a popular poet, beloved by the local writing community. Those who knew her still talk fondly about her, and because her death was a tragedy (see her bio under Members of SLWG in 1990s), it appeared as though naming the contest after her allowed many to heal.

During my time on the board in the 2000s, it was suggested we rename the contest, at first, because it had been over two decades and no one remembered Deane Wagner. Then another member passed away, and it was suggested that it could be renamed for a more recent member. However, I argued that history is important. I researched Deane, wrote her history in an article for *The Scribe*, and included a bit about her on the contest form. The contest is at least 26 years old now, and it doesn't appear to be changing anytime soon.

The James H. Nash Memorial Short Story Writing Contest eventually ended. In 1999, many aspects of St. Louis Writers Guild changed to adjust to the situation the Guild was in, the changes in publishing, and the need for change brought by the new millennium. Either shortly before or during this transition, the James H. Nash Memorial Short Story Contest was changed back to the St. Louis Writers Guild Annual Short Story Contest. It also became known as the St. Louis Writers Guild Legacy Short Story Contest. By the time I'd joined the board, people remembered the contest but thought it had been a separate contest.

St. Louis Writers Guild Play Festival

On Friday, May 19, 1995 St. Louis Writers Guild and the Communication Department of St. Louis Community College at Forest Park partnered to hold a Play Festival. Each play was 10 minutes long and was an original work by a St. Louis playwright. The festival began at 7 p.m. in room T-204, Forest Park Community College Theater, 5600 Oakland Avenue. It was free to attend.

The Presidents
1990 – Chuck Hardwick
1991 – Frank Foley
1992 – Julie Keleman
1993 – Jan Shafferkoetter
1994 – Mary Schirmer
1995 – Mary Schirmer
1996 – Terry Gibson
1997 – Terry Gibson
1998 – Terry Gibson
1999 – Terry Gibson

* Information discovered through research; **bold** means it has been confirmed

Board Members in the 1990s
1990
Chuck Hardwick, President
Deane Wagner, Treasurer
Louis Lainer, Secretary

1995 (incomplete)
Mary Schirmer, President
Chris Wayland, Vice president

Members in the 1990s
Thank you to Louis Lanier, St. Louis Writers Guild member in the 1990s. Louis answered all my questions about his time and Deane Wagner.

Guy Bates
Guy Bates, award-winning writer, poet, editor, artist, and graphic designer, founded wysiwyg publishing company in 1991. A co-founder of The Writer's Workshop, he was a board member

of St. Louis Writers Guild, and a founding board member and first elected president of the SLPA, St. Louis Publishers Association.

Guy Bates Books,
Leper and Other Strangers
Lucky Lady Russell Stickney
All of the Roses

Bill Borst

Bill Borst was originally from New York, but he made his home in St. Louis. Known for his baseball history, specifically St. Louis Browns' history, he published several articles and books about the baseball team. In the 1990s, he had a sports radio show on WGNU-AM.

St. Louis Browns: The Story of a Beloved Team (2017), *The Best of Seasons: Celebration of the 1944 St. Louis Cardinals and St. Louis Browns* (1995), *Baseball through a Knothole: A St. Louis History* (1980), *Ohio State Football Trivia* (1988), *October Classic* (1989), *The Brown Stocking* (1985), *Pride of St. Louis: A Cooperstown Gallery* (1984), *Brooklyn Dodgers Fan Memorial 1953-1957* (1982),

Frank Foley – President 1991

A veteran of World War II and the D-Day Invasion, Frank Foley was also a local actor, participating in many local plays held at the Loretto Hilton Theatre and other locations throughout greater St. Louis. He was an extra in several movies shot in St. Louis. He was a lead usher at the Fox Theatre, a tour guide at the Missouri Botanical Garden, a dedicated volunteer at the Missouri History Museum, and a board member of the Carondelet Historical Society. An avid quilter, he donated many quilts over the years. He loved Bingo; he and Louis Lanier even played together on occasion at Notre Dame High School in South St. Louis. During his presidency, he moved the meetings to The Salad Bowl in the Central West End. Frank Foley Jr. passed away on December 1, 2013 at the age of 94.

Terry Gibson – President, 1996, 1997, 1998, and 1999

Terry oversaw the Guild's first modern branding, bringing

a logo, a style guide, merchandise and more to the organization. He still came to a couple of Workshops for Writers Events when they were at the Kirkwood Community Center, around 2010. He oversaw St. Louis Writers Guild at its lowest moment, and kept the Guild together, while inching the organization toward the millennium.

He wrote under the name Terrance K. Gibson. His novel *What's So Great About Sex: A Romantic Comedy* (2006), was described as "Before Hollywood gave us the 40-Year-Old Virgin, Wilbur Klutzheimer was the twenty-nine-year-old virgin in *What's so Great About Sex*? To some people, virginity is a state of sacredness, discipline, and purity. But . . ."

Chuck Hardwick

The Spirit of St. Louis was published by Scribner. The author described the book as being "about flying and an aviator's line in the beginning third of the twentieth century."

Mary Schirmer – President, 1994 and 1995

Mary Schirmer was an actress and writer, known for *St. Louis Paparazzi Inc.* (2009) and *Thursday* (2005). During her time as president, and through her connections, St. Louis Writers Guild held events at the St. Louis Community College at Forest Park.

Julie Kelemen

"Emerged from a maternity ward just outside St. Louis, Mo. Nothing has been the same since." (Julie Kelemen on MuckRack.com)

A journalist, educator, and author, Julie Kelemen was president of St. Louis Writers Guild in 1992. At that time, she was a copy editor for the Suburban Journal, holding that position from 1997 to 2003. After leaving St. Louis, she moved to Wisconsin where she taught English Composition I and II at the University of Wisconsin, Barron County, in Rice Lake, Wisconsin. She went on to be the managing editor and a reporter for the Superior Catholic Herald in Superior, Wisconsin. She has three children's books published by Liguori Publications.

Julie graduated from the University of Kalamazoo with a Bachelor of Fine Arts and went on to receive a Master of Fine Arts from Washington University. She was a member of the Catholic Press Association, American Copy Editors Society, and the Association of Opinion Journalists.

Christopher Kelleher

Christopher Kelleher was a distinguished attorney, specializing in business and copyright. He was also a children's author. Chris was the founder and President of The Law Firm for Businesses. He received numerous awards, including Small Business Lawyer of the Year recognized by the U.S. Senate, and was voted one of the Top 100 St. Louisans to Know by the *Small Business Monthly*. Active in many community service agencies, Chris served as Chairperson of The Missouri Bar Association Business Law Committee, board member of Catholic Community Services, US Bank Small Business Advisory Board, and the Alumni Council for the John Cook School of Business at Saint Louis University. Known as a prolific writer and guest speaker, Chris graduated from Saint Louis University School of Law where he was named to the Order of the Woolsack and earned his MBA, cum laude, from the SLU John Cook School of Business. He graduated summa cum laude from Saint Louis University where he was elected to Phi Beta Kappa. He was married to Shelia Kelleher, and they had a daughter, Shannon, and a son Conor. Christopher passed away in December 2012; he was 52.

Louis Lanier

Louis published his first young adult novel *Rurals and Townies* in 2014, and followed that with *Rurals and Townies, Rurals Rule: Molly's Revenge*, and *Townies' Turn: Molly's Challenge*. All of them are part of the Blanchette High series. A fourth novel in the series, Rurals on Top: Molly's Triumph, launched on April 28, 2018. The fifth novel of the Blanchette High series, *Rurals and Townies Hit the Ice,* debuted in 2019.

He joined St. Louis Writers Guild in 1989, and served as Secretary and editor of *Ins + Outs*, SLWG's newsletter in the 1990s.

He along with Terri Travis (now Terri Blunt) were involved in an online writers' group on the computer service, CompuServe. Included in that group were noted authors such as Daniel Pinkwater and Jane Yolen.

Helen G. McMahon

Helen Griffin McMahon, writer, poet, and editor died of infirmities on Saturday, Sept 25, 1999. She was 88 and lived in Shrewsbury. She was an editorial consultant for Reliable Life Insurance Co. She wrote several books, including, *The Rhyme of My Life*, a book of poems, Portals to Protection, and *Shrewsbury – Of All Places*. She also did some freelance writing and wrote *Neath the Oaks*, an anthology of local authors. A founder of the Shrewsbury Historical Society, she was the unofficial historian of that community. She was a member of St. Louis Writers Guild, the Missouri Writers' Guild, the Webster Groves Monday Club, International Association of Business Communicators, Women in Communications, the Industrial Press Association, and the Press Club of St. Louis. In 1942, she wrote a parody, "A Visit from St. Nicholas," based on "Night Before Christmas," which was published in the *St. Louis Globe-Democrat*. The poem received national headlines when President FDR praised it for its patriotic spirit and good humor about wartime shortages and rationing.

Joan and Ferd Potthast

Every year, at the end of the Season, St. Louis Writers Guild held its annual members' picnic. The event was potluck, and held at the Potthast Farm located in St. Charles County. Joan and Ferd Potthast were longtime members who hosted this highlight of the year. The photos show relaxed members hanging around in small groups, talking, some with plates of food on their laps. Everyone looked happy.

Ferd wrote nonfiction, primarily historical essays, and was the editor of the Didion and Son's Foundry newsletter. Before writing, he served with the St. Charles County Sheriff's Department. Joan was a poet and an English and Drama teacher at St. Dominic High School. They established a small writing nook, a writer's retreat, for those who lived in the city to go to write.

Jan Schafferkoetter (Jan McNichols)
Jan Schafferkoetter was travel writer who visited much of the world. She was a freelance writer who also worked for the *St. Louis Post-Dispatch*. She held many duties within St. Louis Writers Guild, serving on the board of directors and coordinating the writing contests. In March 2000, she hosted an event at the St. Louis County Library Headquarters where she discussed her Travelog Series: Kiss the Blarney Stone.

Chuck Sweetman
Chuck Sweetman served as a treasurer for the Guild when Louis Lanier joined. He worked as an IT specialist for McDonnell Douglas. He wrote science fiction, specifically, dystopian Science Fiction.

Deane Wagner
Deane Wagner was an accomplished writer and poet whose work was published locally and nationally, with pieces in *River Styx, Anthology of Women Writers,* and *Image Magazine.* The first Director of Community Development for the city of Ferguson, holding the position from the 1970s into the 1990s. She oversaw many projects during her years with the city, like the merger of the school districts, the urban homesteader project, revitalization of historic Church Street, and the Three-Fountains Festival. She was a member of the Missouri Arts Council, St. Louis Poetry Center, St. Charles Writers Guild, National Pen Women, and the Wednesday Club. Not only a member, she served as Treasurer of St. Louis Writers Guild in 1990 and 1991.

Always one to share her opinions on the day's headlines, she often wrote the editor and in fact often it was her letter that related to the accompanying cartoon.

In one letter from the January 16, 1980 *St. Louis Post-Dispatch* recounted how she sent a Valentine to her state representative, it had lace doily with a large pink paper heart, and a poem: It's message:

The Yearning heart
Only you can gratify –
Give ERA
Your vote to ratify.

In another letter posted in the *St. Louis Post-Dispatch* in August 1984 she disagreed with the Administration's opinion about a weak dollar overseas being good for agriculture back home, and shared her wittily-worded retort.

She supported several causes important to her by having her name included in a full page newspaper ad for NARAL (National Abortion Rights Action League) and the new R-2 school district, among many others.

Deane Wagner won the Narrative Prize in the annual St. Louis Poetry Center's contest in June of 1980 for her poem, "Before Diagnosis," and the Otto Tomsich Gallery Award from SLPC in May of 1985. She received artwork worth $100 for her poem, "A Courtyard for a Friend."

A lover of poetry she taught workshops, like the one in February 1989, "Framing the Sound: On Writing Poetry," for the Ferguson City Council. Deane Wagner died at home, on Tuesday, July 27, 1993 after a long and courageous fight against cancer. Her death was directly attributable to illnesses related to cigarette smoking. She expressed a fervent wish that any current smokers who read the obituary sense the great loss and devastation for all those involved. In lieu of flowers, memorials in her name were made to the Ferguson Public Library, North County League of Women Voters, and the local multiple Sclerosis Society. Her husband, Frederick J. Wagner, had already passed away in May 1978, and together they had four daughters, April, Adriann, Cynthia, and Maria.

She and her husband included this verse from "Invictus" by William Ernest Henley with their obituaries; apparently it was their favorite:

It matters not how straight the gate.
How charged with punishment the scroll
I am the Captain of my fate
I am the Master of my soul.

Carol Winkler

"Your mom was such a woman of genuine grace, and she seldom had a bad word to say about anyone. She'd always give people the benefit of the doubt when she first knew or met them—not a judgmental bone in her that I could ever see and a heart the size of Australia. If I could be half the woman she was I'd be quite blessed indeed." (A quote from Julie Kelemen, from Carol Winkler's obituary guest book.)

Carol and Ralph C. Winkler had four children. She wrote for the Meramec Community College newspapers while attending the institution. She served as membership director for St. Louis Writers Guild. She even joined Frank Foley and Louis Lanier for bingo.

Carol passed away in November 2017.

Workshops and Events
February 19, 1990

An ad was run in the *St. Louis Post-Dispatch* about the annual writing contest. *"The St. Louis Writers Guild is accepting manuscripts for the annual James Nash Memorial Writing Contest. Entries must be unpublished and between 500 and 2,500 words. Cash prizes range from $100 to $25. Entry fee is $5, and entries must be postmarked by April 5. Information: St. Louis Writers Guild Contest, the 7000 block of Grove Avenue, St. Louis, MO 63119"*

Wednesday, March 19, 1990, 6 p.m.
Travel Writing at Garavelli's Restaurant, 9739 Manchester.

December 31, 1991

A writing contest ad ran in the *St. Louis Post-Dispatch*. *"The St. Louis Writers' Guild is accepting manuscripts for its annual James Nash Memorial Writing Contest. Essays entered in the competition will be judged by Mary Kimbrough, a columnist and author of six books. First prize in the contest is $100. Manuscripts must be postmarked by April 1. Information about the contest may be obtained by writing to the Guild."*

November 18, 1992, 7 p.m.

John Lutz, author of *SWF Seeks Same*, spoke at a dinner program at the Radisson Hotel, 7750 Carondelet Avenue. Reservations had to be arranged by 6pm on Sunday by calling the number provided. The fee was $15 for SLWG Members and $18 for non-members.

Wednesday, Jan 18, 1993

Science-Fiction writer Allen Stelle spoke about his current novel, *Labyrinth of Night*, at a dinner program at the Radisson Hotel-Clayton., 6 p.m. start, dinner was at 7 p.m., and the program began at 8 p.m.

January 18, 1995, 7 p.m.

Fullbright scholar John A. Wright, a local historian and assistant superintendent of the Ferguson-Florissant School District, discussed his latest book, *Discovering African-American St. Louis: A Guide to Historic Sites,* at the St. Louis County Library, 1640 S. Lindbergh Boulevard, Frontenac. For information call Mary Schirmer at the number provided.

Friday, May 19, 1995, 7 p.m.

On May 11, May 14, and May 18 ads were run in the *St. Louis Post-Dispatch* for the Play Festival.

The St. Louis Writers Guild partnered with the Communication Department of St. Louis Community College at Forest Park to offer a 10-minute play festival at the college, 5600 Oakland Avenue. The plays, no longer than 10 minutes were original works by St. Louis writers, and admission was free.

October 12, 1995, 7 p.m.

The Writing World: Live on the Internet presented by fiction writer L.J. Launer in Room L007 Library Building, Forest Park Community College.

Wednesday, January 11, 1996, 7:30 p.m.

Nonfiction writer Eddy Harris, author of *Mississippi Solo*

and *Native Stranger* spoke at St. Louis Community College at Forest Park, Room 007, Library Building.

Wednesday, January 9, 1997, 6 p.m.
True-crime writer Alva W. Busch spoke at the monthly dinner meeting at McNulty's Irish Pub, West Port Plaza. Call for cost.

February 14-16, Feb 22-23, 1997
St. Louis Writers Guild presented **Let Our Words Be Heard and Scene**. Reader's theater featuring poems, short stories and short plays by members. St. Louis Community College at Forest Park theater department. Mildred E. Bastian Center for the Performing Arts. 5600 Oakland Avenue.

March 6, 13, and 27, 1997
Announcements were made in the *St. Louis Post-Dispatch*, about the writing contest.

Artistic Opportunities. St. Louis Writer's Guild: Announces its 1997 writing contest in memory of James Nash and Deane Wagner. Competition is open to writers living within 50 miles of St. Louis. A $5 reading fee is required with each entry. Entries must be postmarked by April 1.

April 3, 1997, 9:30 a.m. to noon
Elements of Short Fiction, SLWG Workshop at the Midtown Arts Center, 3270 Washington Avenue. Reservations required. Fee: $10 members, $20 non-members.

Saturday, May 15, 1997, 10 a.m.
Calvary Cemetery Tour, 5329 W. Florissant Avenue. Sponsored by the St. Louis Writer's Guild. Free for Guild Members, $3 for non-members.

May 15 1997, 6 p.m.
Novelist David Carkeet and poet Louis Jobst were the guest speakers at the SLWG Banquet at the Henry VII Hotel and Conference Center, 4690 N. Lindbergh Boulevard, $20.

July 3, 1997
A call for screenplays for Cinema Spoke, Screenwriter's Reading Session. Held by St. Louis Writers Guild in collaboration with MIMA.

March 12, 1998, 7 p.m.
Publicity with writer and publisher Evonne Weinhaus at McNulty's Pub and Grill, 620 West Port Plaza, Interstate 270 and Page Avenue.

May 16-17, 1998, 10 a.m.
Writers Workshop sponsored by the St. Louis Writers Guild at Barnes and Noble, 9618 Watson Road. Free.

September 19, 1998, 10 a.m.
Writing Workshop sponsored by the St. Louis Writers Guild at Barnes and Noble, 9618 Watson Road. Free.

October 8, 1998
MediaARTS Alliance, in collaboration with the St. Louis Writer's Guild, made a call for screenplays for the third session of CinemaSpoke. The program provided a forum for local screenwriter's scripts to be read aloud by amateur and professional actors. Those interested in an application and information were to call the number provided.

April 27, 1999
The *St. Louis Post-Dispatch* ran an article by Joe Holleman, film critic, on the sessions of CinemaSpoke. *"Folks at CinemaSpoke speak right up if your screenplay is a bomb."*

It was a showcase of the collaboration between St. Louis Writers Guild and the MediaArts Alliance. CinemaSpoke was a local group that met monthly to read screenplays by other group members. Mary Schirmer started CinemaSpoke two years prior, a collaboration between the St. Louis Writers Guild and the MediaArts Alliance.

He described the event which featured a reading and critique of a short play. Six or seven people would read the work aloud, and then 30 or so people gave a critique. The writer was prohibited from speaking.

"For any writer, this potentially frightening," said Mary Schirmer, whose script was featured at the last meeting. "But it doesn't do any good for a writer to have some friend say, 'Oh, honey, it's really good' when it isn't good,"

Schirmer's story, "Losing Battle," a romantic comedy about a security guard who has to lose 50 pounds or lose his job. His battle with his waist kicks off an affair of the heart with a woman who works in the mall our hero guards.

Saturday May 15, 1999, 10 a.m. to noon
Point of View and Style presented by poet and fiction writer, Guy Bates. at Barnes and Noble, 9618 Watson Road in Crestwood. Free.

May 27, 1999, 6 p.m.
Annual St. Louis Writers Guild Banquet with guest speakers Frederick and Patricia McKissack at Henry VII Hotel, 4690 North Lindbergh Boulevard, $21, reservations requested.

Saturday, July 17, 1999, 10 a.m. to noon
Writing Narrative Poetry with local poet Diana Davis; attendees were to bring at least one sample of their writing. Barnes and Noble in Crestwood, $3.

Wednesday, August 18, 1999, 6 p.m.
Writing Biographies presented by Harper Barnes, editor of St. Louis magazine, at McNulty's Bar and Grill, 520 West Port Plaza, Interstate 270 and Page Avenue. $3, dinner separate.

Saturday, August 21, 1999, 10 a.m.
Short Story Writing at Barnes and Noble, 9618 Watson Road in Crestwood, Free.

Wednesday, September 15, 1999, 6 p.m.
Donnybrook host Martin Duggan at McNulty's Irish Pub and Grill, 620 West Port Plaza in Maryland Heights. $3, buy own

dinner.

September 23, 1999, 7 p.m.
Electronic Publishing and Membership in St. Louis Writers Guild presented by Brian Lawrence at Borders Books and Music, 11745 Olive Boulevard in Creve Coeur. Free. (*Not a guild event, it was perhaps his book signing*)

Wednesday, October 20, 1999, 6 p.m.
Mysteries for Literary Snobs: The Plight of Being a Genre Writer with Michael Kahn at McNulty's Irish Pub and Grill, 620 West Port Plaza in Maryland Heights. $3, dinner on your own.

November 11, 1999, 7 p.m.
Electronic Publishing with Brian Lawrence, author of Nightshade, at McNulty's Irish Pub and Grill, 620 West Port Plaza in Maryland Heights, at Page Avenue and Interstate 270. $3

Saturday, November 20, 1999, 11 a.m. to 1 p.m.
The St. Louis Writers Guild presented a book fair with signing and question-and-answer sessions featuring poet Charles Guenther, mystery writers Michael Kahn and Susan McBride, and Romance writer Bobbi Smith at St. Louis Artists Guild, 2 Oak Knoll Parkk in Clayton, Free.

Saturday, December 18, 1999, 10 a.m.
Editing and Revising with Jim Rygeiski, co-author of *The I-55 Series: Cubs vs. Cardinals*, at Barnes and Noble, 9618 Watson Road Free.

85th Anniversary Members Booklet from 2005

19 |
St. Louis Writers Guild, 2000-2005, David Motherwell, President

After 80 years, the turn of the millennium brought about an interesting time for St. Louis Writers Guild. The organization had to deal with a changing publishing industry, dwindling opportunities for writers, and a world quickly moving into the future but constrained by the methods of the previous century.

Sure, everyone survived Y2K, but the millennium brought the emergence of technologies that reshaped the publishing industry. However, they weren't yet integrated into the publishing industry or the individual writer's life.

Writers at this time still sent queries via snail mail or by parcel. Certainly, typing had improved. Most used Microsoft Word or would be moving soon from similar programs, like Word Perfect or Microsoft Works. No longer was handwriting or typing the only options for writers. If their muses demanded, handwriting and typewriters were still available, but increasingly, computers became the main tool of the writer.

However, it was not quite the digital age, just yet.

Writers and members of this time sent newsletters via the mail, and used phone numbers to gather information. However, the price of stamps was ever increasing, as were printing costs and other fees. Email existed but most people didn't have it. Querying was accomplished with paper query letters and submission pages stuffed into an envelope and sent to a literary agent. Requests meant printing the whole manuscript and sending it via UPS or FedEx to the literary agent. Then writers waited weeks to get the return of their own self-addressed, stamped envelope with folded creases from having been stuffed into the original envelope—inside, a cutoff strip of paper a couple of inches wide with a form rejection paragraph. Writers lived for those strips. Often, they were posted on the wall of an office, or collected together in a box.

Leading the Guild through this time was David Motherwell, the longest consecutively serving President of St. Louis Writers Guild. He guided the Guild through its toughest years and then passed the mantle on to Robin Moore Thiess, who was the Vice President at the time. Born in Chicago, he moved to a sixty-acre farm in Arkansas when he was 3 months old. With a degree in civil engineering, he worked all over the world on projects from nuclear power plants, the Saudi power grid, NASA rockets, the first skyscraper built in the USA using the metric system, and the St. Louis MetroLink light rail extension. In 1999, he penned a memoir, *Life on Sunnyside Farm.*

David Motherwell, who once climbed Mt. Kilimanjaro, is a tall and thin man with a calm demeanor. He was described by more than one member as being, "sharp as a tack."

The Monthly Meeting in the 2000s

St. Louis Writers Guild continued the tradition of meeting on the third Wednesday of the month. However, they began a new tradition with an event on Saturday mornings. At the Wednesday dinner meeting, the meal was now the guest's responsibility, instead of being included in the price. The fee to attend the meeting was $3. The program started at 7 p.m. In January 2000, St. Louis Writers Guild met at McNulty's Irish Bar and Grill, in West Port Plaza, Interstate 270 and Page Avenue. Interested people could call for more details. Programs consisted of an author talking about their books or a topic of interest to writers.

In the early 2000s, St. Louis Writers Guild started to hold events at the Crestwood Barnes & Noble on Watson Road. At first it was a chance to sell books; SLWG held a book fair at the store, but soon they held a workshop on the first Saturday of the month, from 10 a.m. to noon in the Community Room.

For a time in the early 2000s, the events all were free to attend. It corresponded to the time when SLWG was at its lowest membership and was done to attract the interest of the public. By about 2003, the fees had returned. It is at this time that the $5 fee for non-members came into use and has continued to the current meetings.

A Drop in Membership

When David Motherwell took over the presidency in 2000, SLWG Membership had fallen to the lowest number since 1920. There were many reasons for the decline, but it had much to do with the transitioning world. Email, the internet, and the modern independent publishing movement were in their infancy. St. Louis Writers Guild struggled to find its identity as the publishing world lost so many publications. Newspapers and magazines were dwindling in numbers and had yet to be replaced by anything. Writing hadn't taken off as one of America's pastimes, and the idea of joining a writers' group wasn't on many people's minds.

Thirty members—that was it, maybe less. Dues were lower than they are today, and they met in a restaurant once a month to discuss a writing topic and have lunch. Given the size the Guild would become, it might sound really small, but these were *writers*. I know many of these members, and they were a tight-knit group of friends. I almost envy that time: the personal attention they directed toward each other, the bonds that lasted for decades. Most were working writers, the backbone of any significant writers' group. St. Louis Writers Guild could have collapsed at any moment. It had been around 80 years, a good run for certain, but it didn't fold. These amazing writers innovated, held the mantel of tradition high, and eventually grew the Guild.

Some great stories, lasting friendships, and lifetime members came from this time. Hats off to each of them. They preserved the Guild in its most dire hour. They endured because they loved not only the organization, but also the St. Louis literary community, and most of all they believed in helping other writers.

The History of St. Louis Writers Guild

The Most Epic Story in SLWG History –
The Run to Save the St. Louis Writers Guild

One might try and claim hyperbole, some might call it exaggeration, but there are moments one can point to and say ... this day mattered, this day changed the future of St. Louis Writers Guild... One such day was August 22, 2004.

With only a handful of members, and a number of expensive costs incurred over the year, the Guild was running out of money. They cut the number of pages in *The Scribe* to four, but it wasn't enough. St. Louis Writers Guild had little money, and much of it went to the contests and newsletters, not to mention the monthly meeting. So, when the time came to buy a software package in order to send out an electronic newsletter on a regular basis through the new email format, there simply wasn't enough money in the budget.

Thus, Donna Springer, Treasurer at the time, raised the money by running a marathon. Yes, a marathon. Donna volunteered to participate in what was dubbed the St Louis Heritage (pledge) Run. She was already training for the Lewis & Clark Marathon on Sept 19, so this became part of her training. People from St. Louis Writers Guild and across St. Louis pledged money, and she was able to raise enough to buy the software. On August 22, she ran 15 miles round trip from the Kate Chopin star on University City's Walk of Fame to poet Eugene Field's House near the riverfront. Her route included Forest Park, the Central West End, and parts of St. Louis University and Washington University campuses.

Coincidentally, August 22nd was the birthday of authors Ray Bradbury and Dorothy Rothschild Parker. Also, on that date in 1762, Ann Franklin became America's first newspaper editor – of the *Newport Mercury* (Rhode Island). In 1932, it was the date of the first experimental TV broadcast in England. A note regarding St. Louis Heritage: Ulysses S. Grant and Julia Dent were married on this day in 1848.

Donna Springer ran a total of 15 miles and raised $325!

Once SLWG was able to send out a monthly email, the numbers began to rise. It wasn't a crazy amount, but it attracted a few more members who continued to carry the torch.

David Motherwell wrote a touching tribute in *The Scribe*—"We're Running on Empty!" and Donna Springer wrote of her own experience in *St. Louis Reflections* with "Run Across the Mississippi River."

The 85th Anniversary

By September 2005, money was okay and membership had risen from 60 to 140 members. The organization grew to the point of needing to become a more formal group. David Motherwell held the first Business Meeting on September 3, 2005. It didn't replace the monthly meeting, but became an addition to the meeting. The business meeting started at 9:30 a.m., and the board discussed St. Louis Writers Guild's affairs. The goal was to talk for 30 minutes, but the first meeting ran long. After the business meeting, a 5+5 critique workshop was held. The first one was such a success that they decided to hold them quarterly. The business meeting took only 30 minutes, maybe a slight bit of the meeting. Eventually though, business became too much to discuss before a meeting, and a separate board meeting was created in 2006.

At that meeting, the executive board discussed final details of the start of a young writers' program in conjunction with St. Louis Writers Studio, plus, details about the St. Louis Book Festival on Oct 21-23, 2005, where they hosted an author's book table and featured a presentation by Walter Bargen, as well as a presentation on the features of a new website.

The 85th Anniversary Celebration

St. Louis Writers Guild Membership Chairman Peggy Haldeman wrote about the event for *The Scribe*:

Sunset 44 provided an elegant setting and scrumptious dinner for 120 friends and supporters of the literary arts who gathered on Thursday, September 15 to celebrate St. Louis writing in honor of the St. Louis Writers Guild's 85th Anniversary.

It was wonderful for me as membership chairman to meet many long-term Guild members who came out in droves to honor three-time Guild President, Charles Guenther, our keynote speaker. Charles delighted us with anecdotes of Guild history and his tale of a family outing that inspired his award-winning poem, St. Genevieve: Memorial Cemetery. We were privileged to hear a few of his translations and original poems as well. David Motherwell, Guild President, presented Charles with an engraved pen and picture frame for his vast and varied contributions to Missouri's literary history and the Guild.

The evening was a rich collaboration of some of St. Louis' finest literary arts organizations, magazines, and individual authors. Featured speakers included Nan Sweet from River Styx, Richard Burgin from Boulevard, Denise Pattiz Bogard from St. Louis Writers Workshops and Ruth-Miriam Garnett from First Civilizations, as well as Michael Castro, Colleen McKee, and Harry Jackson, Jr. Poetry and prose readings ran the gamut from poignant and intense to profound and comical.

Success!

As David Motherwell stepped down, he penned this for *The Scribe*:

I am particularly pleased with the progress we have made this year. It has always been my intention to vacate this position on a positive note. As is true of other presidents from time to time in the long history of the Guild, we have experienced ups and downs. Sometimes our low points seemed especially grim. In my folder of Guild correspondence, I have a letter from a former board member proclaiming, "St. Louis Writers Guild is in danger of folding!" While I knew at the time that this was only one person's pessimistic outlook, there is no question that we have sometimes struggled to maintain our membership in order to further our mission for St. Louis Writers. Thank God, we did not fold; in fact, we have once again risen like Prometheus from his ashes. – David Motherwell, *The Scribe* 2005

The Annual St. Louis Writers Guild Members' Picnic

For many years, St. Louis Writers Guild annual members' appreciation picnic was a highlight of the summer. Usually held in June as the last event before the summer break, a potluck picnic was held from 1994 to 2005 at Ferdinand and Joan Potthast's farm.

(More on this event on page 189, Chapter 18 St. Louis Writer's Guild in the 1990s.)

St. Louis Writers Guild's First Website

Before the days of GoDaddy, Network Solutions, and well before Squarespace, if a community organization wanted to have a web presence, it had to use a service. For St. Louis Writers Guild, that was Postnet.com.

The page had information on the Guild and perhaps a bit more. It would be fascinating to see a screen shot, but sadly none exists.

The URL for the SLWG website was communities.postnet.com/stlouis/writersguild

The President
2000 – 2005 David Motherwell

The Executive Board Members
2005
David Motherwell, President
Robin Moore Theiss, VP of Programs
Peggy Haldeman, Membership Coordinator

Members in the 2000s
Susie Meyer

We should all aspire to be Susie Meyer, a sweet woman who has been an ardent supporter of St. Louis Writers Guild. Susie Meyer was secretary and treasurer for the Guild, but her biggest role was as the program chairman, scheduling many of the speakers during the late 1990s and early 2000s. Having joined the Guild in the 1990s, she remains an active member to this day.

I remember the first time I met her; we were at a workshop. As a new board member, I was helping the author with their book signing. Susie asked me to take a picture of her and the author. She told me she had her picture taken with every author who spoke and showed them to her grandchildren. Susie always had a smile on her face in spite of the many trials she had faced, from a tornado that struck her house to the broken foot she hobbled to every workshop on. She wrote poems, short stories, and essays, and often entered the writing contests.

At her very first meeting, which was at the restaurant next to a bowling alley, she arrived in her nicest suit. The waitress dumped the tray of food all over her, ruining her suit, and yet, Susie became a member.

Dorothy Schertel

Dorothy R. Hussmann Schertel was a columnist for the old *Naborhood Link News* and the author of several historical books. She passed away on Thursday, January 17, 2002 at the age of 83 from kidney failure brought on by complications from Alzheimer's disease. She lived most of her life in Lemay, before spending her last days at the Lutheran Convalescent Home in Webster Groves. She listed herself as a member of St. Louis Writers Guild.

Donna Springer

Donna Springer, a registered nurse, writer, and former board member of St. Louis Writers Guild, famously ran across St. Louis to raise money for SLWG. In 2004, she ran 15 miles and raised $325. A longtime fixture at all SLWG events, she joined in 1986 and is still a member in 2020. A member of the St. Louis Camera Club, the St. Louis track Club, was on the board of directors for the St. Louis Poetry Center, and a former Treasurer, Membership Chair, and 2006 Member of Distinction for St Louis Writers Guild. Her poem "Mid-time, Six A.M. Saint Louis" won an honorary mention in the 2006 Deane Wagner Poetry Contest and was published in *St. Louis Reflections*.

Workshops and Events
January 13, 2000, 7 p.m.
Publishing Trends in the 21st Century, St. Louis Writers Guild kicked off the new millennium with a panelists Lisa Greening of Left Bank Books, Jeffery Fister from Virginia Publishing Co., and local writer, Guy Bates at McNulty's Irish Bar and Grill, 620 West Port Plaza, Interstate 270 and Page Avenue. $3.

February 17, 2000, 10 a.m. to noon
The monthly meeting featured Connie McIntyre, designer of *Make Your Own Book* kits, who demonstrated her kits and discussed making individual books. at Barnes and Noble, 9618 Watson Road. Reservations are required. $5 guests, free for members.

Wednesday, Feb 16, 2000
Persistence presented by Susan McBride, author of *And Then She Was Gone*. Dinner (on your own) at 6 p.m. with the program commencing at 7 p.m. McNulty's Irish Bar and Grill, 620 West Port Plaza, Interstate 270 and Page Avenue. $3, free for members.

Wednesday, March 15, 2000
How Books are Chosen for Review with Jane Henderson, book review editor for the Post-Dispatch at McNulty's Irish Bar and Grill, 620 West Port Plaza, Interstate 270 and Page Avenue. $3 guests, free for members.

Saturday, April 15, 2000, 10 a.m. to noon
How to Find Markets for Your Work on the Web, led by Brian Lawrence. Reservations are required. Barnes & Noble, 9816 Watson Road in Crestwood. Free for members, $5 for others.

Saturday, May 20, 2000, 9 a.m. to 1 p.m.
Book Sale: The St. Louis Writers Guild hosted a book sale of more than 500 hardbacks and paperbacks of all genres as a fund-raiser for the guild. The sale was held in the offices of RealtyNET Walsh, 4924 Hampton Avenue. Free

May 3, 2000
For an unknown amount of time or regularity, an ad was placed at the top of the Everyday section of the St. Louis Post-Dispatch.

"Postnet.com – Begun in 1920, the St. Louis Writers Guild is the oldest organization for writers in the region. To find out more about this and other local arts organizations, go to communities.postnet.com/stlouis/

writersguild"

Saturday, May 27, 2000, 7 p.m.
Annual banquet featured guest speaker, Pauline Laurent, the author of *Grief Denied – A Vietnam Widow's Story*. Laurent detailed the process she used to writer her story, discuss the book's evolution and explained how her perspective had changed. Henry VII Hotel, 4690 North Lindbergh Boulevard in Bridgeton. Free.

Saturday, June 17, 2000, 10 a.m. to noon
An Open Mike for Writers and Poets sponsored by St. Louis Writers Guild. Call to confirm your time at the mike or just stop by and listen. Barnes and Noble, 9618 Watson Road in Crestwood. Free to members, $5 for others.

September 16, 2000
Luella Turner, wrote about author Dusty Richards and his latest book, *The Lawless Land*, for the *St. Louis Post-Dispatch*, "Circle the wagons. Dusty Richards is coming to town on his book tour."

Thursday, September 14, 2000
Book signing at Barnes & Noble, 11952 Manchester Road, Des Peres, 3-5 p.m.
Workshop for Liar's Link at Cultural Arts Center in St. Peters, 7-9 p.m.

Friday, September 15,
Book signing at B Dalton Books at Mid Rivers Mall in St. Peters, 3-6 p.m.

Saturday, September 16,
St. Louis Writers Guild's monthly workshop at Barnes & Noble, 9618 Watson Road, Crestwood, 10 a.m. to noon with a book signing at the store from noon to 1 p.m.

Tuesday, October 23, 2000, 7 p.m. to 9 p.m.
Mystery Writers Susan McBride, Letha Albright will meet fans at the Brentwood Library, 8765 Eulalie Avenue. *Uncover many more events of interest to writers old and new at the St. Louis Writers Guild's postnet.com Community Website, http://communities.postnet.com/stlouis/*

writersguild.

Wednesday, November 15, 2000
The Craft of Poetry with local educator Joan Potthast. Dinner (on your own) at 6 p.m. and the program started at 7 p.m. McNulty's Irish Pub and Grill, West Port Plaza, Page Avenue and Interstate 270 in Maryland Heights. Free Admission.

January 2001, Each Thursday at Noon throughout January
A Brown-Bag Noon Hour Writers Group sponsored by The St. Louis Writer's Guild. in the Community Room next to the Café at the Barnes and Noble, Crestwood. *Bring your lunch and your writing to share for critiquing.*

Saturday, January 20, 2001, 10 a.m.
Workshop allowed each participant to give a five-minute presentation of his or her works and get five minutes of constructive feedback. Barnes & Noble, 9618 Watson Road in Crestwood. Free.

Wednesday, February 21, 2001, 6 p.m.
Home is Where the Heart Is with author, Daniel Williamson. McNulty's Irish Pub and Grill, West Port Plaza, Page Avenue and Interstate 270 in Maryland Heights. Free for members; $3 others.

Saturday, March 3, 2001
Using the Right Word a hands-on workshop from The St. Louis Writers Guild. 10am to Noon, Barnes & Noble, 9618 Watson Road in Crestwood. Free for members, $5 others.

This was the first listing found for the $5 for non-members, a fee that continues at that same price in 2020.

Wednesday, March 21, 2001, 6 p.m.
Ches Schneider discussed his new book, *From Classrooms to Claymores*. McNulty's Irish Pub and Grill, West Port Plaza, Page

Avenue and Interstate 270 in Maryland Heights. Free for members, $3 guests.

Saturday, April 7, 2001, 10 a.m.
Writer's Open Mike and Critique Session: Participants presented old or new work for feedback. Sponsored by the St. Louis Writers Guild. at Barnes & Noble, 9618 Watson Road in Crestwood. Free for members, $5 guests.

Wednesday, April 18, 2001
Award-winning author Jeanie Ransom discussed her novel, **I Don't Want to Talk About It**, which dealt with divorce from a child's point of view. McNulty's Irish Pub and Grill. $3, free for members.

Saturday, May 5, 2001, Noon to 3 p.m.
Sidewalk Book Fair: A reading and book signing with a variety of local authors, presented by Left Bank Books and the St. Louis Writers Guild. on the sidewalk outside Left Bank Books, 399 North Euclid Avenue. Free.

Saturday, July 7, 2001, 10 a.m. to noon
5+5 Workshop for writing, sharing work in progress and networking. Barnes & Noble, 9618 Watson Road, Crestwood. Free for members, $5 for guests.

Wednesday, July 18, 2001
Chris Scribner, discussed his most recent book and the fine art of being a father. Dinner (on your own) at 6 p.m. and the program started at 7 p.m. McNulty's Irish Pub and Grill, West Port Plaza, Page Avenue and Interstate 270 in Maryland Heights. Free for members, $3 guests.

Wednesday, August 15, 2001, 7 to 8 p.m.
Author Jim Jackson. Barnes & Noble 8871 Ladue Road in Ladue. $3. Free for members.

September 1, 2001, 10 a.m. to noon
Tools to Trim the Fat From Poetry and Prose presented by Guy Bates. at Barnes & Nobles, 9618 Watson Road in Crestwood. $5 guests, free for members.

Wednesday September 19, 2001, 7 p.m.
Writing the Query Letter and Synopsis presented by Shirley Kennett, author and member of the Mystery Writers of America. Barnes & Noble, 8871 Ladue Road in Ladue. $3 guests, free for members.

September 26, 2001
The James Nash Memorial Short Story Contest was announced. First prize was $150. Stories should be no more than 5,000 words. Up to three stories per writer may be submitted, and the entry fee was $15 per manuscript. Deadline was October 20. Send manuscripts to: Guy Bates at the P.O. Box address provided.

Wednesday, October 17, 2001, 7 to 8 p.m.
Top 10 Things That Never Change in a Writer's Life presented by best-selling author Bobbi Smith. Barnes & Noble, 8871 Ladue Road in Ladue. Free.

Saturday, October 13, 2001, 2 to 4 p.m.
Published local authors signed copies of their books. Barnes & Noble, 9618 Watson Rd in Crestwood. Free.

Wednesday, January 16, 2002, 7 to 8 p.m.
The group's monthly meeting featured Scottie Priesmeyer who spoke about issues writers must deal with before they write a story. at Barnes & Noble, 8871 Ladue Road in Ladue. Free.

Saturday, January 5, 2002, 10 a.m. to noon
Guy Bastes led a **5+5 Workshop on Creating Settings**. Barnes & Noble, 9618 Watson Road in Crestwood. Free.

Wednesday, February 20, 2002, 7 p.m.
E-Publishing presented by Brian Lawrence. Barnes and Noble, 8871 Ladue Road in Ladue. Free.

Wednesday, March 20, 2002, 7 p.m.
Writers' rights and wrongs – a guide to meeting legal and ethical expectations, and protecting your own rights, too with attorney Mark Sableman. Barnes & Noble, 8871 Ladue Road in Ladue. Free.

Saturday, May 4, 2002, 1 to 3 p.m.
St. Louis Writers Guild members signed copies of their books. Waldenbooks, St. Louis Galleria, Clayton Road and South Brentwood Boulevard in Richmond Heights. Free.

Saturday, June 1, 2002, 10 a.m. to noon
5+5 workshop participants shared a piece of work in progress and receive feedback from the workshop leader and other members in the group. Barnes & Noble, 9618 Watson Road in Crestwood. $5, free for members.

Saturday, July 6, 2002, 10 a.m. until noon.
Infinitives and Gerunds. Barnes & Noble, 9618 Watson Road in Crestwood. $5, free for members.

Wednesday, August 21, 2002, 7 p.m.
Organizing Your Sources presented by author Julie Beard. Barnes and Noble, 8871 Ladue Road in Ladue. Free.

September 4, 2002
The James Nash Memorial Short Story Contest was announced with a first prize of $150. Stories with a maximum of 5,000 words, had to be submitted by October 31, 2002, to Donna Springer c/o St. Louis Writers Guild, to the P.O. Box address provided.

Writers were requested to attach a 3-by-5inch card to the front of each manuscript with name, address, phone number, title and number of words. The announcement also mentioned that writers must have the title on the front page of the manuscript. The entry fee was $15 per manuscript, and up to three manuscripts were allowed.

Wednesday, September 18, 2002, 7 p.m.
Dorthea Fuller Smith, author of *Two Codes for Murder: A True Crime Story*. Barnes & Noble, 8871 Ladue Road in Ladue. Free.

Saturday, October 5, 2002, 1 to 3 p.m.
Meet the Authors Day with St. Louis Writers Guild at the Barnes & Noble, 9618 Watson Road in Crestwood. Free.

Wednesday, November 20, 2002, 7 p.m.
Who Done It? Use of Scientific Tools to Solve Crimes, presented by Reena Roy. Barnes & Noble, 8871 Ladue Road in Ladue. Free.

Wednesday, February 19, 2003, 7 p.m.
Local author, Albert Montesi. Barnes & Noble, 8871 Ladue Road in Ladue. Free.

Wednesday, March 19, 2003, 7 p.m.
Conevery Bolton Valencius discussed her book *The Health of the Country* at Barnes & Noble, 8871 Ladue Road, Free.

Saturday, April 5, 2003, 10 a.m. to noon
5+5 Critique Workshop, *participants were invited to read five minutes of a work-in-progress, which would be followed by five minutes of critique*. Barnes & Noble, 9618 Watson Road in Crestwood. $5.

Saturday, June 7, 2003, 10 a.m. to noon
Bookmaking, presented by Connie McIntyre. Barnes & Noble, 9618 Watson Road in Crestwood. $5

Saturday, August 2, 2003, 10 a.m. to noon.
5+5 Session, led by Connie McIntyre. *Participants are invited*

The History of St. Louis Writers Guild

to bring a work-in-progress to read to the group for 5 minutes followed by a 5-minute period of critique and suggestions. At Barnes & Noble, 9618 Watson Road in Crestwood. $5.

Saturday, September 6, 2003, 10 a.m. to noon
Writing Short Stories, presented by Lester Pope. Barnes & Noble, 9618 Watson Road in Crestwood. $5.

Saturday, November 1, 2003, 10 a.m.
Punctuate with Confidence presented by Fran Hamilton. at Barnes & Noble, 9618 Watson Road in Crestwood. $5.

November 16, 2003 (third wed), 7 p.m.
Journalist, Monika Kleban at Barnes & Noble, 9618 Watson Road. Non-members $5.

2005
June 2005 – Edward Boccia, presented the monthly workshop.

September 15, 2005 – A Celebration of St. Louis Writers

October 2005 – The 85th Anniversary
Author and educator, Cathi LaMarche, presented the monthly workshop.
Also,
St. Louis Book Festival and Arts Fair
A book fair event at Jamestown Mall to support Battered Women in St. Louis. Mel Meyer operated the SLWG member book table for the event.

Tuesday, October 11, 2005, 7-9 p.m. – The second open mike event was held at Sunset 44 in Kirkwood.

November 17, 2005 – Lecture: John Bricuth, presents the at the Barnes & Noble, Ladue.

December 2005 – SLWG Holiday party at Marv Schneider's house, the Member of Distinction Award presented.

The History of St. Louis Writers Guild

SLWG Promotional Bookmarks

20 |
StlWritersGuild, 2006 to 2009, Robin Moore Theiss (now Robin Moore), President

In 2006, as the new Busch Stadium opened, David Motherwell stepped down and Robin Moore Theiss became president of St. Louis Writers Guild. She had served as a board member since 2004, having joined the year before, and was one of the architects of St. Louis Writers Guild's amazing growth. The year 2006 started off with 226 members. Having served in the corporate board room of a health care company, Robin brought a business acumen to her time as president. In treating SLWG as a corporation, she instilled the idea of it being a business and operating like a business to the rest of the board members. Robin oversaw the creation of the Guild's first true website and shifted the focus to email communication, something many of the older members at the time objected to. SLWG still sent out *The Scribe*, the paper newsletter, but *Here's News!* became the emailed newsletter.

Robin started an online book selling business, with a focus on rare books. Eventually, she opened a bookstore in downtown Kirkwood. STLBooks was on Jefferson Avenue. It was a wonderful bookstore with a glass case devoted to books by St. Louis Writers Guild members from the past and some other cool editions as well.

In her 2006 SLWG Member Spotlight it was said of Robin, "Her passion for Missouri's literary heritage borders on obsession. "I have a profound regard for Missouri authors and, in particular, for the St. Louis Writers Guild," she said, "Its founders' and early members' contributions to national literature were substantial. They deserve public recognition."

Though novelists still dominated SLWG membership, the genres were interesting. Memoir was the biggest genre at that time, followed by thriller and mystery writers. Then there were also a large number of freelance writers and poets.

St. Louis Writers Guild Workshops at Barnes & Noble

With an increase in membership came a need for a new meeting space. Restaurants no longer had enough space, and members' living rooms weren't really an option anymore. Robin reached out to Barnes & Noble in Crestwood, 9618 Watson Road. St. Louis Writers Guild had used the venue several times before to host author events, such as when Western author Dusty Richards came to St. Louis on his book tour. Now, Robin sought to make the change permanent.

This also shifted the meetings from the third Wednesday of each month to the first Saturday of each month, as well as moving the time from the evenings to the morning.

Barnes & Noble-Crestwood offered the Community Room, a long rectangular room in the back of the store. For each meeting, they set up a few rows of chairs facing the long wall. A table was set up near the door, where name badges were set out along with any handouts and the two-month calendar. Posters of Mark Twain, Amy Tan, Kurt Vonnegut, and other literary greats watched over the crowd that usually numbered about thirty. The Barnes & Noble Café provided coffee, juice, and pastries for people to enjoy during the meetings. Barnes & Noble-Crestwood ordered the speaker's books, if warranted, and after the workshop, members got their books signed and then took them out to the register for purchase before they left. St. Louis Writers Guild was an excellent venue for authors with books for sale.

Each month a speaker or panel presented a workshop on a variety of subjects, from...

"Beyond Myths and Old Wives' Tales: Copyright, Contracts, and Law for Writers" presented by Mark Sableman, Esq, of Thompson & Coburn.

Dwight Bitikofer, poet and publisher of the Webster-Kirkwood Times, presented tips for writers on how to effectively read their work aloud before a live audience.

"Publishing A-Z" with best-selling author, Bobbi Smith.

Ryan D. Jones and Julie Earhart presented, "Convince Your Readers You Know What You're Talking About."

A new format came to the workshop, one that continues to the current day. Most people arrived about thirty minutes early to talk, network, gab, or whatever. Then a mad rush of people arrived about ten minutes before the event. The room swelled. The membership committee chairman ran the front table, handing out nametags to members, signing non-members in and collecting the $5 fee, which could always be applied to membership if they joined in the following thirty days. Robin then took the center of the room, made certain everyone had a two-month calendar, and began the announcements.

This was when the famous start to every meeting began. Robin Theiss asked, "Has anyone submitted their work this month?" It could be a query to a magazine, literary agent, publisher, blog site, or other submission. Members raised their hands, sometimes half the room, other times it was only one. Then Robin asked, "Did anyone receive a rejection?" Some hands fell, but many remained, and she called for applause. Honoring this painful process had always been a part of St. Louis Writers Guild. Then finally she asked if anyone received an acceptance. Those who raised their hands announced where their work would be published. News was also called for, and if a member had a new book, they showed it off. Lastly, any last-minute announcements were made.

The workshop lasted about two hours, with a ten-minute break about 11a.m. to allow people to move around and get more coffee if they wanted. A question and answer session followed, with a book signing for the author. The room was usually cleared out by about 12:30 p.m.

Membership was raised to $42 for a regular single-year, and $27 for seniors. It was in 2007 that the first student price was added. For $27, any currently enrolled university student could be a member. The thought was not only to attract new members but to help those who were trying to get a job in the publishing industry or wanted to be a better writer. Also, at this time, they create a prorated membership fee: prior to May 1 - $40/year, Senior/Student $25; After May 1, $42, $27.

Occasionally, for special guest speakers or special workshop events, St. Louis Writers Guild utilized Chesterfield Arts, 444 Chesterfield Center, right across the parking lot from Chesterfield Mall, sometimes in association with the Chesterfield Writers Guild.

After her March 2007 workshop, Suzann Ledbetter sent this message,

Robin et al,

Y'all are amazing! The energy zipping around the room Saturday could have powered the city for a week. An F5 brainstorm, as it were, and of all the groups I've spoken to, your guild is by the" far the most creative, intuitive, and flat-out smart, not to mention inspiring. Just the boost I needed to get my own book-in-progress off its duff and rolling! Thank you so much for inviting me...

All our best,
Suzann Ledbetter

Wednesday Night monthly Meeting Becomes the Thursday Night Lecture Series

In the early 2000s, the Wednesday night meetings at McNulty's Pub and Grill moved to the Ladue Barnes & Noble, but by Robin's presidency, the night changed to Thursday, and the meeting was held every other month. It became known as the St. Louis Writers Guild Lecture Series. As the monthly workshop at the Crestwood Barnes & Noble became the primary event, the lecture series fundamentally changed from the meetings at the restaurants that dominated the last several decades of the writer's organization. The lecture format still focused on an author, but the event became more of a cross between a book signing and a lecture. The bookstore handled the sale of many of the authors' books, and they sold very well as the events grew to hold 30 people or more.

St. Louis Writers Under the Stars – September 30, 2006

One of the first big events Robin presided over was "Writers Under the Stars," a night of poetry readings in the Kirkwood Park. A number of poets and authors read from a podium at center stage in Lion's Amphitheater, including Richard Burgin, Mark Tiedemann, Rick Skwiot, Michael Castro, Michael Nye, and three emerging writers, Kenneth Harrison Jr., Olivia Ayes, and Gregory Otti. Music was provided by the GMan's First Person Blues Groove with refreshments from Mount Pleasant Winery and Fitz's Root Beer. The originally scheduled night, July 29 was cancelled as storms doused the event, but it was quickly rescheduled and everyone agreed to participate again. When Robin arrived with the newly purchased sound equipment, the amphitheater was completely dark. There were no lights on stage or in the amphitheater. Robin and her husband rushed home and gathered all the Christmas tree lights they could find. They strung them down the aisles and dotted the main stage, providing just enough light for those attending to see. The effect created an ethereal atmosphere, adding to the literary ambiance. Dwight Bitikofer interviewed Robin for the *Webster-Kirkwood Times* in a story about the event. People spoke for years about how the event was a magical night.

Here's News! listed these members to say thank you to: Peggy Haldeman, Jeff Haldeman, Gwen O'Brien, Connie Garcia, Julia Gordon-Bramer, Marianne Blake, Erin Hibbard, Robin Theiss, Dane Marti, Vanessa Theiss, Taylor Menke, Mary Menke, Jud Miner, Doreen Hulsey, Diana Baird, Dianna Graveman, David Motherwell.

St. Louis Writers Guild Thrives!

Ending 2005 at 140 members was astounding, but under Robin's guidance and the changes she made, by 2007, membership rose to 293! These writers represented all aspects, from New York Times Bestsellers to those who were just starting out.

In 2007, SLWG still took summers off, holding fewer events during the summer months. Open mics continued, but there were no lectures. It all resumed in September along with the announcement of the annual short story contest.

Another change was the replacement of the picnic with a Volunteer Luncheon instead. It was still a picnic, but the focus was less on getting all the members together and more about honoring those who had worked so hard. One year, instead of a separate picnic, SLWG got sandwiches, and everyone stayed after the workshop.

The Longest Day

For a time, the board meetings were held after the monthly meeting. Often it was a lunch; everyone ate and then SLWG business was discussed. It usually meant a 3 p.m. finish. In 2008, however, came the never-ending day, a good day for certain, and it set a precedent still followed to this day.

Robin Moore Theiss, president at the time, decided it was time to finish the Guild restructuring. It had grown in an unorganized way, expanding as needed. The time had come to set an organizational chart, and finish the new bylaws. Robin secured the basement of a church; a member offered up the space. The entire board and all the committee members met after the monthly workshop. The workshop was near the church and everyone decided to eat lunch after the organizational meeting. Everyone assumed it would be a short meeting.

About fifteen people sat around several long rectangular tables pushed together. Robin had a couple of large blue poster boards with colored foam tags marked with each job. Everyone defined their positions and duties. The secretary recorded everything. Hours passed as the structure and rules of the organization took shape. Logic won out over anything else, as similar duties were grouped together and any overlap or conflict was removed. It created a streamlined organization chart that is still used over a decade later.

After hours and hours of working on organizational structure, job duties, and member benefits, everyone was starving. A few board members had already fallen by the wayside. Then we all finally broke for dinner. Everyone met up at a nearby St. Louis

Bread Co./Panera. At the end of the day, St. Louis Writers Guild had a clear structure, lines of communication and responsibility, and completed bylaws that only needed to be typed up and signed.

It came at a cost… two died that day… not really, but it did become infamous and dominated meeting planning for years to come. However, knowing what came from that day, everyone in attendance gave of themselves, so SLWG would thrive. In an odd twist, four presidents were in the room that day, Robin Moore Theiss, Rebecca Carron, David Lucas, and me.

Tennessee Williams and the SLWG Short Story Contest

In 1935, Tennessee Williams entered the St. Louis Writers Guild's Short Story Contest—the oldest in the Midwest—and won the grand sum of ten dollars. This is what we advertise, though to be truthful, we didn't have the story. It was lost.

Robin Theiss had talked to Dakin, Tennessee's brother in 2007 at the presentation ceremony for the Tennessee Williams' bust statue in the Central West End. She'd also discovered two clues: one was a letter written by the Guild to tell him he had won, and second, the story didn't appear in any list of Tennessee Williams short stories.

As the new Historian, I turned my attention to finding this story that was such a part of the Guild's legacy. I found the largest collection of Tennessee Williams' papers in the archives of the Harry Ransom Center at the University of Texas at Austin, and spent a few hours going through the catalog of their archives. Then in Box 43, Folder 5, I found a title, "Stella for Star." I immediately inquired about the folder and asked to hire a proxy researcher to see exactly what it contained. There were two manuscripts, and a number of fragments. That was when I jumped for joy and yelled "I found it!" which sent both my cats scurrying for the other room. The board decided to copy the entire file, all the fragments and both manuscripts, about 70 pages in all.

Then just before June, an ordinary white box arrived at my door. The pages weren't in order, which made discerning the final draft a bit difficult, but it was a joy to go through. Most of the pages were annotated by his hand, and it was amazing to see his mind at work. Everything was typed on a typewriter, so when he made a correction, he started a separate piece of paper, and later included them in his next draft. That's one reason why there were so many fragments in the file, and he made me appreciate my computer. Most fascinating were his corrections, his editing process laid bare. He struggled with plot points and smoothing out characters like writers do today, but even then, it was excellently written and fascinating to read. He even scrapped his first draft and rewrote most of the story, as shown by the two different beginnings. It is classic Tennessee Williams: his incredibly deep and complex characters are expressed with artful and poetic detail.

The final version of the story, the version he submitted, was also in the collection. It even retained the crease marks from where it had been folded in thirds and placed in an envelope.

"Stella for Star," is a wonderful short story, the fictional account of a real-life mystery. A lock of hair was found in the personal effects of Jonathan Swift, the Dean of Saint Patrick's. Labeled, "Only a woman's hair," Thomas L. Williams threaded his story around the idea of unrequited love between the cleric and a woman who lived on the grounds. In the story, Swift walks down a street and through a garden where he encounters different people and then ghosts that challenge him about his beliefs. He then has a poignant conversation with Esther in the garden.

An author's note accompanied the submission which explained his reason for writing the story, and a hand-written note at the top of the cover page which suggested sending it to the *Atlantic Monthly* and mentioned that it was "well written." It is uncertain who wrote the note, but it could have been one of the judges or contest coordinators.

I would love to have included it in this collection, but St. Louis Writers Guild, nor I, have the rights for that, and they're not easily obtained. However, SLWG did hold a reading at the open mic night with a full house for that evening.

One of the best parts of this whole experience was finding out that "Stella for Star" was written by Thomas Lanier Williams while he was attending Washington University. He wouldn't become

Tennessee for a few more years. Nothing else could emphasize more why St. Louis Writers Guild needs to encourage writers.

There's more. Research proved much of the story, but as with all things, the truth had changed over time. Read more in the Writing Contest Section on page 383.

SLWG's First Official Website

Robin Moore Theiss oversaw the creation of St. Louis Writers Guild's first website—www.stlwritersguild.org. Seeking the hosting and webmaster services of Doreen Hulsey, they created a website, a central hub for all things for the organization. Created on the beginning WordPress-style site, it had pages for a variety of information, from rules and guidelines, to information on events and how to join. Since it was the mid-2000s, chat rooms and forums were all the rage, and St. Louis Writers Guild had a robust forum. Topics covered everything from FAQs to dialogue, and other writing topics. One of the big topics of the day was a discussion of the different writing rules and which were more appropriate—AP Style or the Chicago Manual of Style. A large discussion took place on the forums. Critique Groups could be signed up for, and there was documentation, like contest entry guidelines, membership application, and more.

The site had a patterned maroon color scheme with silver trim. The classic logo sat in the corner. The website came right as the internet started ruling everyone's life and became the number one-way people discovered the organization.

Loud Mouth and Wired Coffee

The Loud Mouth and Wired Coffee Open Mics during this time reached the height of their popularity.

The first SLWG Open Mic of the current incarnation happened during Robin Theiss' presidency, was held at Kaldi's Coffee in Kirkwood. The event quickly moved to Sunset 44, a restaurant in Kirkwood, but as the meetings moved away from there, so did the Open Mic. Wired Coffee, a trendy little café on Lindbergh Boulevard. in Sunset Hills, was selected as the new venue. A charming place, they had plenty of seating at small tables or comfortable chairs around a fireplace, and ice cream. They had other food, but ice cream was always key. The first Open Mic Night @ Wired Coffee was held on Tuesday, August 08, 2006.

Wired Coffee always had a family-friendly audience. Loud Mouth Open Mic was started to allow a more mature content. The Mack, a bar at 4615 Macklind Avenue 63109, provided the perfect venue for the event. A room in back was the setting for the Guild's new open mic. Many a curse word or raunchy subject was spoken. It honestly wasn't as crazy as it sounds, but it was a chance to not worry about one's language. The first Loud Mouth Open Mic Night was held on March 27, 2007.

Each open mic took on its own identity but they had very different endings. This tale is told in detail in Chapter 27 The Epic Saga of the SLWG Open Mic Nights.

The Big Read and The Big Write

To continue St. Louis Writers Guild's community outreach, the organization joined with Cultural Festivals, an organization in Clayton that held several large community events, a music festival, the book festival, and what they were most known for, an art festival. St. Louis Writers Guild served as the logistical organizers for the book fair's writing contest and provided speakers for the writing workshops at the book fair. The festival, held every October, was called The Big Read, and the kids' writing contest associated with the event was called The Big Write.

The event moved between downtown Clayton and the circle drive in front of Clayton High School. When they shut down North Central Avenue for the festival, the workshops were held in the restaurants, and the main tents were at the intersection of Forsythe and North Central. When in Shaw Park, the high school became the workshop location. Every year, St. Louis Writers Guild had two booths next to each other. One was used for providing information about the Guild, its events, and membership. The second booth had a table where members signed and sold their books. Members signed up for hour-long sessions and there were usually two to three authors in the booth.

St. Louis Writers Guild collected and coordinated, then

sorted and vetted all the entries. They secured several judges for the multiple rounds of judging and the two different divisions of the contest and served as Master of Ceremonies for the award ceremony held at the book fair. It was never hard to find a judge for The Big Read; every member wanted to participate in judging. Cultural Festivals received grants to hold these events and handled all the prizes and printing costs. They also had a more extensive network of educational contacts.

Though it started under Robin's time as president, Rebecca Carron carried on until the festival ended.

SLWG Bookmarks (pictured on page 216)

Bookmarks were created for several years around 2005-2008 every year. They incorporated different designs and author quotes but had a similar color theme so they looked cohesive. The major color was maroon, then shades of green, yellow, red, purple, and white. They were handed out when people inquired about the Guild.

One design depicted people reading on benches under trees, with the logo, and two phrases: "Please Keep Your Place! Read St. Louis Authors." On the other side, it had a quote from Mark Twain, "Really great people make you feel that you, too, can become great," and a fact about the author.

Another bookmark showed two hands holding a book with the logo on a golden background, it had the same two phrases, and then on the reverse, a quote from Tennessee Williams, "When I stop working the rest of the day is posthumous. I'm only really alive when I'm writing."

One marked 2007, had two brightly colored people reading on one side with the logo and the same two slogans. The other side had the website, a short bio, and a quote from T. S. Eliot, "Only those who risk going too far can possibly find out how far one can go."

The 2008 bookmark had four people on the front, two adults and two children, each with a book in their hands. The colorful people are blue, red, purple, yellow, orange, and other vibrant colors on a flowing background of maroon, gold, and navy blue. It contained the two slogans, but on the back was information about Maya Angelou, along with a quote, "Words mean more than what is set down on paper. It takes the human voice to infuse them with shades of deeper meaning."

Special Event Workshops
Harvey Stanbrough

Award-winning author, poet, and editor, Harvey Stanbrough was most relaxed in his home in the deserts of Arizona, but after meeting him at the Missouri Writers' Conference, the decision was made to ask him to come to talk with the members of St. Louis Writers Guild. He came in for two events: on April 8, 2007, he spoke at the regular monthly SLWG meeting. He returned that summer, and on July 15, 2007, Harvey held a second, paid event, teaching everyone how to edit, punctuate, and improve a manuscript. The regular monthly meeting was held at the Crestwood Barnes & Noble, but the second event took place at Chesterfield Arts. Harvey was a character at both events; a retired marine, he commanded the room, and charmed every writer there.

There is an epic tale that goes along with these events. It started on Harvey Stanbrough's way into town. I was at work when I received a call. I had agreed to serve as Harvey's point of contact while in town. Harvey was calling from the side of the highway. Upon arriving in St. Louis, two motorcycles stopped on the highway. The cars behind them stopped. Harvey stopped. The car behind Harvey did not stop. He was fine, but the car was not. I left work and drove to pick him up from the tow truck lot. We went to dinner that night at the restaurant at his hotel to forget about the day's craziness. Harvey, ever the trooper, refused to forgo his event. Eventually, a rental car carried Harvey back to Arizona, but SLWG had made its mark on him as well. Harvey remained a member long after his honorary membership had ended.

The President
Robin Moore Theiss – 2006, 2007, and 2008

Board Members at this Time
2007
Robin Moore Theiss, President
Mary Ward Menke, Vice President
Gerry Mandel, Secretary
Alicia Lundstrom, Treasurer
Doreen Hulsey, Webmaster

Committee Chairs
Robin Moore Theiss, Programs
Claire Applewhite, Publicity
Marianne Blake, Membership
Katie Shanahan, Newsletter
The Scribe Staff – Managing Editor Mary Menke, Editor and Layout, Katie Shanahan,

2008
Mary Ward Menke, Vice President of Operations
Rebecca Carron, Vice President of Programs
Secretary Open
Alicia Lundstrom, Treasurer
Faye Adams, MWG Rep.
Brad R. Cook, Historian

2006 Members of Distinction
Julia Gordon-Bramer, Peggy Haldeman, Maurice L. (Bud) Hirsch, Doreen Hulsey, Jeff May, Connie McIntyre, Mary Menke, Jud Miner, David Motherwell, Donna Springer, Robin Moore Theiss, and Thelma Urich.

2007 Members of Distinction
Lind O'Connell, David Motherwell, Rebecca Carron, Elaine Abramson, Gerry Mandel, Robin Theiss, Mary Menke, Peggy Haldeman, Marianne Blake, Doreen Hulsey, Paul Wittmer, Diane Marti, Will Bereswill, Kathi Buescher, Jud Miner, Thelma Urich, Peggy Chumbley, Julia Gordon-Bramer, Diana Graveman, Meg Bergmann, Faye Adams, Pat Detrick

Members from 2005-2009
Faye and Billy Adams

Faye Adams, poet, author, and tax consultant, was a longtime member of St. Louis Writers Guild, who served as Contest Coordinator for years.

Faye Adams was an award-winning writer of poetry, children's books, nonfiction, and short fiction. She was published in anthologies, newspapers, poetry journals and magazines, like *IDEALS* and *The Ozark Mountaineer*. Faye served as Advisory Board Member to the Missouri State Poetry Society, as Co-editor of the *On the Edge Annual MSPS Poetry and Prose Anthology*, a member of the Society of Children's Book Writers and Illustrators, and as St. Louis Writers Guild Representative to the Missouri Writers' Guild. Faye won many awards, between 2005 and 2006 she won seven first place awards and several second and third places including the AWC Prose Award for fiction. This continued with the Senior Poet Laureate Award in 2010 and in 2012, and was honored as a featured poet in *Lucidity Poetry Journal*, Summer of 2011. Her books may be viewed at: www.fayeadams.com

Billy Adams was a fighter pilot in WWII and never climbed out of the cockpit. He loved flying and planes, but it was nature that most often influenced his poetry. He published a number of books, including a collection of The Big Write Finalists for SLWG in 2009.

Faye and Billy were longtime members and advocates for the Writers Society of Jefferson County. They lived in DeSoto, MO, for many years but were fixtures of the St. Louis literary community.

Faye Adams

Poetry Anthologies: *Pearls of the Pen* 2003, *Lost and Found* 2004, *Life on the Edge* 2005, *Gems From the Past* 2007, *HERSTORY* 2007, *HIMS* 2007.

Books

Pathways—A Book of Poetry, Illustrated by Aimee Wegescheide 2005

Chester, the Lonely Crow, Illustrated by Aimee Wegescheide 2005

Cookies & Blackberry Wine, Poetry and Nonfiction Illustrated by Aimee Wegescheide 2006
- *Breath of Heaven*
- *On the Lighter Side*
- *Verses for Kids of All Ages*

Claire Applewhite

Claire Applewhite mystery author, songwriter, publisher, and past-president of Missouri Writers Guild. She owned Smoking Gun Publishing and served on the board of the Midwest Mystery Writers of America, and as Publicity Chairman for St. Louis Writers Guild. As a member of the St. Louis Metropolitan Press Club, she coordinated their efforts at Gateway Con. Claire was also a member of Sisters in Crime, Ozark Writers League, and created the Voices of Excellence program.
- *The Wrong Side of Memphis*
- *Crazy For You*
- *St. Louis Hustle*
- *Candy Cadillac*
- *Tennessee Plates*
- *The Doctor's Tale*

Marianne Blake

Membership Committee Chairman – The keeper of the book of nametags.

Doreen Hulsey

Doreen owned a web design company and became SLWG's first official webmaster in 2005. Her teenage daughter joined in 2002 and a second daughter joined in 2005, they attended many meetings at a time when SLWG didn't have many resources for young writers.

Alicia Lundstrom, (Alicia Janechill Beard)

Alicia was a writer who spent her day job as an accountant. A whiz with numbers, she was a disciplined treasurer of St. Louis Writers Guild who made certain every bill was paid and accounted for.

Gerry Mandel

Gerry Mandel was one of the initial open mic MCs at Wired Coffee and a longtime regular at all the iterations of the open mic. He spent years in advertising before channeling his love of Charlie Chaplin into a novel, *Shadow and Substance: My Time with Charlie Chaplin* (2010).

Mary Ward Menke

Mary Menke was the vice president of operations for St. Louis Writers Guild for a number of years. She acted as a liaison between the venues and the organization and handled the organization's logistics. She became the editor and publisher of *The Scribe* in 2002, having joined the Guild in 2000. She and Robin were the core of this era. Her first book, published in 2005, was titled, *The Light at the End of the Tunnel: Continuing Back to Life After a Spouse Dies*, a collection of stories from people who had survived the death of their spouses. A writer and editor, she runs an editing service called WordAbilities.com. She is also an adjunct instructor of Oral Communications and Intercultural Communications for Ranken Technical College.

Thelma Urich

A fiction writer, essayist, poet, playwright, and novelist, Thelma was President of the National League of American Pen Women St. Louis Branch, Secretary of the Missouri Association of Playwrights, a member of Missouri Writers Guild, and an SLWG member since 2004. Her first love was poetry and tried many different styles including her Ethereen in honor of Ben Franklin's 300th Birthday. An Ethereen is a 10-line stanza with each line having an additional syllable.

Workshops and Events
2006
February 2006
Tuesday, February 14, 6:30 p.m.- 9:30 p.m. join us for a

Literary Valentine's Day Party and Open Mike Night! "What Love is Like" was the theme for the evening. At the Kirkwood Community Center room 302, 111 S Geyer Road. Kirkwood 63122. No fee to attend. $5 donation asked to cover the room. Register in advance to read.

Thursday February 16, 7-8 p.m. – Lecture: **Great Beginnings: Essential Qualities of a Good First Chapter** presented by John Dalton author of Heaven Lake published by Scribner. Barnes and Noble Ladue, 8871 Ladue Road, Ladue 63124

March 2006
Saturday March 4, 10 a.m. to Noon – Workshop: **Enthrall Your Audience: Show, Don't Tell!** presented by Dorry Pease at Barnes and Noble Crestwood.

Tuesday, March 7 from 7-9 p.m. – Open Mike Night at Sunset 44 Bistro, 118 W. Adams in Kirkwood.

Thursday, March 16, 7-8 p.m. – Lecture Series: **Why 1984 is Literature, but Star Troopers is Not** presented by Sci-fi author Mark Tiedemann, president of the Missouri Center for the Book.

April 2006
April 28-30 – MWG Conference: Mastering the Craft held at Hilton Hotel, Kansas City Airport.

April 1 – Workshop by Julie Earhart, freelance writer, columnist, fiction writer.

April 20 – Lecture by Richard Newman, poet and editor of *River Styx magazine.*

May 2006
May 6 – Workshop with Ruth Miriam Garnett. Kickoff of the annual Deane Wagner Poetry Contest.

May 18 – Lecture by Ron Bechtel of the Great Hollywood Story Search. He discussed how to break into writing for film.

June 2006
Saturday June 3, 10 a.m. to Noon – Workshop: **Deadline is my Middle Name: Insights From A Veteran Newspaper Reporter, Freelance Feature Writer, and Book Author**

The History of St. Louis Writers Guild

presented by Patricia Corrigan.

June 13, 7-9 p.m. – Open Mike Night, at PJ's Tavern, 123 W Jefferson Ave in Kirkwood 63122. Carol O'Dell read from *Southern Revival: Deep Magic for Hurricane Relief*. An anthology to raise money for rebuilding and restocking America's Gulf Coast Communities.

Thursday June 15, 7-8 p.m. – Lecture series: **Breaking the Rules: How to Write What you Love and Sell Big** featuring award-winning mystery author Susan McBride at Barnes & Noble, Ladue 8871 Ladue Road in Ladue 63124.

July 2006

No Regular Events – but two Very Special Events

Sunday July 16, 4-8 p.m. – **Annual Summertime Picnic** at Kirkwood Park – *Dust off that lawn chair. Just food, fun, and friendship for all you literary kindred spirits! Bring a dish to share and your favorite beverage. The burgers and dogs are on SLWG! All are welcome.*

July 14 & July 21 – *Webster Kirkwood Times* published two stories on **Writers Under the Stars** and an interview with Robin Moore Theiss on a look back at SLWG through the ages.

July 29, 7 p.m. – the original date for **Writers Under the Stars.**

August 2006

Saturday August 5, 10 a.m. – Workshop Panel: **What is Good Writing? Let's Argue!** Paul Thiel hosted a panel with John Lutz, Richard Burgin, Colleen McKee, and Harry Jackson Jr.

Tuesday August 8 – **Open Mic Night** at the brand-new location, Wired Coffee, 3860 South Lindbergh Boulevard in Sunset Hills. *Gorgeous décor and sumptuous food and drink fare, including iced and hot coffees, teas, smoothies, gelatos, pastries, and more! Register in advance if you want to read!*

September 2006

Saturday September 9, 10 a.m. to noon – Workshop: **Critiques: How to Dish 'Em Out and Take 'Em** presented by Carol O'Dell author of *Mothering Mother*.

Saturday September 9, 2-4 p.m. – Two workshops for

young writers interested in entering the Big Write. Jud Miner at Barnes & Noble, Chesterfield, and Julie Earhart at the Schlafly Library in the Central West End.

Tuesday, September 12, 7-9 p.m. – **Open Mike Night** at Wired Coffee 3860 S. Lindbergh Boulevard, Sunset Hills, 63127

Thursday September 21, 7-8 p.m. – Lecture Series **Structuring the Memoir** presented by Rick Skwiot at Barnes & Noble Ladue.

A Very Special, Special Event

Saturday September 30, 7 p.m. to 10:30 p.m. – **St. Louis Writers Under the Stars**

Come Sample the works of five nationally acclaimed St. Louis award winning authors Richard Burgin, Michael Castro, Mark Tiedemann, Rick Skwiot, and Michael Nye – three outstanding emerging writers Kenneth E. Harrison Jr., Olivia Ayes, and Gregory Otti! Enjoy music by GMan's First Person Blues Groove and refreshments from Mount Pleasant Winery and Fitz's Root Beer AND… if you're lucky enough, you could take home a raffle basket valued at $200 in donated books, gift certificates, free subscriptions, wine, and other tantalizing items (and more are still expected!)

Just because weather doused our day doesn't mean it doused your interest! The event has been rescheduled. All seven authors have agreed to try it again and the event promises to be better than ever in the cooler, hopefully drier fall season.

Thank you to Peggy Haldeman, Jeff Haldeman, Gwen O'Brien, Connie Garcia, Julia Gordon-Bramer, Marianne Blake, Erin Hibbard, Robin Theiss, Dane Marti, Vanessa Theiss, Taylor Menke, Mary Menke, Jud Miner, Doreen Hulsey, Diana Baird, Dianna Graveman, David Motherwell.

October 2006

Saturday October 7, 10 a.m. to 5 p.m. – **Big Read Literary Festival** – *No workshop just the big read. The first year of this festival in the central business district of Clayton. Big Write award Ceremony at 12:30 p.m. – SLWG authors sold 72 books!*

No open mic, instead National Welsh Pasty Toss Day! St. Louis Writers Guild and Dressel's Pub will commemorate this dubious holiday with short readings by Welsh heritage authors, Jud

Miner, Jack Owen, and a special mystery guest. Dressel's Welsh Pub, 419 N. Euclid, St. Louis, 63108

Thursday October 19, 7-9 p.m. – **Loving the Unlovable: Being True to Your Characters** presented by Mary Troy, author of *Cookie Lily*, and director of the MFA program at UM-STL.

October 1 – The Annual James Nash Memorial Short Story Contest opened for submission, judge was Mary Troy, deadline was November 10.

November 2006
Saturday November 4 – Finishing Lines: How and When to End Your Story presented by Valerie Vogrin. *There is a brown bag critique group luncheon afterward to learn about the program.*

November 9 (one week earlier) 7-8 p.m. – SLWG Lecture Series: Stranger than Fiction presented by Ridley Pearson, Barnes & Noble, Ladue

November 9 – November 12 – Barnes & Noble Book Fair Benefit for SLWG, 15% of all sales on November 9 using the voucher benefited the Guild. All sales on which mention SLWG during this time

December 2006
December 3, 4-8 p.m. – **SLWG Members' Annual Holiday Party** – *You Should bring (1) a finger food to share (2) a beverage of your choice (3) a wrapped new or like new book on writing (4) a spouse, significant other, friend (5) humorous or holiday themed reading. Member only.*

December 12, 7-9 p.m. – A Very Special Open Mike Night with readings by the 2006 James Nash Memorial Short Story Contest winners.

2007
January 2007
January 6 – Workshop – **Ready, Set.... Go! How to Set Achievable Writing Goals for 2007!** Presented by Julie Hood author of the *Organized Writer*, *she will lead a workshop aimed at launching your success strategy for 2007. Be sure and register for event – we expect a crowd. We have a lot to cover at our 1st / 1st Saturday workshops so*

plan on sticking around until 12:30 p.m.
Cycle Critique Groups launched in Jan 2007.

The Volunteer Luncheon, the second annual, meet everyone and learn about their roles, help pick the Members of Distinction and how to volunteer. Held at Barnes & noble. Preregistration is required
SLWG Sponsors Best Essay Contest for MWG Conference.

February 2007
February – Workshop presented by Suzann Ledbetter
February – Lecture presented by Richard Bargin

March 2007
March – Workshop presented by Patsy Zettler Margo Dill-Balinski, March Workshop
March – Lecture presented by Dan Dillon

April 2007
April – Lecture presented by Richard Beban,
April 20 – Deane Wagner Poetry Contest Opens
April 24, 8-10 p.m. – Loud Mouth Open Mic At the Mack
April 30 – Online Elections Open For Votes for SLWG Officers

May 2007
May 5, 10 a.m. to Noon – Workshop: **Some Things Change: Storytelling remains the Same** presented by Dick Weiss. Also, live Elections
May 8, 7-9 p.m. – Open Mic at Wired Coffee
May 17, 7-8 p.m. – Lecture: **Forget About Fame: Confessions of a Ghostwriter** presented by Bobbi Linkemer.
May 22, 8-10 p.m. – Loud Mouth Open Mic Night at the Mack.

June 2007
June 2, 10 a.m. to Noon – Workshop: **Convince Your**

Readers You Know What You're Talking About presented by Ryan D. Jones and Julia Earhart at Chesterfield Arts

June 12, 7-9 p.m. – Open Mic at Wired Coffee

June 16 – Deadline for the Deane Wagner Poetry Contest Submissions

June 26, 8-10 p.m. – Loud Mouth Open Mic Night at the Mack

June 30 – SLWG at the Science Center with Jud Miner, Fran Hamilton, and Connie McIntyre.

July 2007

July 7, Round-Up Workshop: **Beyond Myths and Old Wives' Tales: Copyright, Contracts, and Law for Writers** presented by Mark Sableman Esq, Thompson & Coburn

July 8 – Critique Groups Cycle #3 begins

July 10, Open Mic at Wired Coffee

July 24, Loud Mouth Open Mic at The Mack (must be 21)

August 2007

August 14, Open Mic Night at Wired Coffee

August 28, Loud Mouth Open Mic (must be 21)

September 8, Workshop: **Tips for Writers on How to Effectively Read their Work Aloud Before a Live Audience** presented by Dwight Bitikofer, poet and publisher of the *Webster-Kirkwood Times*.

September 11, Open Mic at Wired Coffee

September 20, Lecture Series with John Lutz

September 25, Loud Mouth Open mic at The Mack (must be 21)

October 2007

Saturday, October 6 – The Big Read Literary Festival in Central Business District of Clayton – *Build a Bear Workshop and cash prizes for the top three in each category of the Big Write.*

October – Lecture presented by Eleanor Sullivan

November 2007

November – Workshop with Julie Failla Earhart

November – Lecture series with Barri Bumgarner

2008
January 2008
Saturday, January 5, 10 a.m.–12 p.m. – Workshop: **From To Do to Ta-Da: Overcoming Blocks and Barriers to Reach Your Goals** presented by Joanne Waldman @ Barnes & Noble Crestwood

Tuesday, Jan 8, 7-9 p.m. – Open Mic @ Wired Coffee – Wired Art Writing Contest Begins

Tuesday, Jan 15, 7- 9 p.m. – Loud Mouth Open Mic @ The Mack

Thursday, Jan 17, 7-8 p.m. – Lecture Series: **Distance and Perspective in Writing** presented by Qiu Xiaolong @ Barnes & Noble, Ladue

February 2008
Saturday Feb 2 – Workshop: **Publishing A-Z** presented by Bobbi Smith

Saturday, Feb 2, 12:30 p.m. – **2nd Annual SLWG Luncheon**

Tuesday, Feb 12, 7-9 p.m. – Open Mic @ Wired Coffee

Tuesday, Feb 19, 7-9 p.m. – Loud Mouth Open Mic @ The Mack

Tuesday Feb 26 – Wired Art Writing Contest Ends

March 2008
Saturday, March 1, 10 a.m. – 12 p.m. – Workshop: **Networking Secrets for the Professional (or would-be professional) Writer** presented by Trisha Grisham and the Missouri Writers Guild.

Tuesday, March 11, 7-9 p.m. – Open Mic @ Wired Coffee

Tuesday, March 18, 7-9 p.m. – Loud Mouth Open Mic @ The Mack

Thursday, March 20, 7-9 p.m. – Lecture: **7 Years + 300 Rejections Letters + One Published Novel!** presented by Judy Merrill Larsen

April 2008
Saturday, April 5 – **Special Workshop: Poetry** presented by Harvey Stanbrough, (4hrs, fee)
Tuesday, April 8 – Open Mic @ Wired Coffee – Gerry Mandel MC, Dwight Bitikofer Sound
April 11-13 – MWG Conference at Stoney Creek Inn in Columbia, MO
April 15 – Loud Mouth Open Mic @ The Mack

May 2008
May 3 – Workshop: **Internet** presented by Damian Farnworth and Shawn McDonald– plus a SwiftTech presentation.
May 13 – Open Mic at Wired Coffee, Jeff May MC and sound equipment
May 15 – Lecture presented by Kevin M. Mitchell, humor writer
May 20 – Loud Mouth Open Mic @ The Mack

June 2008
June 7 – Workshop: **Poetry** presented by Walter Bargen, Missouri Poet Laureate
June 10 – Open Mic @ Wired Coffee
June 28 – **The Big Write – Write a Story Workshop** at Chesterfield Arts, Jud Miner presented

July 2008
July 8 – Open Mic at Wired Coffee
July 12 – Special Workshop: Fiction presented by Harvey Stanbrough at Chesterfield Arts – Fee Required
July 15 – Loud Mouth Open Mic

August 2008
August 2, 10 a.m. to noon – Workshop: **Feed Your Head: What good writers should read to become great writers**, presented by Dr. Rebecca Carron & Brad Cook
August 12 – Open Mic Night @ Wired Coffee

August 19 – Loud Mouth Open Mic @ The Mack

September 2008
September 6 – Workshop presented by David Crespy, playwright
September 9 – Open Mic @ Wired Coffee
September 16 – Loud Mouth Open Mic @ The Mack
September 12 – The Big Write Contest Entry Deadline

October 2008
October 11 – The Big Read and Big Write Awards
October 14 – Open Mic Night @ Wired Coffee
October 21 – Loud Mouth Open Mic @ The Mack

November 2008
November 1 – Workshop: **Screenwriting for Television** presented by Paul Guyot
November 11 – Open Mic Night @ Wired Coffee
November 15 – Short Story Contest Deadline
November 18 – Loud Mouth Open Mic @ The Mack
November 20 – Lecture and B&N Book Fair

December 2008
December 6, 10 a.m. to noon – Holiday Party at the Barnes & Noble, Crestwood
December 9 – Open Mic @ Wired Coffee with the Short Story Contest Winners
No Loud Mouth or Lecture

The History of St. Louis Writers Guild

Poet, Michael Castro and Jazz Muscian, J.D. Parran
sketches by Peter H. Green

Final version of the Classic SLWG Logo

21 |
StlWritersGuild, 2009-2011,
Dr. Rebecca Carron Wood, President

As the digital age overtook the publishing industry and Amazon ushered in the self-publishing boom, St. Louis Writers Guild found itself once again in a state of transition. Overseeing this time within the Guild, including the 90th Anniversary, was Dr. Rebecca Carron, soon-to-become Dr. Rebecca Carron Wood, as she married during her time as president. Rebecca was by far one of the friendliest presidents of St. Louis Writers Guild. Having recently seen her at Workshops for Writers, people were still drawn to her aura. With a bright smile and curly white hair, she was a vibrant force.

As an adjunct professor, she taught composition and literature classes at St. Louis Community College, Southwestern Illinois College, SIUE, and as a professor for St. Louis University. She worked in the corporate IT world where she wrote several technical manuals. Her romantic paranormal novel, *The Full Moon Hotel* won first place at the 2006 Ozark Creative Writers Conference.

It can't be easy to follow some of the most influential presidents of SLWG history, but Rebecca not only rose to the job, her laid-back approach ushered in a new era for the organization. By maintaining the traditions and keeping it low-key, the organization not only celebrated its history and had some great guest speakers but became a group of friends, despite its large size.

Rebecca was a regular at the Open Mics, and during her era,

the open mic had its greatest run. Several changes were made to the format and location, but Rebecca always had a funny poem or a political limerick to entertain. Whether at Wired Coffee, The Mack, Schlafly Tap Room, Kirkwood Train Station (the restaurant), or the Kirkwood Amtrak Station, she attracted large crowds who returned every month.

With a robust board and Rebecca's friendly demeanor, the Guild thrived for its 90th Anniversary. The organization remained around 200 members.

Monthly Meetings During This Time

At first the meetings were at the Crestwood Barnes & Noble, but as the bookstore lost their Community Relations Managers, the time came to move and a new place was found, one that had more than enough space for all the people who attended each month. St. Louis Writers Guild's new home was the second or third floor of the Kirkwood Community Center, 111 S. Geyer Road.

Vice President of Programs

When Robin Moore Theiss had to step down because of business commitments and her daughter's wedding, she turned to the board, but everyone had day jobs and was already doing a number of jobs within the organization. Rebecca was the brand-new Vice President of Programs and wasn't certain she wanted the job of President so quickly, but she did have an interest in the position and wanted to help the members. SLWG carried on, and for a short time Rebecca Carron served as VP of Programs, showing her passion for the organization by bringing in some great speakers. The board unanimously voted to make Rebecca the President, and Peter Green took over her programming duties.

The 90th Anniversary – the Year of Festivals

Dr. Rebecca Carron Wood oversaw the Year of Festivals to celebrate the 90th anniversary. The decision was made not to have one event, but a year's worth of events to honor St. Louis Writers Guild. There were five festivals in total with a number of other events.

Kokopilau: An Evening of Poetry and Music with Michael Castro and J.D. Parran

(pictured on page 250.)

The year of festivals began with "Kokopilau: a Night of Music and Poetry" with jazz musician J.D. Parran and warrior poet Michael Castro. It was a throwback to the beatnik poets of the '60s, with about 90 people in attendance at Cicero's, 6691 Delmar, in the University City Loop. It was held on Saturday, September 12, 2009, 6:30-8:30 p.m. Admission was $10.

Michael Castro, a local guerilla poet and warrior poet, along with other cool titles, teamed up with famous jazz saxophonist J.D. Parran to create an album. SLWG secretary Dianna Graveman knew Michael and was the liaison between the Guild and the poet. The back room at Cicero's served as the venue. Castro and Parran played two sets, and then Cicero's regular Saturday night entertainment was scheduled to perform. The event was a huge success, standing room only, and an inspiring evening. Not only did people talk about the event for years, but the music and poetry inspired Peter Green to sketch Michael Castro and J. D. Parran. He captured their likenesses quite well and they were displayed at the following SLWG workshop and in *The Scribe*.

Robert Randisi

Having held several successful paid workshops with Harvey Stanbrough and Suzann Ledbetter, the board decided in 2010 to hold another. Robert Randisi, author of over 500 novels under 15 different pen names, agreed to speak. On May 1, 2010, he presented "Writing True Fiction." He talked about his writing process, and how he handed over a mostly polished manuscript to his editor (his wife) and then it went to his publisher. A pulp novelist, he wrote several series, and obviously, multiple novels a year. Once again, Chesterfield Arts was packed with writers eager to hear about his remarkable career.

Writers in the Garden

On June 5, 2010, members of SLWG met in the Boxwood

Garden of the Missouri Botanical Garden. Dwight Bitikofer led a discussion on poetry, and then members spread out through the garden for 30 minutes to write. Many wandered through the trails of the English Woodlands or along the bridges of the Japanese Garden. Inspired by beauty, members returned 30 minutes later, in the Children's Bird Garden for readings.

2nd Annual Writers Throwdown— Writers Under the Sun

Come one, come all to a test of literary might! Poets and Flash Fiction writers are invited to a Throwdown: a contest to determine the best poem and flash fiction story of the day! Cash prizes and great writers – exactly what SLWG has been doing for the past ninety years—only with a bit more flair.

Poets and Flash Fictionists were invited to a Writers Throwdown. Catherine Rankovic was the judge, and she declared two winners, one for each category. David Lucas was the master of ceremonies for the Throwdown which was held on July 10, 2010 from 1-4 p.m. The event replaced the monthly workshop, which had to be moved due to the holiday. The entry fee was $10 for the first poem or flash fiction, and $5 for each additional entry. This was pooled, and the winners and SLWG split the pot. The event was free for members to attend and $5 for non-members. The rules were simple: no more than two pages/ three minutes per piece, and it had to be family-friendly.

The event was held in a small theater, The Focal Point, 2720 Sutton Boulevard, Maplewood, Missouri. Participants stood on stage and performed, while Catherine sat halfway back in the audience. The chipped wooden stage and old theater style of seating without cushions gave the day a rustic vibe, and Peter H. Green even dressed up in a bright white wig and beard to match his poem. The competitive nature of the event provided a raucous atmosphere, but the writers remained friendly and it ended up being a fun event.

Based on the poetry slams of the day, it was hoped the event would catch on, but it never did.

Writers in the Park

Writers in the Park was a free writers' Festival held in Kirkwood Park. Eight speakers gave ten workshops on a variety of subjects, like editing, genre writing, and publishing. STL Books sold novels and t-shirts while Big Bear Grill provided the food. It was an amazing August afternoon with about 85 people in attendance.

A full account can be found in Chapter 28: Writers in the Park on page 359.

An Evening with Ted Kooser

With Dwight Bitikofer's connection to St. Louis Poetry Center and Peter H. Green's connection to Maryville University, an idea was hatched to bring in a poet of note, specifically the Poet Laureate, Ted Kooser. At the time, his speaking fee was $10,000, more than anyone one organization could afford. By pooling our resources, using the university's facilities, and grant money from a foundation, the three entities were able to bring in an outstanding guest from Nebraska.

"An Evening with Ted Kooser" was held on October 22, 2010 in the auditorium at Maryville University, part of The Medart Lecture Series Sponsored by Maryville University, with participation of St. Louis Writers Guild & St. Louis Poetry Center.

A book signing and meet-and-greet started the evening, *The Times Newspapers* arranged for a caterer, and people paid extra to attend and get their book signed. The Maryville University library hosted the meet-and-greet, and then everyone headed over to the auditorium, with multi-level seating and a giant stage. About 100 people attended the main event.

Dwight introduced Mr. Kooser, who spoke and read to over a hundred people. He talked about his poems, his life, and his experience as US Poet Laurate. A humble, soft spoken, and intelligent man, it was a wonderful evening that members and others talked about for years afterward.

One of the most distinguished writers of our time, Ted Kooser served as the United States Poet Laureate Consultant in Poetry to the Library of Congress from 2004-2006. A Presidential Professor of English at the University of Nebraska-Lincoln, he published twelve books of poetry, including *Delights and Shadows*, which won the Pulitzer Prize for Poetry in 2005.

Voices of Valhalla: A Hayride Through Time

St. Louis Writers Guild partnered with Valhalla Cemetery and the St. Louis Genealogical Society to write scripts for "Voices of Valhalla: A Hayride Through Time."

Read the complete tale on page 279 of Chapter 22.

Literary Agent Chris Richman of Upstart Crow

On November 6, 2010, St. Louis Writers Guild brought literary agent, Chris Richman of Upstart Crow Literary, to St. Louis to talk about query letters and contacting literary agents, and to take pitches from participants. "Making the Perfect Pitch," captivated a packed house at Chesterfield Arts.

The Winter Gala

The 90th Anniversary capped off with The Winter Gala, a dinner event held at Orlando Gardens on December 5, 2010. The evening was themed around the 1920s and members were encouraged to dress up. Evelyn Buretta and Butch Drury and his wife showed up in period-themed attire. Everyone was encouraged to wear their finest.

TKO DJs provided the music, and the food was catered by Orlando Gardens, which itself was a fixture on Watson Road, having hosted weddings, bar mitzvahs, birthday bashes, family reunions, and more. A Guild-themed cake provided dessert and members danced the night away. There is a great photograph of that night with Dr. Rebecca Carron Wood on the dance floor with Marcel Toussaint and others, a fond memory from a rather raucous evening.

Bill McClellan, the famous columnist for the *St. Louis Post-Dispatch*, gave the keynote address and brought the same wit and humor as in his columns. Then the first of the Robin Moore Theiss Award for Service were handed out. It was a way to honor those who volunteered their time for St. Louis Writers Guild. Dwight Bitikofer, Lynn Obermoeller, and Brad R. Cook were honored that night.

It was decided to hold the Winter Gala as an annual event, a chance to get together not in the confines of a workshop, to get away from the words and have fun. To cut down on costs, the following year, SLWG turned to Llywelyn's Pub in Webster Groves. They had a large room downstairs for group events and the Guild had a blast. Author Ridley Pearson gave a truly inspiring keynote address. The second year, David Lucas, Mary Ward Menke, and Rebecca Carron were honored with the Robin Moore Theiss Award for Service.

A Letter from the Governor

In 2010, two letters were sent out to see if St. Louis Writers Guild could get any acknowledgement of its anniversary. The first letter went to the Missouri Governor, and the second went to the White House. The President never responded, but I did learn that the White House will send a letter on the 100th birthday. Perhaps 90 wasn't enough.

However, Governor Jay Nixon did respond. The governor sent a letter, thanking and acknowledging St. Louis Writers Guild for its commitment to the literary community of St. Louis.

A New Website

The second biggest project Rebecca oversaw was the new website. In 2009, there was a time when the board members were locked out of the website. In part because of this, the organization has never handed complete control over to a third party. Rebecca called in a friend from work. Renie had designed the St. Louis Police Department's website for looking up cases and criminals; he was a programmer far beyond what SLWG could ever afford, but he was happy to help. Renie was a really nice guy from the Philippines and an expert with computers. He designed a new website for SLWG, and it was gorgeous, too—a modern, full-page design at a time when the WordPress blog format was 90% of websites.

There were only two problems with Renie: 1) he was expensive, even with his discount for the non-profit, and 2) he was constantly traveling, which made uploading files and information troublesome. Renie even designed a new logo, a square one, as the rectangular one, the classic logo, was no longer the right format for the web. A quill coming out of an inkwell, the logo was never made public.

While all of this website drama was happening, the Guild switched to a temporary website, stlwritersguild.net. It was a simple site that basically continued to push out information about events, contests, and the workshops. The confusion of the two websites was a nightmare to manage, but the .net site allowed the Guild to continue moving forward as it settled the new stlwritersguild.org.

Changes, Lots of Changes

The last major hurdle Rebecca had to overcome as President was the decline of the bookstore industry and its constant effect on SLWG. It started as soon as she stepped into the role of President. The Barnes & Noble in Crestwood, which had been the home of the workshops for years, began filling the Community Room with storage. After a couple of the area stores closed, half the room was filled with shelves, tables, and fixtures. Members sat jammed against the stuff, which was annoying and a bit unsightly, but SLWG adapted.

SLWG was always good at selling books. Several members got their yearly reading material from SLWG speakers. However, as multiple managers departed and no one took their place, the room filled up, and communication became more difficult. The final straw came when they neglected to order any books for a New York Times Bestselling Author who spoke to the Guild.

SLWG's board voted to move.

The hunt was on for a room that could hold 40 people comfortably, where we could be guaranteed a spot every month, and which would allow SLWG to collect the $5 admission fee for non-members. Easy, right? Unfortunately, none of the other bookstores could handle 30-40 people, and all said no. The public library was welcoming, but all library events had to be free. Plus, the library couldn't guarantee the room on a monthly basis; any library events superseded the SLWG meetings. Quickly, the board realized that the workshop would require having to rent out a space every month. Luckily, the budget could already handle a modest rental fee, and membership was rising.

The search was on and many places were considered, but then SLWG discovered the Kirkwood Community Center. Centrally located, it offered classroom-like rooms with tables and chairs. They had a large parking lot, and it sat on the edge of picturesque Kirkwood Park. The expanded space was a hit, but people did miss the café right outside the door. St. Louis Writers Guild started making coffee. There was a large pot for every Workshops for Writers, usually brewed by David Lucas. He and I arrived early to set up the tables, chairs, and lectern.

St. Louis Reflections—*An SLWG Anthology to celebrate the 90th Anniversary*

In 2010, as part of the 90th Anniversary, it was decided to publish members of St. Louis Writers Guild in an anthology. The book centered around stories of St. Louis. Each story had to be about a person, a place, or an event that had happened in St. Louis. Everyone who submitted was accepted, and it made for a wonderful collection of memories and an ode to the city that had hosted everyone. Next came the idea of how to put the book together and publish it. This was long before the self-publishing explosion, and the rise of e-books. Luckily, Robin Moore Theiss, after leaving the Guild, set up a publishing company as part of STL Books.

Working with Robin, the anthology came together quite easily. Renie Gemzon, the webmaster, was also a photographer and had taken a gorgeous photo of the Arch that he thought worked great as a cover. He was right. If you haven't seen the cover, it is stunning. David Alan Lucas II took a photo of the sun cutting through the clouds which was used for the back cover. Robin Moore Theiss and Mary Ward Menke edited the anthology.

Forty-seven short stories and poems from 36 different members were included in the anthology. There was about a three-month window for members to turn in their work. Two pieces were commissioned for the anthology: an opening by President Dr.

The History of St. Louis Writers Guild

Rebecca Carron Wood, and an overview of SLWG history from me. Faye Adams had written a poem about St. Louis Writers Guild when the inspiration struck, and it was the perfect ending to the anthology.

The members who were in the anthology all received a free copy, and then the remaining run of 75 books sold out within a month. SLWG ordered 100 more, and those sold well, too. *St. Louis Reflections* was 103 pages, and cost $9.99. Currently, there are only a few copies left, and that's it. There is no ability to print more, so the copies that are in people's collections are the only ones that exist.

St. Louis Reflections included:

St. Louis Reflections: A journey through history, friendship, and writing by Rebecca Carron Wood, Ph.D.

Ninety Years and Thriving! By Brad R. Cook
And Where Did You Go To High School? by Pat Bubash
The Rise and Fall of a Famous Name by Linda O'Connell
Meeting Mister Buck by Deborah Marshall
Sportsman's Park by Billy Adams
On the River's Edge by Faye Adams
Mama Mississippi by Niki Nymark
Seven by Dwight Bitikofer
There's No Place Like Home by Claire Applewhite
A Little Guy Who Lived Up to His Name by Peter H. Green
She Belonged There by Marcel Toussaint
Home to St. Louis by Dr. Rebecca Carron Wood
A Two-Season Town by Mary Ward Menke
Clayton: The Little City by Brad R. Cook
Handel's Market by Lynn Obermueller
An Intimate Acquaintance by Debbie Fox
Cahokia Mound 72 by Alice M. Azure
Butterflies at Hartford Coffee by Dwight Bitikofer
Atop St. Mary Magdalene by Dwight Bitikofer
The House Call by Morton Levy
Concert on a Stormy Sunday by Astrid Stahnke
Childhood Memories by Jeanine Dahlberg

A Walk in the Park by Rebecca Davis Keller
Duet With Egret – Forest Park by Marilyn Probe
Dinner at Fred Harvey's by Morton Levy
Places Remembered by Billy Adams
Remember St. Louis by Marie Jantzen
Mid-Time Six A.M. St. Louis by Donna Springer
Road to the World by Hal Simpkin
How I Learned to Swim Underwater by Morton Levy
Over a Blanket and a Pillow by Marcel Toussaint
Three A.M., Franklin Avenue on My Mind by Niki Nymark
Run Across the Mississippi River by Donna Springer
Horseradish Blues by Alice M. Azure
Caught in the Current by Thelma Urich
A Small Slice of St. Louis History by Faye Adams
A City of Memories by Kris Dalpiaz
A Hasty Decision by Marie Jantzen
Racism the Gateway Drug by M.B. Duffy
Light Perspective to St. Louis Airport by Marilyn Probe
Conch Shell by Alice M. Azure
The Making of a Poet by Marie Jantzen
Torn Flag in the Wind by Marcel Toussaint
A Scent of Honeysuckle by Ross Braught
Obit: Dominic Williams by Thelma Urich
St. Louis Writers Guild by Faye Adams

The Big Read and The Big Write

St. Louis Writers Guild was a partner in The Big Read festival. In 2010, the event was held in downtown Clayton. The city shut down Central Avenue from Maryland Avenue to the courthouse. A main stage at Central and Forsythe had great literary speakers provided by Maryville University. St. Louis Writers Guild held a couple of workshops for writers in a restaurant around the corner. The SLWG booth was a double because we were a partner of the festival. The booth was separated into two parts. One held all the promotional material for SLWG and was staffed by members who answered questions, and the other side was for SLWG Member book signings. A schedule was created, and members got one hour to sign books and answer questions about their work. Other organizations like Sister in Crime were there as well, along with all kinds of vendors. The restaurants along the book fair acted like food vendors with special foods and other fare. The public turned out, and members sold a lot of books.

The previous year, 2009, the event was held in the circle drive in front of Clayton High School. The booths wrapped from one end to the other and even into the parking lot, where the main stage was set up. Clifford the Big Red Dog and Curious George walked around entertaining the children. They set up food vendors on one end and had a variety of events going on throughout the day. St. Louis Writers Guild had the same booth design, with one for promoting the organization and the other for member book signing. SLWG also started to retain the books while the authors were not there to continue selling. SLWG never took a fee for this, only recorded the sale and passed along the money. A wonderful way of showcasing all the great books by SLWG Members.

The SLWG workshops were presented by various members and held in Clayton High School. On a side note, as one of the presenters that day, it was interesting to get to teach in a classroom I had once sat in as a student.

Book Booth Blurb for The Big Read and Writers in the Park

A book selling opportunity!

St. Louis Writers Guild has once again reserved a booth at The Big Read Festival. This annual tradition is an exceptional way for members to sell their books. In addition to The Big Read, October 9, this year you will also be able to sell your books during Writers in the Park, August 28, at a discounted rate.

Reservation fee for members is $25 for one or $35 for both events. For non-members, the fee is $35 for one or $45 for both events. Reservation Forms and booth rental fee must be postmarked by August 21, 2010 to be included in both events. Books must be mailed by that date or may be brought the morning of the event. SLWG will store the books between events but they must be picked up at the end of The Big Read Festival.

Writers in the Park – Saturday August 28, a writer's festival at Kirkwood Park

Writing Workshops, a Children's Workshop, and Readings in the Amphitheater,

The Big Read Festival – Saturday October 9, annual event in downtown Clayton presented by Cultural Festivals. SLWG is a partner in the Big Write Contest.

Cost this year is $25 for one or $35 for two events for SLWG/Missouri Writers Guild/Saturday Writers /Chesterfield Writers/ Writers Society of Jefferson County/Sisters in Crime members, or $35 to non-members for one or $45 for two events. Each additional title is only $5 extra.

The fee covers SLWG's cost (only) to rent and equip the booth. It provides you with featured space for your book(s) on our back wall shelving, stock space for browsers on the merchandise tables, storage of your extra books beneath the tables (for replenishment of stock), a photo feature of you or your book cover on the back wall, and an optional scheduled book signing. SLWG will also promote the event and our booths, display your photo, list your name and book signing timeslot on a large easel sign, provide you with a central cashier for sales, and include attractions designed to bring the festival visitors to our booth. Autograph sessions will only be provided at the Big Read Festival.

You may bring promo materials (bookmarks, postcards, etc.) that will be available on the signing table during your book signing. Booth attendance is strictly scheduled by SLWG. There is simply not enough room for all exhibitors and needed volunteers to be in the 16x20' booth all day. Your books will be sold in your absence by volunteers. Remaining books will need to be picked up by the end of the Big Read Festival. SLWG will store books until then.

Exhibitors agree to volunteer to assist with manning either of the SLWG booths (if needed) around the time of their scheduled book signings (not during their signings, of course!).

For more information, please review the Book Booth Exhibitors Reservation Form at www.stlwritersguild.org.

Branding St. Louis Writers Guild

As advertising became more important to St. Louis Writers

Guild, a need to inform people about everything the organization was doing, branding the events became more important.
- Twitter created November 2010
- Facebook Group created on August 10, 2008
- Instagram June 5, 2016

The SLWG Cell Phone and the End of the SLWG Phone Number

SLWG had a Motorola flip phone with a black leather case. Styling!

At first, board members passed it between each other, usually taking it for a month until the next board meeting when they happily handed it over. Board members carried the phone on them in a purse, on a belt, or just within arm's reach. Some board members answered every call, but most of the time callers had to leave a message and then they would be called back. It meant a lot of admin time for whoever had the phone and led to many awkward phone calls in strange places. Increasingly, it was the President who carried the phone, and SLWG did get some weird calls. There were people asking for the name of the Guild's literary agent or others wanting to know how long it took to get published through the Guild. Most, though, were after basic information, either about the Writers Guild—I had a good five-minute speech down about the organization—or wanting to know about the next meeting. Those were easy, but more and more, email became the main way members communicated.

Eventually, as the cost of the phone was increasing, and fewer people wanted the duty of carrying the phone, St. Louis Writers Guild switched to email-only communication, and the long era of a board member having to man the phones ended.

The President
2009 – Dr. Rebecca Carron
2010 – Dr. Rebecca Carron Wood
2011 – Dr. Rebecca Carron Wood

Board Members and Locations 2009-2011
Board meetings were held in several places. For a time, they were held at Growler's Pub, 3811 S. Lindbergh Boulevard or Borders on Olive Boulevard in Creve Coeur.

2009
Mary Menke, VP of Operations
Peter Green, VP of Programs
Dianna Graveman, Secretary
Alicia Lundstrom, Treasurer
Fay Adams, MWG Rep
Brad R. Cook, Historian

August 2009
Mary Menke, VP of Operations
Peter Green, VP of Programs
Ashley Lawlor, Secretary
Dwight Bitikofer, Treasurer
Faye Adams, MWG Rep
David Alan Lucas II, Membership Chairman
Brad R. Cook, Historian

Members from 2009-2011
Sherrie Hill
Sherrie Hill, author, realtor, operated the SLWG table at many events. Her warmth was often one of the first things new members were greeted by at the workshops.

Sherrie published her first novel, *Hickory Hill*, a historical fiction novel set in Illinois, in 2013

Peter H. Green
In his career as an architect, Peter has witnessed enough close calls, suspicious acts and outright skullduggery to lure him into writing mysteries.

A writer, architect and city planner reared in a family of journalists, Peter found his father's 400 World War II letters, his humorous war stories, his mother's writings and his family's often hilarious doings too good a tale to keep to himself, so he launched a second career as a writer.

Peter earned a Certificate in Creative Writing and Bachelor of Architecture degree from Washington University, St. Louis, and a B.A. from Yale University. He is Vice President, Programs, for St. Louis Writers Guild (SAME), a member of Sisters in Crime, St. Louis Publishers Association and Missouri Writers Guild. Among design organizations, he is a member of the American Institute of Architects, American Planning Association, American Institute of Certified Planners and past St. Louis Post President and Fellow of the Society of American Military Engineers. Awards include the Distinguished Service Award, St. Louis Post, SAME, and a 2010 Robin Moore Thiess Award for Outstanding Volunteer Service from St. Louis Writers Guild. He lives in St. Louis with his wife, Connie, and has two very young, married daughters and three small grandchildren. (from Peter's Amazon.com bio)

Ben's War with the U.S. Marines (2014)
Crimes of Design (2014)
Fatal Designs (2015)
Radio: One Woman's Family in War and Pieces (2016)
Chicago's Designs (2019)

Dwight Bitikofer

Dwight Bitikofer is a poet and was the co-founder and for over forty years has published *The Webster-Kirkwood Times*, which expanded to include the other *Times Newspapers* – *the South County Times*, and *the West End Word*. He served as Treasurer of St. Louis Writers Guild for many years where his frugal nature ensured the Guild's funds were always well spent. Dwight was a longtime member and board member of the St. Louis Poetry Center. His vocal poetic styling was sought by others and he performed readings all over the region. He was the recipient of the 2003 Kirkwood Area Chamber of Commerce Lifetime Achievement Award. He has received numerous accolades over his career including awards from the Missouri Press Association and the Independent Free Papers of America.

Linda O'Connell

Linda O'Connell is a successful freelancer and multi-genre

writer with more than 250 publishing credits. Her personal essays, poetry, and articles have appeared in diverse regional, national, and international publications.

Linda's nonfiction essays have been published in 28 *Chicken Soup for the Soul* books. She is a frequent contributor to *Sasee Magazine*. Linda has published creative nonfiction in *Saturday Evening Post, The War Cry Magazine* (Salvation Army), *True Love, The Good Old Days,* and *Reader's Digest*. Her work also appears in numerous literary magazines, in print and online.

Linda published a book, *Queen of the Last Frontier,* and an anthology, *Not Your Mother's Book On Family,* for a publisher in Northern California. She is a three-time recipient of Metro Lines/ Poetry in Motion. Her winning poems were posted on local buses and MetroLink trains for one year each.

As a columnist for a local sports paper, Linda wrote parenting articles for two years. She has written articles for *Writers Journal* and also for an educational publication.

Lynn Obermoeller

Lynn Obermoeller is a writer and poet who was active in St. Louis Writers Guild. For a time, she was the editor of the newsletter, *Here's News!*

Ashley Lawlor (Ashley Jones Wood)

Ashley Lawlor is a writer and blogger who served as Secretary of St. Louis Writers Guild.

Marcel Toussaint

Marcel Toussaint was an award-winning poet who was a fixture of the open mic nights and even presented at the SLWG Lecture Series. He published numerous books of poetry and in 2013 his novel, *Terms of Interment*. Marcel passed away on July 26, 2018.

Workshops and Events
2009
January 2009

January 3, 10 a.m. to noon – **Secrets & Lies – The Truth Behind What it Takes to Write and Produce a Television Series** presented by Paul Guyot, at Barnes & Noble, Crestwood, 9618 Watson Rd. Crestwood, 63126. Free for SLWG Members; $5 for non-members Please register in advance.

January 13, 7 to 9 p.m. – Wired Coffee Open Mic Night at Wired Coffee, 3860 S. Lindbergh, Sunset Hills 63127. Free.

January 15, 7 to 8 p.m. – Lecture: **The Evolution of Television News** presented by Don Marsh, at Barnes & Noble – Ladue, 8871 Ladue Rd., Ladue 63124. Free. Please register in advance.

January 20, 8 to 10 p.m. – Loud Mouth Open Mic Night, at The Mack, 4615 Macklind, St. Louis 63108. Free. Please register in advance.

February 2009

February 7, 10 a.m. to noon – **The Future for the Nonfiction Freelancer (Your yellow pad and pen just won't get it any more)** presented by Harry Jackson Jr.

February 10 – Wired Coffee Open Mic Night

February 17, 8 to 10 p.m. – Loud Mouth Open Mic Night, at The Mack, 4615 Macklind Ave., St. Louis 63108. Free. Must be over 18.

March 2009

March – Lecture Series presented by Barri Baumgarner

July 2009

Saturday, July 11, 7-10 p.m. – **SLWG Movie Night: Single White Female** with Author John Lutz at the Engineer's Club

Tuesday, July 14 – Open Mic @ Wired Coffee

Thursday, July 16, 6-8 p.m. – **SLWG Picnic**, George Heidman Shelter @ Creve Couer Park

Tuesday, July 21 – Loud Mouth Open Mic @ The Mack

August 2009
Saturday, August 1 – Workshop: **Critical Elements of the Short Story** presented by Rebecca Carron.
  Tuesday, August 11 – Open Mic @ Wired Coffee
  Tuesday, August 18 – Loud Mouth Open Mic @ The Mack

September 2009
Saturday, September 5 – Workshop: **Business Fundamentals for Writers** presented by Faye Adams
  Tuesday, September 8 – Open Mic @ Wired Coffee
  Saturday, September 12, 6:30-8:30 p.m. — A Night of Poetry and Music with Michael Castro and J. D. Parran. Cicero's 6691 Delmar Blvd., St. Louis, MO 63130.
  Tuesday, September 15 – Loud Mouth Open Mic @ The Mack
  Thursday, September 17 – Lecture: **Finding my Voice and Writing from the Heart: From Unpublished to Sold in Less than a Year** presented by Angie Fox, New York Times Bestselling Author.

October 2009
  Saturday, October 3, 10am to noon – Workshop: **Get the Right Gun for Your Murder: A Firearms Primer for Writers** presented by Thomas Applewhite, M.D.
  Saturday, October 10, 9am to 4pm – **The Big Read Festival**, Clayton
  Tuesday, October 13 – Open Mic @Wired Coffee
  Tuesday, October 20, 2009, 8-10 p.m. – Loud Mouth Open Mic @The Mack

November 2009
  Saturday, November 7 – Workshop: **Stage Write: What Happens Before the Curtain Goes Up** presented by Gerry Mandel
    Tuesday, November 10 – Open Mic @Wired Coffee
    Tuesday, November 17 – Loud Mouth Open Mic @The

The History of St. Louis Writers Guild

Mack

Thursday, November 19 – Lecture: **Writing Regional Histories: How One Book Contract Morphed into Four presented** by Dianna & Don Graveman authors of *St. Charles* with the Arcadia Press. Gift wrapping by SLWG members.

December 2009
Saturday, December 5 – Members Only Holiday Party
10 a.m. to noon at the Kirkwood Community Center
Tuesday, December 8 – Open Mic @Wired Coffee
Tuesday, December 15 – Loud Mouth Open Mic @The Mack

2010 – 90th Anniversary
January 2010
Saturday, November, 10 a.m. to noon – Workshop: **Writing Literary Commercial Fiction, Rejection and Publication** presented by Jeffery Penn May author of *Where the River Splits* – Kirkwood Community Center, second floor. 111 S. Geyer Rd. Free for members, $5 for non-members.

Thursday, January 20, 7:30 p.m. – 9:30 p.m. – SLWG Lecture Series: **How to get a Book Reviewed/What to Expect** presented by Jane Henderson at the Barnes & Noble, Ladue.

February 2010
Saturday, February – Workshop: **Living History: Capturing the Stories of WWII Veterans** presented by Matt Lary.

March 2010
Saturday, March – Workshop: **Freelance Writing and the Missouri Writers Guild Conference** presented by Margo Dill of the Missouri Writers Guild.

Thursday, March – SLWG Lecture Series: **Why aren't I Published?** presented by Claire Applewhite, author of *The Wrong Side of Memphis*

April 2010
Saturday, April 3 – **Discovering the Story within Non-fiction Materials** presented by Jeffery Copeland, author of *Inman's War*

April – The Missouri Writers Guild's Annual Conference, "Just Write"

2010 Deane Wagner Poetry Contest winner Niki Nymark, judge John Hahn

May 2010
Saturday, May 1, 1-4 p.m. – **Writing True Fiction** presented by Special Guest Speaker Robert Randisi, at Chesterfield Arts, 444 Chesterfield Ctr #130, Chesterfield, MO 63017.

Thursday, May 7-9 p.m. – SLWG Lecture Series: **Promoting Yourself on a Shoestring Budget** presented by Joanna Campbell Slan

June 2010
Saturday, June 5, 9:30-12:30 p.m. – **Writers in the Garden,** a Writers Retreat to the Missouri Botanical Garden, with Dwight Bitokofer.

July 2010
Saturday, July 10, 10-1 p.m. – **Second Annual Writers Throwdown "Writers Under the Sun"** with judge, Catherine Rankovic, at the Focal Point in Maplewood.

July, SLWG Lecture Series: **Preparing a Manuscript for Submission** with Mary Menke, Faye Adams, and Gerry Mandel.

August 2010
Saturday, August 7 – Workshop: **Contracts, Copyrights, and the Quirks of Protecting your Creativity in the Digital Age** presented by Mark Sableman.

Saturday, August – **Writers in the Park** – A free Writers Festival at Lions Amphitheater in Kirkwood Park with Dr. Rebecca Wood, Cole Gibsen, Judy Moresi, Faye Adams, Peter Green, Mary Menke, David Lucas, Jaclyn Devey, STL Books, and food by Big

Bear Grill.

September 2010
Saturday, September 4, 10 a.m. to noon – Workshop: **Get Critiqued! A 5+5 Workshop** moderated by SLWG's Cycle Critique Groups, Mary Menke and Brad R. Cook – Kirkwood Community Center, Second floor.

Thursday, September 16 – SLWG Lecture Series: **Researching Your Novel** presented by Brad Cook. Barnes & Noble, Ladue.

October 2010
90th Anniversary – An October to Remember
Saturday, October 9 – The Big Read Festival, Big Write Contest Winners, in downtown Clayton

Multiple Weekends – Voices of Valhalla: A Hayride Through Time – at Valhalla Cemetery

Friday October 22 – Friday Night Reading and Reception with Special Guest Ted Kooser, Poet Laureate of the US, at the Maryville University Auditorium. Reception had a fee, but the reading was free.

Saturday, October 23, 10 a.m. to noon — **Poetry Workshop** with Ted Kooser, Buder Hall at Maryville University.

October 26, 7:30 to 9:30 p.m. – **The first Writing to the Edge Open Mic Night – A Classy, Yet Edgy, Open Mike Experience** – *in the Eliot Room at the fabulous, historic Schlafly's Tap Room 2100 S. Locust St. 63103. Join MC Mike McGuire and the exceptionally creative members and guests of St. Louis Writers Guild.*

November 2010
Saturday, November 6, 10 a.m. to 1 p.m. – **Making the Perfect Pitch** presented by Special Guest Speaker Chris Richman of Upstart Crow Literary — at Chesterfield Arts, 444 Chesterfield Ctr #130, Chesterfield, MO 63017. *Preregistration required. The fee is $25 for members of SLWG and its affiliated chapters, $35 for non-members. You may request one pitch session that will last no longer than 5 minutes. There are a limited number of pitch sessions available and priority will be*

given to the genres that Mr. Richman represents.

Thursday, November – SLWG Lecture Series – **Success in Genre Fiction** presented by Eileen Dryer

December 2010

Saturday, December 4, 7-10 p.m. – **90th Anniversary Winter Gala** with Keynote Speaker Bill McClellan of the *St. Louis Post-Dispatch*, with dinner and dancing at Orlando Gardens. Music provided by TKO DJs.

2010 Short Story Contest with judge Angie Fox

2011

January 2011

Saturday, January 8 – Workshop: **Write Away: Start the New Year Writing** presented by Patricia Bubash author of *Psychology of Writing*

Thursday, January 20 – Lecture: **Several Deadly Sins for Creative Writers** presented by Rick Skwiot

February 2011

Saturday, February, 5 – Workshop: **Missed Opportunities & Misunderstandings in Writing Fiction** presented by Steve Lattimore

Tuesday, February 8, 7-9 p.m. – **First Highlands Family-Friendly Open Mic at the Highland Brewing Co.** in downtown Kirkwood

Tuesday, February 22, 7:30 to 9:30 p.m. – Writing to the Edge Open Mic, Eliot Room at Schlafly's Tap Room, 2100 S. Locust St. 63103

March 2011

Saturday, March 5, 10 a.m. to noon – Workshop: **Missouri Writers Guild**

Tuesday, March 8, 7-9pm – Kirkwood Highlands Family-Friendly Open Mic

Tuesday, March 22, 7:30 to 9:30 p.m. – Writing to the Edge

Open Mic

May 2011
Thursday, May 19 – Lecture: **Writing for Young Adults** with Anthony John, author of *5 Flavors of Dumb*

June 2011
Thursday, June 2 – 2nd Annual SLWG Picnic and Volunteer Appreciation Event at Tillis Park

Saturday, June 4 – Workshop Panel: **Mastering the Big Four—Facebook, Twitter, Websites and Blogs** with Cole Gibsen, Shawntelle Madison, and Sarah Whitney,

July 2011
Saturday, July 9, 1-4 p.m. – **Poetry and Prose Throwdown** at The Focal Point in Maplewood.

Thursday, July 21 – Books for Joplin, transporting thousands of books to tornado ravaged Joplin.

Thursday, July 21 – Lecture: **Seven Common Blunders Developing Screenwriters Make** with Dave Trottier. *Give your script the competitive edge by dodging these common errors and writing compelling dialogue and action that create memorable movie moments and maximize your script's marketing potential. Author of* The Screenwriter's Bible, *(now in its 5th edition), nearly 300,000 sold.*

August 2011
August 6 – Workshop Panel: **Bait Your Hook: Critiquing your Best Stuff** – Brad Cook, moderator.

Saturday, August 20 – Writers in the Park a mini-conference with Angie Fox – **Lining Up the Bones**; Kim Lozano – **Poetry Workshop**; Robin Thiess – **Publishing**; Debbie Marshall – **Introduction to Wounded Warrior Oral History Program**

September 2011
Saturday September 10, Workshop: **Screenwriting** with Annene Tressler-Hauschultz, Emmy award-winning, TV scriptwriter.

Thursday, September 22 – Lecture: John Lutz, discussing his recent novels, *Serial*, and *Tropical Heat*. (Location to be announced)

October 2011
Saturday, October 1 – Workshop: Jeff Copeland, author of *Inman's War*.

October 14-23 – 2nd Voices of Valhalla, *Halloween hayride at Valhalla Cemetery reviving the cemetery's inhabitants to tell their stories. Several weekends, but October 14 and 15 were managed by SLWG.*

November 2011
Saturday, November 5 – Workshop: **Publicity and Promotion** presented by Claire Applewhite

Thursday, November 17 – Lecture: Richard Burgin, discusses and signs his new novel, *Shadow Traffic*, after checking several locations SLWG held the event at the Kirkwood Community Center.

December 2 – Winter Gala: Keynote Speaker, Ridley Pearson at C.J. Muggs, Webster Groves

December 13 – St. Louis Reflections Anthology Release Party at the Kirkwood Amtrak Station

The History of St. Louis Writers Guild

WALTER
BARGEN

DAVID
CLEWELL

WILLIAM
TROWBRIDGE

Poet Laureate 2008-2009   *Poet Laureate 2010-2011*   *Poet Laureate 2012-13*

FRIDAY, MARCH 15, 2013 · 7:30 P.M.
Maryville University Auditorium, Anheuser Busch Academic Center
Maryville University Drive • 63141
Admission is free ~ A reception and book signing will follow the reading

The Modart Lecture Series
SPONSORED BY MARYVILLE UNIVERSITY
with the participation of the St. Louis Writers Guild and St. Louis Poetry Center

22 |
SLWG, 2011 to 2014, Brad R. Cook, President

As NASA's Curiosity Rover soared toward Mars, I became president of St. Louis Writers Guild. In June of 2011, the board meetings were held at the Highland Brewing Company/The Kirkwood Train Station, a restaurant and craft beer brewery in downtown Kirkwood on Jefferson Avenue. This meeting was slightly different. The SLWG Picnic replaced the workshop that month, so we were meeting on a different Saturday in June. Dr. Rebecca Carron Wood pulled me aside before entering the restaurant and told me she had to step down due to increased duties at work, part of which was teaching refugees via remote lectures. She asked if I was interested in the presidency. To be honest, I hadn't thought about it. I was still trying to get my books published. However, I had been doing a lot behind the scenes, especially for the 90th Anniversary. When she announced she was stepping down at the board meeting, I asked if anyone else wanted the job. No one did, and they voted unanimously to make me president.

I must admit, I wasn't expecting it when it happened, and that's probably best. I don't know if anyone actively seeks the office. It's more of an honor you accept than something to be sought.

I went home that night and created a document—**My Time as President**—and wrote several pages of notes on what I wanted to accomplish, from programs and special events, to new member opportunities. Plus, I made notes on how to improve the organization, changes I'd always wanted to make, and in the end, how to honor the 62* (64*) presidents before me.

*I was the *63 president of St. Louis Writers Guild at the time, and since then it changed to 65, and could be updated again—there are still two unknown years.*

The first words I wrote were a philosophy, a three-pronged approach on how to move forward with St. Louis Writers Guild: **1) Focus on Helping Writers Who Are Starting Out, 2) Empower Writers Who Are Querying or Publishing, and 3) Showcase the Authors Who Are Already Published.**

The plan was to cut SLWG's overhead while expanding member benefits, to clarify communication with members, and to connect with the literary community more deeply. In September, at my first official board meeting (the July and August board meetings were about Writers in the Park), I set the course with the first item on the agenda—*a new era that feels just like the old.*

Workshops for Writers, the monthly meeting of St. Louis Writers Guild

The Kirkwood Community Center was the home of St. Louis Writers Guild during my presidency. Centrally located within the zip codes of SLWG and with several members living in the district, SLWG was able to get lower rates on all our rentals. The meetings were held on the first Saturday of most months (January, July, and September could be moved due to holidays) in the long rectangular rooms on either the second floor, with the attached kitchen, or the third floor with the mirrored wall and ballet bar. Occasionally, dance practice disturbed the workshop, but usually SLWG was the only group. However, there was almost always a trade or craft show going on, and hockey practice at the rink. The Kirkwood Community Center was a hub of activity.

Board members arrived about 9 - 9:15 a.m. to set up the tables, chairs, and the SLWG table. Six-foot tables were set up with three to four chairs, and an aisle down the middle. By the door, an L-shaped arrangement formed the SLWG table, where registration was set up and books were laid out, along with handouts and other promotional material. David or one of the other board members would start making the coffee. Many members arrived about 9:30 a.m. to talk with others and get a good seat. Shortly before 10 a.m. came a rush of members and guests who formed a line as they signed in, and non-members paid the $5 fee. There was always a buzz to the beginning of the meeting; people had questions, old friends were reuniting, and the first timers were attempting to soak it all in.

At 10 a.m., announcements started, and I continued the tradition of asking if any had submitted in the last month, if anyone had been rejected in the last month, and if anyone had seen success in the last month. I always tried to be encouraging to those who had submitted or been rejected and celebrated everyone's successes. If I forgot, I'd kick myself, and stick it in during the 11 a.m. break. The program ended at noon; however, people often stuck around to talk to the speaker, one or more of the board members, or their friends. Thus, the room never cleared out until 12:30-1 p.m.

The New stlwritersguild.org

One of the biggest projects for me—finish something Rebecca had started—a new website. We were using stlwritersguild.net at that time while stlwritersguild.org was still under construction. We were all set to move forward, but a series of typhoons struck Renie's family back in the Philippines. He traveled back and forth and wasn't able to work on the website as much. Then in September 2011, Typhoon Nesat, or Typhoon Pedring, as it was known in the Philippines, impacted the region. It was the most powerful tropical storm since 2005 and killed 83 people. Eight major typhoons struck the region that year, devastating the area and killing over 3,000 people. In the end, Renie had to return to help his family, and SLWG was left without a webmaster.

I had already created several websites by this point, including stlwritersguild.net, and wasn't certain the Guild needed to pay an expensive webmaster. I put forward a plan for a new website, and once approved, I created a nice website that anyone on the board could update and modify. We used Network Solutions, and created a really cool website . . . for 2013. We also upgraded the newsletter, *Here's News!*, from an old text-based email to a new graphic and color block design. Right away, SLWG started receiving praise for the more modern and fancy designs. The website grew over the next several years as new programs and features were added, until the little website became a robust resource for writers.

St. Louis Writers Guild Reaches Out

One thing I wanted to accomplish was more outreach and communication with the other St. Louis literary organizations. I'd heard tales of angst between the various organizations since I'd joined, but no one from those stories were still part of the different groups. I figured it was time to reach out. We started simple and slowly, and today, SLWG has deeper and closer relationships with Missouri Writers' Guild (MWG), St. Louis Publishers Association (SLPA), Saturday Writers (SW), Greater St. Louis Chapter of Sisters in Crime (SiC), Missouri Romance Writers of America (MORWA), The St. Louis Press Club, and more, thanks in large part to the efforts of the presidents that followed me.

St. Louis Writers Guild did hold events by partnering or collaborating with the other literary organizations. We worked with Nancy Hughes, Margert Donnelly, and Dwight Bitikofer of the St. Louis Poetry Center and with Maryville University to bring in the three Missouri Poet Laureates, and Ted Kooser. We held events and shared speakers with the St. Louis Publishers Association, working with its members, Bob Baker, Warren Martin, and Linda Austin. At this time, SLWG also worked closely with Missouri Writers' Guild to help with their yearly conference.

Budget Cuts

The other achievement I am proud of was cutting spending, freeing up budget money for other projects, including bigger events, and top-quality speakers. One way was by making *The Scribe* electronic, another was to not hire a webmaster, and still another was to look at where the Guild could cut spending through modernization. It allowed us to continue holding great programs, to begin routinely paying speakers, and renting the meeting rooms without raising membership fees.

Books for Joplin

The first thing I did as president was team up with the President of Missouri Writers' Guild for Books for Joplin. A massive EF5 tornado struck the town of Joplin, Missouri on May 22, 2011. A mile wide, with winds of almost 200 miles an hour, it tore through town, devastating the city, killing 158 and injuring 1,150 people, and did $2.8 billion in damage—the costliest tornado in US history. Not only did it destroy a hospital, but it damaged the library and a couple of schools. So many books were destroyed that Deborah Marshall, President of Missouri Writers' Guild, took action. She sponsored a book drive with several of the St. Louis literary organizations and chapters of MWG. Members of St. Louis Writers Guild responded in droves, collecting enough books to fill my living room and office.

Deb rented an F-150 pickup truck. I brought all the books SLWG had collected and took them over to her house. We loaded those books and all the books MWG and other organizations had collected into the bed of the truck, thousands of books, and jumped on I-44 West, headed for Joplin.

The devastation was intense. A somberness hung over the city like a storm cloud, despite the sunny day we arrived on. Joplin was still cleaning up. The city was trying to rebuild, but if a city could look sad, Joplin was despondent. We passed the volunteer tent cities, including the giant Tide tent where everyone could do a load of laundry, and drove past streets lined only with tree trunks, stripped bare of branches and leaves.

Arriving at the Middle School, the least damaged in the system, we found a flurry of activity as every teacher from the district worked to get the schools back up and running. This place served as the collection and sorting spot for all books and supplies for the schools and libraries. Immediately, we had volunteers helping us unload the boxes of books. With industrial-sized dollies and flat-bed carts to hold the boxes, we wheeled them into the school cafeteria. The room was stacked with boxes of books and towers of unboxed books that went from floor to ceiling. Several people worked at a table in the center, cataloging each book, and sorting them into orderly piles that formed walls of books.

I've been in few rooms with as many books as I saw that day. The teachers and librarians were grateful, and everyone thanked us numerous times. It was a cool moment when the St. Louis Literary Community came together to help devastation in the state.

St. Louis Reflections Release Party

St. Louis Reflections: An Anthology by St. Louis Writers Guild in Honor of Its 90th Anniversary was the culmination of a lot of work. (See details on page 251 of Chapter 21 about 2010 and the 90th Anniversary.) To celebrate, St. Louis Writers Guild held a book launch at the Kirkwood Amtrak Station on December 13, 2011. The night was a great success. Wine and hors d'oeuvres were provided by One-19 North, a Kirkwood restaurant. Contributors to the anthology read their pieces in front of the holiday decorations, giving the event a celebratory feel. The train station was packed, and every seat was taken. SLWG sold a lot of books that night and gave each contributor a copy. As president, I acted as MC. Dr. Rebecca Carron Wood opened the night with her piece, "St. Louis Reflections: A Journey Through History, Friendship, and Writing," which had also opened the book. I read my poem, "Clayton: The Little City." Peter H. Green, Linda O'Connell, Faye Adams, Billy Adams, Dwight Bitikofer, and more, read throughout the evening.

A Night of Poetry and Jazz

"A Night of PoJazz," as it was called, was one of the more interesting events during my time as president, and one I was proud SLWG held. "A Night of Poetry and Jazz" was the collaboration of Dwight Bitikofer, who was SLWG Treasurer at the time, and Raven Wolf C Felton Jennings II, a musician and artist, who melded his unique brand of spiritual jazz with the poetic beats of six local poets. I hoped it would be a good continuation of the "Writers Under the Stars" event that Robin Moore Theiss held during her presidency.

Poets like Treasure Shields Redmond, Gerry Mandel, Nicky Rainey, Jason Braun, and Erin Chapman, joined Dwight and Raven

Wolf on stage. While the poets read, Raven Wolf provided musical accompaniment by playing various drums, flutes, a saxophone, and other instruments. The Higher Education Channel (HEC), set up cameras and lights to film the event for their State of the State segment. They interviewed the poets and Raven Wolf, and talked to me about St. Louis Writers Guild.

The event was held in the Kirkwood Amtrak Station. It was free to attend, and we had a packed house of 30-plus people. Its success allowed Dwight and Raven Wolf to take it on tour, performing PoJazz throughout the area.

A Special Event! The Poets Laureate of Missouri

With the success of the Ted Kooser event, the three entities—Maryville University, the St. Louis Poetry Center, and St. Louis Writers Guild—decided to hold another event. Missouri had recently started selecting state-wide poet laureates, and the third Missouri Poet Laureate, Walter Bargen, had recently been selected. The decision was made to get all three together for a single night of poetry. "A Special Event! The Poet Laureates of Missouri: An Evening with David Clewell, William Trowbridge, and Walter Bargen," was held at 7:30 p.m. on Friday, March 15, 2013 in the auditorium at Maryville University. This was another collaboration between The Medart Lecture Series, Sponsored by Maryville University; with participation of St. Louis Writers Guild & St. Louis Poetry Center.

Below are the biographies of the three Missouri poet laureates used for the event:

David Clewell

"David Clewell is the author of eight collections of poetry—most recently, Taken Somehow By Surprise (University of Wisconsin Press, 2011)—and two book-length poems. His work regularly appears in a wide variety of national magazines and journals—including *Poetry, Harper's, The Georgia Review, New Letters, The Kenyon Review,* and *Boulevard*—and has been represented in more than fifty anthologies. Among his honors are several book awards: the Felix Pollak Poetry Prize (*for Now We're Getting Somewhere*), National Poetry Series selection (*for Blessings in Disguise*), and the inaugural Four Lakes Poetry Prize (*for Taken Somehow By Surprise*). He served as poet laureate of Missouri from 2010 to 2012.

"Clewell teaches writing and literature at Webster University in St. Louis, where he also directs the English Department's creative writing program. His collection of Charlie the Tuna iconography is now the largest in private curatorship."

Sadly, David Clewell passed away in August 2020 at the age of 65.

William Trowbridge

"The current Poet Laureate of Missouri, William Trowbridge holds a B.A. in Philosophy and an M.A. in English from the University of Missouri-Columbia and a Ph.D. in English from Vanderbilt University. His poetry publications include five full collections: *Ship of Fool* (Red Hen Press, 2011), *The Complete Book of Kong* (Southeast Missouri State University Press, 2003), *Flickers, O Paradise*, and *Enter Dark Stranger* (University of Arkansas Press, 2000, 1995, 1989), and three chapbooks, *The Packing House Cantata* (Camber Press, 2006), *The Four Seasons* (Red Dragonfly Press, 2001) and *The Book of Kong* (Iowa State University Press, l986). His sixth collection, *Put This On, Please: New and Selected Poems*, was published in 2014 by Red Hen Press. His poems have appeared in more than 30 anthologies and textbooks, as well as in *The Writer's Almanac* and in such periodicals as *Poetry; The Gettysburg Review; Crazyhorse; The Georgia Review; Boulevard; The Southern Review; Columbia; Colorado Review; The Iowa Review; Prairie Schooner; Epoch*; and *New Letters*. He has given readings and workshops at schools, colleges, bookstores, and literary conferences throughout the United States. His awards include an Academy of American Poets Prize, a Pushcart Prize, a Bread Loaf Writers' Conference scholarship, a Camber Press Poetry Chapbook Award, and fellowships from The MacDowell Colony, Ragdale, Yaddo, and The Anderson Center. He is Distinguished University Professor Emeritus at Northwest Missouri State University, where he was an editor of *The Laurel Review/GreenTower Press* from 1986 to 2004. Now living in the Kansas City area, he teaches in the University of Nebraska Low-residency MFA in Writing Program."

Walter Bargen

"Walter Bargen has published fourteen books of poetry and two chapbooks of poetry. Recent books are *The Feast* (BkMk Press-UMKC, 2004), *Remedies for Vertigo* (WordTech Communications, 2006), *West of West* (Timberline Press, 2007), *Theban Traffic* (WordTech Communications, 2008), *Days Like This Are Necessary: New & Selected Poems* (BkMk Press-UMKC2009), and *Endearing Ruins* (Illiom-Verlag, Germany, 2012). His work has appeared in hundreds of magazines and anthologies. He was the winner of the Chester H. Jones Foundation prize in 1997, a National Endowment for the Art Fellowship in 1991, the Hanks Prize, and the William Rockhill Nelson Award. He is the first poet laureate of Missouri (2008-2009)." (www.walterbargen.com)

About 125 people attended the free event at Maryville University. They laughed more than any other poetry event I've attended, as poems about Sasquatch and UFOs were read alongside the usual poetry about nature and beautiful seasons. Afterward, the three poet laureates held book signings, and each had a line across the lobby floor. They sold every book, over three hundred copies of their books in all.

SLWG Events at this time

After the unceremonious end to the Loud Mouth Open Mic, SLWG's slogan became: "St. Louis Writers Guild, it's as easy as 1…2…3…": Workshops for Writers on the First Saturday of Every Month, The SLWG Open Mic Night on the Second Tuesday of Each Month, and The SLWG Author Series on the Third Thursday of every other month." This slogan remained in use until the end of the SLWG Author Series.

Worked great, too. Rolled off the tongue and made it easy to remember.

The SLWG Author Series

The SLWG Author Series formed out of the desire to not let the long-running lecture series disappear. The end of the lecture series is outlined in depth later on, in Chapter 26: "The SLWG Lecture Series," but to summarize, after Borders closed, the audience dwindled, but technology was advancing. SLWG began streaming the lectures and posting them to YouTube. This meant a switch from an author talking for an hour to a 10-to-30-minute interview with an author. I hosted each episode, using my laptop as the camera and a service called Livestream to send it out over the internet. Members could sit back and watch from the comfort of their own home. The online audience could even ask questions via Twitter @stlwritersguild, or through the Livestream chat box.

For a time, it was like an every-other-month television show.

At first, this was a successful format. Authors didn't sell as many books, but more people saw them speak. About 12-15 people showed up in the beginning, with usually no more than a handful watching live online, but the videos often received hundreds of views.

Two shows that really defined what the SLWG Author Series became were a tribute show and one of the biggest episodes of all. While the SLWG Author Series was still held at All On The Same Page Bookstore in Olivette, MO, two people connected to SLWG passed away suddenly. Wilfred "Will" Bereswill and Linda Houle of L&L Dreamspell died within a month or so of each other. Will Bereswill was a mystery author, and a popular member of the Guild. He worked for Anheuser-Bush as an environmental engineer and often spoke of his travels to China. Linda Houle of L&L Dreamspell was a publisher in Texas, who brought several SLWG members, like T.W. Fendley, Peter H. Green, Claire Applewhite, and Judy Moresi to bookshelves. On July 25, 2013, I interviewed Peter, Claire, and Judy for an episode called, *A Night with Authors of L&L Dreamspell*. We shared memories of Will and Linda and talked about their influences on the publishing world and St. Louis Writers Guild.

The most viewed episode ended up being the interview with New York Times Bestselling Author, Ann Leckie in July 2015.

Another episode of note was held on March 21, 2014, and featured New York Times Bestselling Author Angie Fox at STL Books in Kirkwood, MO. By this time, the SLWG Author Series had a format and a flow to each episode. We arranged Angie's posters behind her and her books in front of her. We had a small crowd but enough to fill STLBooks to capacity. The online audience asked several questions and the interview went great. Angie was charming as always, and everyone had a great night. She even sold books, so, she and STLBooks were happy. The episode was one of the best in terms of flow and the discussion, and the video received many views.

The format for the SLWG Author Series consisted of an author sitting in a chair beside mine. The camera was focused on the guest – no need to see the guy asking questions every month—plus, the hope was to have different interviewers, with the focus always on the author. Because we livestreamed the event, people could watch all of the before and after parts. They never made the posted video, but I always said they were the best parts of the episodes.

Once settled, I began recording. First came the introductions and the promotion of their latest book, their most popular book, and then I asked writing-focused questions about their process or opinions on certain topics. Did they outline every plot point or write as they went, by the seat of their pants? The questions were given to the authors ahead of time, so they knew what would be discussed and could prepare their answers. There was one question I asked of every guest—"Which was easier to write, the first line or the last line?"

The SLWG Author Series ended when it became too difficult to interview the speakers. Often, they left right after the workshop, and schedules were difficult to coordinate. Also, it may not have been smart to focus on the speakers. We were hoping it would be a way to get a little more time with them and more information about the workshop topic, but often if people had attended the workshop they didn't need to watch, and if they didn't go, there was less incentive to search for it. Also, many authors objected to being filmed.

Voices of Valhalla

In 2010, Valhalla Cemetery Contacted St. Louis Writers Guild with a proposal. They were creating a haunted hayride through their historic cemetery and needed writers to write the monologues for some of the famous people interred there. A local director and local actors took care of the performance. St. Louis Writers Guild accepted, and we were given a list of people they wanted to feature, and members of the St. Louis Geological Society researched each person, giving some details. Then the writers did a little more research and wrote the page-length monologues.

I wrote a couple of them, and about a dozen SLWG members participated. The pieces were edited by the director, who structured and ordered them the way he wanted, and picked the monologues, based off the actors he had available.

SLWG Members acted as volunteers on Halloween Weekend, too. Voices of Valhalla ran for the two weekends before Halloween and sold out every hayride. The *St. Louis Post-Dispatch* and other outlets ran stories on the event and even mentioned my monologue. SLWG Members helped park cars and take tickets and got to take an all-SLWG hayride later that night. Despite the cold, everyone had a wonderful time as we called out who had written which pieces.

The second year was just as successful, only the St. Louis Genealogy Society didn't help us with research, but the cemetery had information and each writer researched their subject. The crowds showed up again, and the second year they even added another weekend.

Sadly, that was the end for SLWG's involvement in Voices of Valhalla. Once informed that they could not use the monologues written by SLWG members without SLWG involvement, the relationship ended. Voices of Valhalla continued for a year or two, but never had the size or excitement of those first two years.

Writers in the Park

Writers in the Park is one of my favorite memories of St. Louis Writers Guild. It began as a way to celebrate the 90th Anniversary and thrived for the next seven years. Tasked with creating the first event, I ended up coordinating all of them.

Each year was an adventure unto itself. Each event took on some personality and earned a nickname.

8/22/2010 – A Celebration of the 90th Anniversary
8/20/2011 – Writers in the Rain
8/25/2012 – A True Writers Festival
8/24/2013 – Young Writers in the Park
8/23/2014 – Writers Melting in the Park
8/29/2015 – Writers Freezing in the Park
8/6/2016 – The Last Writers in the Park
3/7/2020 – Writers at the Lodge
(Read about Writers in the Park in Chapter 28 on page 343.)

SLWG at The Missouri Writers Guild Conference

St. Louis Writers Guild aided Missouri Writers' Guild with its annual conference for much of the late 2000s and early 2010s. As I learned researching this book, though, SLWG had assisted MWG as speakers, as planners, and as attendees, since the beginning.

SLWG performed many duties while assisting Missouri Writers Guild with their conference, especially when the event was held in St. Louis. Whether it was transporting speakers to Cape Girardeau in 2009, or serving as Speaker Shepherds (people who escorted the conference speakers throughout the weekend, to and from the airport, and occasionally the Arch or the Art Museum), for conferences at the 2010 Chesterfield Drury Inn, 2011 Westport Plaza Sheridan, 2012 Chesterfield Double Tree, 2013 Westport Plaza Sheridan, and the 2014 Downtown Ramada.

One year, rain at Westport meant the speaker shepherds helped ferry people through village under umbrellas, and in 2012 David Lucas and I hosted an Open Mic on Friday night. The SLWG Author Series interviewed the speakers for multiple years and SLWG and the STL Literary Consortium even operated a bookstore in 2014. Many of the SLWG presidents presented workshops at the conference.

I made videos consisting of funny memes created from photos of the conference mixed with shots of the year from all the MWG chapters, the videos played during the banquet dinner as entertainment.

End of The Big Read / Beginning of the Young Writers Awards

As The Big Read Festival continued, the Guild became more and more involved, meeting with Cultural Festivals, the company that ran the festival, on multiple occasions to discuss not only The Big Write Contest, but also the writing workshops track, awards ceremony, and more. Cultural Festivals also held several other events, like a jazz festival and the Clayton Art Fair. They operated off several federal grants and provided wonderful events for the city. However, in 2010, funding was cut. The first to fall was the jazz festival, as they focused on The Big Read and the Clayton Art Fair.

In 2011, word came that without the National Endowment for the Arts grants, the festival could not continue. Due to budget constraints, they focused on the Clayton Art Fair. The Big Read and The Big Write had to end. Cultural Festivals was crushed, SLWG was devastated. No one wanted to see it end, especially when the previous year generated 700+ entries. All of us loved the event, but we understood; however, SLWG didn't want to lose the contest. So, I went to the board with a proposal. SLWG would never be able to match the financial commitment of The Big Write, which had sent flyers and entry forms to every school in several states and a couple of countries. However, SLWG could hold the contest and reach out to every school in the St. Louis area. Thus, the Young Writers Awards became the newest annual writing contest.

Young Writers Awards

The Young Writers Awards copied the format of The Big Write, and did so with permission from Cultural Festivals, with the understanding that SLWG couldn't use The Big Write name. For the contest, the board came up with the first sentence, and the young writers had to write the next 500 words. It had to be an original work by the student. *(You can always tell when Mom or Dad has a hand in the storytelling and writing.)*

Jennifer Stolzer, Secretary for SLWG, took over the coordination of the writing contests, and I designed a fun certificate for the winners. SLWG paid the winners a cash prize and for the first two years, notebooks, pens, and journals were included. In the early years, the contest never reached the numbers of The Big Write, but it had the same impact on tomorrow's writers. Every year, young writers in 4th and 5th or 6th through 8th grades discovered that they were writers. Some simply enjoyed writing a story in class that day, but others showed real talent.

Without a doubt, the Young Writers Awards was my favorite contest of the year. Reading the stories was inspiring. Untethered, their imaginations flowed to every corner possible. It was raw, unrefined by years of English composition classes. Spotting the future writers was easy. They shined like diamonds. Their stories were interesting, funny, had true characters, and left the reader with an impression.

SLPA Vendor Showcase

In support of the new relationships that SLWG had formed with the other literary organizations, when SLPA, the St. Louis Publishers Association, asked if we wanted to partner with them for their big event, a Vendor Showcase the board said, "yes."

They had rented The Lodge Des Peres, for a day in August 2013. The Guild was invited to be a part of the event, to encourage our members to partake, and to have a presence at the event.

The SLPA Vendor Showcase was filled with publishers, book layout experts, cover designers, illustrators, and more. SLWG had a table and it was a great networking opportunity.

The event became a regular feature of St. Louis Publishers Association's year.

Lit in the Lou

Lit in the Lou was a book festival held on October 11, 2014 along Ackert Walkway in Ackert Park, in University City Loop. St. Louis Writers Guild was one of the organizers and arranged some of the programming for the event.

The Transformation of the Lecture Series

St. Louis Writers Guild used to hold three events a month.

As the saying went, "SLWG is as easy as 1…2…3…" Workshops for Writers was on the first Saturday of the month. The Open Mic was on the second Tuesday of the month, and the SLWG Lecture Series was on the third Thursday of every other month, the odd months. However, as the years passed, each of the events changed. The Lecture Series had the most drastic changes and dwindled until it ended unceremoniously.

The lecture series was a part of my presidency to look back on and study. At the time, it felt like nothing we did had any effect on the lecture series. There was an obvious mood change in the people, plus a change in the industry itself.

The Lecture Series started at Barnes & Noble in Ladue and went through four other incarnations before ending as the SLWG Author Series, an online interview after Workshops for Writers that was posted to YouTube.

The complete tale of the SLWG Lecture Series can be found in Chapter 26.

The Highest Membership in SLWG History

St. Louis Writers Guild, building on what David Motherwell, Robin Moore Theiss, and Dr. Rebecca Carron Wood had done before, grew to the largest membership in its history in 2012, with over 340 members by the end of the Season. The Guild had a strong board; each position was filled, and everything flowed well. David Lucas, the VP of Membership, not only dealt with all member issues but also reached out into community seeking new members. The Guild advertised through colleges, libraries, and other organizations around town. The year was packed with informative workshops and events. Most importantly, no matter what events the Guild held, the focus remained on how to best help its members. Plus, the boom of e-book readers was in full swing, and many people were interested in writing a book.

Membership always fluctuated throughout the year, and from year to year, but since the mid-2000s the Guild averaged about 200 members, with several members spread across the nation. In addition, SLWG reached about 1500 satellite members, the name most commonly used for the local and regional writers not part of the Guild but who got the newsletter or were part of the social media reach, plus former members who still stayed connected. The city at this time was a hub of Midwestern writers, from freelancers to New York Times Bestselling authors.

The President
August 2011 to March 2015 – Brad R. Cook

Board Members and Meeting Locations from 2011 – 2015
Board Meetings were held at Wired Coffee, Growler's Pub, Highland Brewing in Kirkwood, Barnes & Noble – Ladue, Borders Books in Creve Coeur, Kaldi's Coffee House in Kirkwood, Followed by a Programs and Publicity meeting

2011
Brad R. Cook, President
David Alan Lucas II, VP of Membership
Dwight Bitikofer, Treasurer
Peter H. Green, VP of Programs & Publicity
Faye Adams, MWG/Contests
T.W. Fendley, Secretary
Renie Gemzon, Webmaster

2012
Brad Cook, President
David Alan Lucas II, VP of Membership
Dwight Bitikofer, Treasurer
Historian
Peter Green, VP of Programs & Publicity
Faye Adams, MWG Representative/Contest Coordinator
T.W. Fendley, Secretary
Rebecca Wood, Past-President
Renie Gemzon, Webmaster

2013
Brad Cook, President

The History of St. Louis Writers Guild

David Alan Lucas II, VP of Membership
Dwight Bitikofer, Treasurer
T.W. Fendley, VP of Programs & Publicity
MWG Rep and MWG Contest Coordinator, Faye Adams & Peter Green
Jennifer Stolzer, Secretary
Rebecca Wood, Past-President
Renie Gemzon, Webmaster

2014
Brad Cook, President
David Alan Lucas II, VP of Membership
Jamie Krakover Treasurer
T.W. Fendley, VP of Programs & Publicity
Peter H. Green, MWG Rep
Jennifer Stolzer, Secretary

Members from 2011-2014
T.W. Fendley

T.W. Fendley is an award-winning author of historical fantasy and science fiction for adults and young adults. Her debut novel, *Zero Time*, is a 21st Century Celestine Prophecy that melds ancient Mayan history with New Age spirituality and time travel. Readers chose *Zero Time* as the 2011 Best Science Fiction/Fantasy Novel. Fendley's short stories have earned national recognition, including a *Writer's Digest* award. She began writing fiction full-time in 2007 after working more than 25 years in journalism and corporate communication. Fendley serves on the board of the St. Louis Writers Guild and belongs to various other writing organizations. When she's not writing, she travels with her artist husband and tests practical uses of precognition. Learn more at www.twfendley.com.

Zero Time (2011)
The Labyrinth of Time (2014)
Moonblood (2020)

Jamie Krakover

Growing up with a fascination for space and things that fly, Jamie turned that love into a career as an Aerospace Engineer. Combining her natural enthusiasm for Science Fiction and her love of reading, she now spends a lot of her time writing Middle Grade and Young Adult Science Fiction and Fantasy.

Jamie has two female in STEM (Science, Technology, Engineering, and Mathematics) short stories published in the *Brave New Girls* anthologies and two engineering-centered nonfiction pieces published in *Writer's Digest's Putting the Science in Fiction*. She is a member of SCBWI (Society of Children's Book Writers and Illustrators), the treasurer of St. Louis Writer's Guild, and she blogs for a Middle Grade group blog, titled Middle Grade Minded.

Her debut young adult novel, *Tracker220*, was published in 2020.

Steven Langhorst

Steven Langhorst was a writer and poet who was one of the main photographers for St. Louis Writers Guild events and the Gateway to Publishing Conference & Convention. A former principal and school administrator, he captured the feel of the meeting in his work and was the best at capturing little moments between members. In 2015, his logo design was combined with one designed by Brad R. Cook and became the modern SLWG Logo. A regular at the open mics, he was known for writing a train poem or two as they interrupted the speaker. Steven was the bartender for the SLWG Virtual Speakeasy; each month he talked about some historical point and taught everyone how to make the featured cocktail.

Hal and Chris Simpkin

At the age of 80, after retiring from Flight Test at McDonnell Douglas Corporation, Hal D. Simpkin published two books, *G-Eye and The Log Cabin Gas Station*. He also wrote several short stories.

Chris Simpkin attended every meeting with Hal and the two were not only popular members but also participated in various aspects of the Guild.

Jennifer Stolzer
Jennifer Stolzer is an author/illustrator living in the St. Louis area. She graduated from Webster University with a degree in interactive digital media and animation and uses these skills to create bright and engaging characters, both in words and images. Her illustration company, Jennifer Stolzer Illustration, has served the St. Louis area and its authors for six years. You can see samples of her work at www.jenniferstolzer.com or on Facebook under Jennifer Stolzer Illustration.

Jennifer was voted Top 5 Local Children's Book authors by readers of the *St. Louis Post Dispatch* in 2017. Her first picture book, *Dog Park* (2014) is based on her award-winning animation by the same name. Her debut YA Fantasy, *Threadcaster*, was released in 2017.

Workshops and Events
2012
Saturday, January 7 – Workshops for Writers: **Editing/Proofreading: A Do-it-Yourself Job?** presented by Mary Menke

Thursday, January 19, 7-8 p.m. – **First SLWG Lecture at Buder Hall, Maryville University** – TW Fendley and Sarah M. Anderson spoke.

Saturday, February 4 – Workshops for Writers: **The E-Revolution: Creating, Promoting, and Selling your Work Online** presented by Bob Baker, President of SLPA

Saturday, March 3 – Workshops for Writers: **Perfecting Your Pitch to Agents, Publishers, and Editors** presented by Margo Dill, Steve Wiegenstein, and Peter Green

Thursday, March 15 – SLWG Lecture Series – Cole Gibsen at Buder Hall, Maryville University

Saturday, March 31, 7-9 p.m. – **A Night of Poetry & Jazz** at the Kirkwood Amtrak Station with Dwight Bitikofer and Raven Wolf, along with Gerry Mandel, Treasure Shields Redmond, Erin, and Niki. The event was showcased on HEC (Higher Education Channel)

Saturday, April 7 – Workshops for Writers: **A Publisher's View of Publishing** presented by Lisa Miller, Bill Adams, and Kristina Makansi

Saturday, May 5 – Workshops for Writers – **To Blog or Not To Blog is No Longer a Question** presented by David Alan Lucas II

Thursday, May 17 – SLWG Lecture Series with Gerry Mandel at Buder Hall, Maryville University

Saturday, June 2 – Workshops for Writers: **Too Busy, Too Tired, Too Left-Brained to Write Creative Non-Fiction? Think Again!** Presented by Linda O'Connell & Dianna Graveman

Saturday, July 7 – **July Cooler! Annual SLWG Members Appreciation Picnic**, indoors at the Kirkwood Community Center, *and featured the giant letters S-L-W-G made by Gus' Pretzel Shop, and members brought food and their books for the members' table.*

Thursday, July 19, 7-9 p.m. – **San Hellman Movie Night & the Founders of SLWG** presented by Brad R. Cook, SLWG President.

Saturday, August 4 – Workshops for Writers: **Worldbuilding: Enriching Your Story with Culture and Setting** presented by Jeannie Lin author of *Butterfly Swords* & Shawntelle Madison author of *Coveted*

Saturday, August 25 – **Writers in the Park**

Saturday, September 8 – Workshops for Writers: **The Author's Guide to Copyright and Fair Use** presented by Paul Lesko, IP attorney with the Simmons Firm.

Saturday, September 29 – **100 Thousand Poets for Change**, SLWG poets joined poets around the world.

Saturday, October 6 – Workshops for Writers: **The Dreaded Synopsis** presented by Brad R. Cook

Tuesday, October 30 – **Dark Visions Halloween Open Mic Night**, at Urban Eats, 3301 Meramec St., South St. Louis, a costumed event. *Everyone came dressed up, except Marcel Toussaint who attended, as always, in his finest suit. T.W. Fendley was an Egyptian pharaoh and I was the Highlander, complete with a plastic sword under my trench coat. Everyone read spooky, or dark themed poems and short stories.*

Saturday, November 3 – Workshops for Writers: **The**

10 Crimes Unpublished Authors Commit and How to Skirt Them presented by Nancy Baumann of Stonebrook Publishing
    Tuesday, December 11, 7-9 p.m. – **Holiday Party** at Kirkwood Train Station

2013
    Saturday, January 5, 10 a.m. to noon – Workshops for Writers: **Write an Essay, Right Here, Right Now** with Catherine Rankovic
    Thursday, January 17, 7-8 p.m. – SLWG Lecture Series: **New Authors Spotlight** with Robin Tidwell, Janet Bettag, and Peter Green at the Buder Family Student Center at Maryville University
    Saturday, February 2 – **Money Saving Tax Tips for Writers** with Faye Adams
    Saturday, March 2 – Workshops for Writers: **Sit Down and Pitch: Preparation for the 2013 MWG Writers Conference** with Brad R. Cook.
    Friday, March 15, 7:30 p.m. – **A Special Event! The Poets Laureate of Missouri an evening with David Clewell, William Trowbridge, and Walter Bargen** at Maryville University Auditorium, The Medart Lecture Series Sponsored by Maryville University with participation of St. Louis Writers Guild & St. Louis Poetry Center
    Thursday, March 21, 7 – 8 p.m. – SLWG Author Series: **An interview with Linda Austin**, author and publisher of *Cherry Blossoms in Twilight* at The Buder Family Student Commons at Maryville University
    Saturday, April 6 – A Special Workshops for Writers: **The 12 Step Program: How to Show, How to Not Tell** presented by noted author and editor, Suzann Ledbetter Ellingsworth
    April 26-28 – The 2013 Missouri Writers Guild Conference: Bringing Writers Together at the Sheraton Westport, Lakeside Chalet Hotel
    Saturday, May 4 – Workshops for Writers: **Focus on Fiction: The Road to Publication** with Lynn Cahoon, Warren Martin, H.C. Beckerr, and Pam DeVoe

Thursday, May 16, 7 – 8 p.m.– SLWG Author Series with **L.S. Murphy** author of *Reaper*, at a new location, All on the Same Page Bookstore!

Saturday, June 1 – Workshops for Writers: **Understanding the Publishing Options with Rocking Horse Publishing**, High Hill Press, and Treehouse Publishing Group

Saturday, July 13 – Workshops for Writers: **Agents: From Hello to Goodbye** with Paula Stokes (aka Fiona Paul) and Cole Gibsen

Thursday, July 25, 7-8 p.m. – SLWG Author Series: **Memorial for Will Bereswill and Linda Houle** of L&L Dreamspell with Claire Applewhite, Peter Green, Judi Moresi –at All On The Same Page Bookstore

Saturday, August 3 – **Workshops for Writers: Weapons in Writing** with David Lucas and Brad R. Cook

Thursday, August 15, 7-8 p.m. – SLWG Author Series with **Nicole Evelina**, author, represented by Jen Karsbaek of Forward Literary at All on the Same Page Bookstore

Saturday, August 24 – **Writers in the Park 2013** *a free mini-conference for writers!* 10am to 2pm Lions Amphitheater in Kirkwood Park

Saturday, September 7 – Workshops for Writers: **Publishing Perspectives** with Lisa Miller, Kristina Makansi, Catherine Rankovic, and Mandy Schoen

Saturday, October 5 – Workshops for Writers: **Becoming an Independent Author** with Kelly Cochran

Thursday, October 17 – SLWG Author Series: **New Book Spotlight!** with authors, Fedora Amis, and Denise Elam Dauw, at All on the Same Page Bookstore

Saturday, November 12 – Workshops for Writers: **Jumpstart your Novel or Memoir** with Linda O'Connell, Donna Volkenannt, Jennifer Shew, and Lauren Miller

Saturday, December 7 – Workshops for Writers – **Part 1: The Power of Email Marketing** with Barry Cozaihr of RESPONSE! Targeted Marketing.

Tuesday, December 10 – Holiday Book Fair at the Kirkwood Community Center

2014

Saturday, January 11 – Part 2: Social Media Made Simple with Barry Coziahr of RESPONSE! Targeted Marketing at the Kirkwood Community Center.

Thursday, January 16 – SLWG Author Series – **Goodbye to All on the Same Page Bookstore?** with Robin Tidwell of Rocking Horse Publishing

Saturday, February 1 – Love Scenes: When to Turn Out the Lights with Lynn Cahoon

Thursday, February 20 – SLWG Author Series with **Jennifer Stolzer** at STL Books

Saturday, March 1 – Sit Down and Pitch presented by author Brad R. Cook

Thursday, March 20 – SLWG Author Series with **Angie Fox** at STL Books

Saturday, April 5 – Get the Most from Writing Conferences presented by Lisa Miller, Kristina Makansi, and Brad R Cook

Saturday, May 3 – Inside the Heart of Darkness with David Lucas

Thursday, May 15 – SLWG Author Series with **Dr. Fred Fausz** at STL Books

Saturday, June 7 – The Five Elements presented by voice coach Sheila Dugan

Saturday, July 12 – The Do's and Don'ts of Writing Query Letters presented by literary agent Whitley Abell of Inkling Literary Agency

Saturday, August 2 – Triple the Mystery with Claire Applewhite, Fedora Amis, and Pam de Voe

Saturday, August 13 – SLPA/SLWG Vendor Showcase – The Lodge Des Peres

Saturday, August 23 – 5th Writers in the Park – Lions Amphitheater in Kirkwood Park

Saturday, September 6 – 5+5 Critique, *a classic SLWG workshop*

**Saturday, September 27 – How to Get Your Book into a

Library or Bookstore at the Kirkwood Public Library

    Saturday, October 4 – Choosing the Writing Life presented by award winning journalist Harry Jackson Jr.

    Saturday, October 24 – Charlie Brennan Book Signing with STL Books — Kirkwood Train Station

    Saturday, November 1 – A Day in the Life of a Beat Cop and Medic presented by Brian L. Bardsley Jr. of the Chicago Police Dept. SWAT Team.

    Saturday, December 6 – Holiday Book Fair with Young Writers Awards Ceremony and Reading

Gateway to Publishing Conference & Convention Programs

23 |
SLWG, 2015-2019,
David Alan Lucas II, President

With the first close up pictures of Pluto, and a number of Solar and Lunar eclipses, the universe was on display, and here on Earth, or more importantly in the STL, 2015 was the 95th anniversary of the Guild. After Lit in the Lou, I asked David Lucas if he wanted the job as president. He did, and the board voted unanimously to make David Lucas the next President of St. Louis Writers Guild.

The Monthly Meetings at this Time

After years of meetings at the Kirkwood Community Center, a change was needed. The rooms were nice, but a large crowd, over 40 people filled it to capacity. Plus, as a long rectangle, those at the back of the room were often unable to see or hear. The sound system started crackling and emitting odd noises – most likely a faulty wire. Then, in 2014, the community center raised its room rates from $60 to $80. SLWG absorbed the cost, but there were bigger rooms at a similar price.

Another issue developed as well: though KCC had a large parking lot, between hockey and all the craft shows, the parking lot was often full. Members had to park on the far side, which was never optimal. The room itself had a clinical look, painted yellow and brown, with wire mesh in the little windows. A new space was needed.

There were two requirements for the monthly meetings:

the room had to be able to hold sixty people and it had to look a little more modern and less institutional than the rooms at the Kirkwood Community Center. The Guild looked at libraries and community centers around town, and The Lodge Des Peres was ultimately chosen.

The Lodge staff set up the rooms, made coffee, and had a wonderful sound system with a wireless microphone. Paradise! After years of slinging tables before every meeting and carting the sound equipment in the backs of cars . . . no more.

The Lodge also had a modern style and welcoming vibe. A fireplace with comfy chairs sat outside the workshop room in the lobby. The main feature of The Lodge was its gym and pool, so people were always coming and going, making for a busy lobby and attracting several new members. The workshop room was large, with a vaulted ceiling and skylights. There was a large drop-down projector screen, and they provided a projector stand, a podium, an easel, and a whiteboard. SLWG set up a table in the back for books and members' promotional material.

The rental fees did increase, but a quick cost analysis was done. In the end, the price of The Lodge Des Peres, which included everything like coffee, sound equipment, and more, was worth the additional money. At this point, the majority of St. Louis Writers Guild's budget was spent on renting the room and paying for speakers.

The change was instantly approved by the membership, and meeting attendance went from 20-30 to 50-60 within months. The room became so full that soon Workshops for Writers was a standing-room-only event. The Lodge took notice and sent a message that SLWG was violating the fire code with the number of people attending. The question arose as to whether to expand into a second room, at double the cost; get rid of the tables, or find a bigger space. None of these were optimal. In the end, we made the decision to remove the back row of tables, which meant St. Louis Writers Guild could accommodate 70 people with ease.

David continued the tradition long set for the meetings, having the announcements at the beginning, and asking the questions – "Did anyone submit in the last month? Did anyone get rejected in the last month? Did anyone get an acceptance or other accolade in the last month?"

Some truly great workshops were held. Several are listed below. The Lodge proved to be a good home for the Guild. Hopefully, it's a place we can settle in for years to come.

The Open Board Meeting

Revisiting an idea started by David Motherwell, David Lucas implemented a yearly open board meeting. St. Louis Writers Guild had always had an open-door policy when it came to members. There have always been multiple ways to contact board members, from addresses, to phone numbers, and finally email, but David took it one step further. The open board meeting was in a public forum, usually before Workshops for Writers, so members didn't have to make a special trip.

Not only did the board conduct its business before an audience, but the floor was open to all members, and any issues, complaints, suggestions, or praises were heard. On average, about 10-30 members attended the open board meetings. They tended to be boring affairs; board meetings were never exciting. However, much humor was injected due to it being an early morning meeting. Plus, it became a time to announce new projects or members' benefits, which made it interesting.

The 95th Anniversary in 2015

95th Anniversary Dinner

On October 24, 2015, St. Louis Writers Guild held the 95th Anniversary Dinner at Llywelyn's Pub, 17 West Moody, in Webster Groves at 6 p.m. Tickets were required for this event as seating was limited. The evening celebrated the past with living past-presidents. The price of tickets was $25 a person, which could be purchased by going to the SLWG website.

Eileen Dreyer was the keynote speaker. A New York Times Best Selling author, she had published 31 romance novels, 8 medical-forensic suspense novels, and 7 short stories. She was a multi-award-winning author of many books including her *Drake's Rakes* historical romance series.

The History of St. Louis Writers Guild

As Historian, I spoke about the long history of the Guild and the success of the Legacy Project. David Lucas then provided a glimpse of the future, as he finally let the cat out of the bag and announced the Gateway to Publishing Conference & Convention.

Recording Workshops for Writers

One thing David brought to the monthly Workshops for Writers was recordings of the events for members who missed the meeting. SLWG had been writing up articles on each event for *The Scribe* for years. David took it a step further, first by filming the event. The video files were so big that they were impossible to upload, and setting up the camera every meeting was a pain. During my time as president, SLWG had tried livestreaming events over the internet, but all the hoops members had to jump through made it prohibitive, and the quality wasn't the best.

David eventually started bringing his digital audio recorder and storing the files, which were huge, on his Dropbox. This allowed SLWG to post the audio from the events. This continued and improved, and in 2018 when SLWG switched to a new website provider, there was finally enough space online to hold several months of recordings. Now, SLWG members can listen to past Workshops for Writers, stretching back almost a year.

Sometimes there will be a recording issue, so they aren't all perfect, but most allow members to listen to past workshops and hear the speaker and the ambience of the event.

David and Melanie

Throughout St. Louis Writers Guild's history there have been many couples who were part of the organization. In the 1920s Elizabeth and Alfred Satterthwait both served as president, then Ruth and Dr. Jerome Grosby guided the organization through the 1950s, which continued into the 70s and 80s with James and Dorothy Nash, and even into the modern day with couples who attend every meeting together like Faye and Billy Adams, Chris and Hal D. Simpkin, or Wanda and Larry Lovan. David Lucas met his future wife, Melanie Koleini, at a writing group that formed from SLWG members who wanted to get together to write. In October

2016, they married. David's groomsmen carried swords, and the bride and groom were not only escorted down the aisle, but also exited under arches of steel. Many of the guests that night were St. Louis Writers Guild members, a testament to the closeness formed by members.

In 2018, David got a job as a martial arts instructor for Tracy's Karate, which meant he had to work every Saturday. Unable to attend Workshops for Writers, he continued working tirelessly behind the scenes, but his presence was missed. Members asked about him at every meeting. Eventually, in 2019, he stepped down as president due to his schedule, which included becoming the fight coordinator for movies as well as forming his own podcast network.

The Write Pack

David Lucas was president of Winding Trails Media, a podcast network that featured not only his own podcast, but also the podcasts of other authors. From a group of writers who met once a week to write came the idea of a writers' round-table, a forum where writers discussed topics about the publishing industry. Thus, Write Pack Radio met every Sunday to record an hour-long show, or occasionally two shows. Though a couple of regular Write Pack Radio members were also members of St. Louis Writers Guild, it was never a part of the organization. However, with all the guest authors that David had on the show beyond the regular Write Packers who appeared every week, it certainly drew from St. Louis Writers Guild.

For five seasons, Write Pack produced hundreds of episodes on information every writer needed, from fun subjects like world building to hard-hitting topics like how to write about sensitive causes. With Kathleen Kayembe as co-host, and regular Write Pack Members like Melanie Koleini-Lucas, Jennifer Stolzer, Chanèl Etienne, Leigh Savage, George Sirois, Fedora Amis, and me, plus, guest authors like Angie Fox, Meredith Tate, LaShaunda Hoffman, James Young, Rob Howell, Bob Baker, and more, episodes were thought provoking, informative, and injected with the humor that comes from locking a bunch of writers in one room. After five seasons with each episode getting hundreds of listens from around the world, David ended the podcast in 2018. There was a reunion episode at the last Gateway to Publishing Conference & Convention in June 2019. Write Pack Radio is still available online, but be certain to check out the new content from David.

David Alan Lucas II, the Legal Expert of St. Louis Writers Guild

With a background as a paralegal, David would be the first to give the legal disclaimer that he is not a lawyer, and what he said was not official legal advice. However, with a mind that understood bureaucracy and the law, he was an asset who dealt with many of the Guild's legal issues.

One of the first was the official listing with the State. Missouri required the Guild to renew its status every couple of years, but no one knew that until David went to verify. He spent his first year as president ensuring that St. Louis Writers Guild was up-to-date with all its paperwork.

He also worked with the VLAA, the Volunteer Lawyers and Accountants for the Arts, to take care of the legal issues for the organization. Occasionally, SLWG needed a lawyer to review official documents or ran into an issue where it needed legal advice. VLAA is a wonderful organization, and they were always so incredibly helpful to St. Louis Writers Guild.

Seriously, if you are a writer or artist and need a lawyer or accountant, please visit VLAA.org

Community Outreach

One major thing David did during his tenure was extend St. Louis Writers Guild into the community. The Guild had always participated in community events. The organization strived to be a part of all the literary events in the city, and if not at the event, then by promoting and bringing awareness to the event.

Penned Con

One of these events was Penned Con. David arranged to be one of the event sponsors for two years. Penned Con was the largest indie author convention in St. Louis, held every September at the City Center Hotel in downtown St. Louis, the one painted with a 1920's art deco design. SLWG had a table in the organizer's hall both years and several members of St. Louis Writers Guild operated the table. They discussed the organization and its events with attendees, and had tons of free promotional material from SLWG members to pass out. David and I also presented for their writers' workshops. Both years there was little clean up as all the promotional material was snatched up by the end of the day. They even sold some *Scribe* books, bound issues of *The Scribe* from the current year.

Archon

Another place St. Louis Writers reached out to was Archon, the science fiction convention held every October in Collinsville, Illinois. A popular convention with authors, many SLWG members had attended the event for years, to the point where committee chairs would have to host the monthly meeting if the events were on the same weekend, but the organization hadn't officially had a table or been represented. T.W. Fendley connected with the Archon organizers to provide authors for their writing workshops at the convention. SLWG members with tables in Booksellers Row and the main tables for the convention had information about SLWG.

The Burbs

When Chesterfield contacted St. Louis Writers Guild about participating in their arts festival, The Burbs, David brought it to the board and everyone agreed. SLWG had a large booth on the main walkway and gave numerous presentations throughout the day. Readings were held by several SLWG members and they signed books as well. The festival was filled with dancers, food trucks, art installations, and an all-day concert series. St. Louis Writers Guild had a prime spot between the parking lot and the amphitheater, catty-corner to the metal statue of a giant rising from the ground. David and I sword fought as part of a workshop on writing fight scenes which drew a crowd. Kathleen Kayembe also had several people stop during her reading. The Burbs was a lot of fun, and one other note, Jennifer Stolzer was commissioned to draw the map of the event. She did an amazing job, and the huge displays that had been printed by the organizers made the piece impressive.

Shortly after, SLWG asked her to create the map for Gateway Con.
NaNoWriMo
Another way David reached out was through NANOWRIMO, the National Novel Writing Month, a challenge to write 50,000 words in the month of November. David teamed SLWG with the St. Louis Public Library (SLPL) and the St. Louis County Library (SLCL) for a series of events and write-ins. In my final years as president, the organization had held a number of write-ins for NANOWRIMO, but David made it more of a feature of the year. NANOWRIMO was a popular event, and many people came out to the workshops and write-ins presented by the NANOWRIMO organizers and St. Louis Writers Guild.

Hannibal Writers Guild
David stayed in close contact with Ryan P. Freeman, the first president and founder of the Hannibal Writers Guild. The organization came about from Ryan's experience with St. Louis Writers Guild, which started with David, Ryan, and me connecting at the Big River Steampunk Festival held every September in Hannibal, Missouri. David and Ryan stayed in touch, and when Ryan formed the Hannibal Writers Guild, David included them in many events, and spoke at their meetings.

Young Writers Awards
Even the Young Writers Awards extended its reach. Beginning with a couple of classes connected to members, it soon grew to more, and through the efforts of Jennifer Stolzer and Cherie Postill, soon every school in the city was receiving word about the contest, and hundreds of kids participated.

Affiliated Literary Organizations
David maintained the connections with the St. Louis Publishers Association and created deeper connections with Saturday Writers, MORWA, SiC, and more, but he also connected with the Midwest Mystery Writers of America and had them partner with Gateway Con. One of David's great achievements was his ability to connect St. Louis Writers Guild with the literary community at large, a dream held by many presidents before him.

1764—A dream never realized

1764 would have been a literary journal produced by St. Louis Writers Guild for the purpose of publishing exceptional prose and other works by writers across the nation and even the world. The name referred to the year St. Louis was founded by Laclede and Chouteau. A few names were thought of for the literary journal, and then a vote was put to the membership who overwhelmingly chose 1764.

When Lauren Miller took over as Director of Communications, she brought the idea of replacing *The Scribe* with a literary journal. The guidelines were set; SLWG would pay a modest rate for short stories, poems, essays, flash fiction, and illustrations. Covers, layout, and uploading were all services the board members would donate. The only expense would be paying the contributors. The hope was that the sale of each literary journal would provide enough to cover the cost of production and maybe even some funding for the Young Writers' programming.

However, as SLWG sought submissions for the literary journal, the editor and champion of the book, Lauren, got a job with a literary agency. After she moved on, there wasn't anyone who could commit to the necessary time. In the end, *1764* was postponed indefinitely, but the groundwork is there . . . ready for someone to pick up.

Gateway to Publishing Conference & Convention (Gateway Con)

Missouri Writers' Guild's 100th Anniversary was in 2015, and President Lisa Miller didn't have a writers' conference but instead invited all the chapters together for a business meeting. Each group got to bring two people. David, as president, represented St. Louis Writers Guild, and I ended up going with him. The two of us drove down to Columbia, Missouri for two days of meetings.

A lot of interesting ideas came out of the meetings, and there was a presentation of MWG's history, which was of particular joy for me. However, they were not bringing the conference back to St. Louis, and the vote indicated that the conference should bounce around the smaller cities of Missouri.

The History of St. Louis Writers Guild

We were disappointed, especially since this meant that St. Louis Writers Guild would not be able to jointly celebrate MWG's 100th and SLWG's 95th Anniversary, which was David's proposal.

On the drive back to St. Louis, David and I discussed what SLWG could do for its members and to honor the organization. The Gateway to Publishing Conference & Convention came out of that drive back. However, it would be a year and a half before the first Gateway Con was held.

The first year, 2017, was the biggest. SLWG claimed the entire hotel and had more rooms than they knew what to do with. David oversaw logistics, I was in charge of programming, and Jessica Mathews handled the Author Hall.

Gateway Con Highlights
2017—Writers at the Rivers

The first year, the literary agents and publishers said that they had requested more manuscripts than at any other conference that year. They praised how prepared and well put together all the people pitching their work had been, and at least one attendee got an agent from the event.

Something funny that took place the first year was the Thursday night pool party with all the organizers. It was a relaxing end to a hectic day.

2018—Writers Assemble

The second year, SLWG teamed with Got Your Six Support Dogs. The Guild raised money for this wonderful charity, and had a couple of dogs at the book fair on Saturday. Kids and dogs meant it was the busiest the book fair would ever be. Cole Gibsen, the founder of Got Your Six Support Dogs, was one of the featured authors.

A funny story from this year came on Saturday night. It started at the bar and then drifted to the tables. By the end, the writers took up a huge portion of the lounge with loud, raucous laughter, so much that other patrons complained, though not enough for the hotel to break it up, and the writers in St. Louis made such a positive impression that they were remembered by staff the following year.

2019—Writers of Tomorrow
The third year featured Ask the Experts. SLWG brought in a lawyer, podcasting experts, a martial arts expert, and more. They ended up being a huge hit, and the most attended workshop was the officer from Chicago SWAT.

This year found writers in another raucous Saturday night at the bar, but we stuffed ourselves in a single room, overflowing with creativity, and much was accomplished, from friendships to the outline for a whole series of inappropriate novels. Unfortunately, a series of thefts put a damper on the event. Also, the St. Louis Blues won the Stanley Cup, which was awesome – Go Blues! – but the parade on Saturday was attended by all of St. Louis, which meant very few came to the book fair. SLWG did stream the parade and hold a watch party, but attendance was greatly impacted.

With David working more, and his martial arts career taking off, along with the losses incurred from the Blues Parade, and the theft of some equipment, the Gateway to Publishing Conference & Convention had to end. Sadly, SLWG only got to kick off the 100th Anniversary at Gateway Con and not end it there, too. However, the lessons learned and the events held at the conference were integrated into a series of events held throughout the year, and that was a hit with members.

The President
David Alan Lucas II, June 2015 to August 2019

Board Members During This Time
Board meetings were held at the Kirkwood Public Library

2017
David Alan Lucas II, President
T.W. Fendley, VP of Programs and Publicity
Jessica Mathews, VP of Events
Jennifer Stolzer, Secretary

Brad R. Cook, Historian
Jamie Krakover, Treasurer
Lauren Miller, Director of Communications
Peter H. Green, MWG Representative

Amy Zlatic, Membership Chairman
Cherie Postill, Kids Contest Coordinator
Ryan P. Freeman, Gateway Con Marketing Coordinator

Members from 2015-2019

Ryan P. Freeman, Marketing Coordinator for Gateway Con
Founder and first President of the Hannibal Writers Guild, Ryan was the author of fantasy novels like *Reinspell* and short stories like "The Trombonist of Munst." He was a publicist for other authors, helping many sell their books, and coordinated the marketing team for Gateway Con. He lived in Hannibal before moving to Santa Fe, New Mexico.

Melanie Koleini Lucas
Melanie was a science and sci-fi writer who worked for Washington University. She often operated the SLWG table at events and coordinated the raffles at Gateway Con.

Lauren Miller, Director of Communications
Worked at Saint Louis Public Library Central Branch, editor of *Here's News!* She went on from St. Louis Writers Guild to become a junior literary agent with the Metamorphosis Literary Agency.

Cherie Postill, Young Writers Contest Coordinator
Cherie Postill was a middle grade author and instructor of young writers. She led the school outreach for St. Louis Writers Guild's Young Writers Contests and worked tirelessly on Gateway Con. A volunteer for a couple of years, when Jessica Mathews became president, Cherie joined the board as the Contest Coordinator. She worked with several of St. Louis Writers Guild's

interns and penned a non-fiction book on beta readers.

Amy Zlatic, Membership Chairman
Amy Zlatic was the Chief Storyteller for Mary Institute and Country Day School (MICDS), and handled all SLWG membership issues for several years. A resident of Des Peres, Missouri, she was instrumental in securing The Lodge for the Guild. She had been a volunteer for years, and when Jessica Mathews became president, she joined the board of St. Louis Writers Guild and even hosted a board meeting at her house.

Workshops and Events
2015 – Kirkwood Community Center
Saturday, January 10 – Reaching Readers via Social Media and Bookstores presented by Robin Theiss and Barry Coziahr
Saturday, February 7 – Fundamentals of Screenwriting presented by writer and photographer Mike Bezemek
Saturday, March 7 – Querying and Pitching - How to "Track"down Literary Agents and Publishers presented by author Brad R. Cook
Saturday, April 4 – Digital Copyright for Analog Writers presented by attorneys Mark Sableman and Mike Nepple of Thompson Coburn LLP
Saturday, May 2 – They Judge Your Book by its Cover presented by author, Catherine Rankovic
Saturday, June 6 – What the Heck is Twitter Good For? Presented by Sarah Coziahr of RESPONSE! Target Marketing
Saturday, July 11 – Journey to the Top presented by Ann Leckie
Saturday, August 1 – Law Enforcement Training For the Arts author and police Capt. Chris DiGiuseppi and Sgt. Paul Bastean
Saturday, August 29 – Writers in the Park aka Writers Freezing in the Park
Saturday, September 12 – Twisting a Story: Nonlinear Plotting Strategies presented by author/illustrator Jennifer Stolzer

Saturday, October 3 – Writing Fact, Creative Nonfiction and Fiction—Differences and Difficulties presented by Authors Gerry Mandel, Patricia Bubash, and Peter Green, along with Mike Stith of One Legacy

Saturday, November 1 – National Novel Writing Month (NaNoWriMo) activities, librarian and author Eric Lundgren

Saturday, December 5 – Road Hazards: The Life of a Touring Writer presented by bestselling author M.R. Sellars.

2016

Kirkwood Community Center & Des Peres

Saturday, January 9, 10 a.m. to noon – **The Empowered Writer** presented by Bob Baker

Saturday, February 6 – Day in the Life of a Trial Attorney presented by Bill Smith, attorney

Saturday, March 5 – Human Fly Fishing: Hand-selling Books presented by Ronald R. Van Stockum Jr.

Saturday, April 2 – Wherever Books are Sold: A Guide to Forming a Lasting Partnership with Independent Bookstores, presented by Emily Hall owner of Main Street Books

Saturday, May 7 – Podcasting Helps Authors Reach Readers presented by David Lucas producer and host of Write Pack Radio

Saturday, June 4 – Learn How to Boost Readership with Mailing Lists & Advertising Campaigns presented by author Eric R. Asher

Saturday, July 9 – Point of View: It's more than First vs. Third presented by author, Brad R. Cook

Saturday, August 6 – Writers in the Park – *the 7th annual Festival for the Writer aka The Last Writers in the Park*

Saturday, September 10 – 5 + 5 Critique Workshop

Saturday, October 1 – Authors: Learn How to Make the Past Relevant to Today's Readers presented by author, Nicole Evelina

Saturday, November 5 – Pictures Speaking: Photographs as Story Prompts presented by short story writer,

Angela Mitchell
> Saturday, December 3 – **Holiday Gathering and Young Writers Awards Readings**

2017
Saturday, January 7, 10 a.m. to noon – **Pulp Fiction Isn't Just a Tarantino Movie** presented by author, Van Allen Plexico at The Lodge Des Peres, 1050 Des Peres Rd., St. Louis, MO, 63131.
Saturday, February 4 – **Poetry/Fiction: The Artistic Language of Horror** presented by Mary Genevieve Fortier and David Schultz II, founders of the St. Louis Area Horror Writers Society
Saturday, March 4 – **How to Pitch & Query Literary Agents & Publishers** presented by Brad R. Cook
Saturday, April 1 – **Step 1: Write, Step 2: ???, Step 3: Profit** presented by McKenzie Johnston Winberry
Saturday, May 6 – **Poisons You Personally Know** presented by Fedora Amis, historical mystery author
Saturday, June 3 – **Making Biography Readable, Salable, and Absorbing** presented by author, Peter Green
Saturday, June 16-19 – **Gateway to Publishing Conference & Convention**, *Writers at the Rivers*, at the St. Louis Renaissance Airport Hotel.
Saturday, July 8 – **Writing a Book is Hard. Publishing is Even Harder** presented by Rick Miles, Red Coat PR
Saturday, August 5 – **Strategies for Critique Partners and Groups** presented by Jennifer Stolzer, Secretary of SLWG and Critique Group Coordinator
Saturday, September 9 – **Writers, Tap into your Intuitive Creativity** presented by Deborah Terra Weltman
Saturday, October 7 – **Taking Your Self-Publishing Career to the Next Level** presented by Liz Schulte
Saturday, November 4 – **Crafting a Successful Synopsis** presented by author, Shawntelle Madison
Saturday, December 2 – **Holiday Gathering and Young Writers Awards Readings**

2018
Saturday, January 6, 10 a.m. to noon – **Landing an Agent (query letter, relationships, and more!)** presented by Justin Wells, literary agent. Remote Workshop at The Lodge Des Peres, 1050 Des Peres Rd., St. Louis, MO, 63131.
Saturday, February 3 – **Novel Revision 101** presented by Meghan Pinson, editor
Saturday, March 3 – **Finish that book!** presented by Allie Pleiter, author.
Saturday, April 7 – **Get Conference-Ready: Perfecting Your Pitch to Literary Agents and Publishers** presented by Brad R. Cook
Saturday, May 5 – **Perspectives on Writing Historical Fiction** with authors, P.A. DeVoe and Ed Protzel
Saturday, June 2 – **The Seven Deadly First-Page Sins** presented author, Arianne "Tex" Thompson – Remote Workshop
June 15-17 – **Gateway to Publishing Conference & Convention**, *Writers Assemble* at the St. Louis Renaissance Airport Hotel
Saturday, July 14 – **Working with an Illustrator** presented by Illustrators Jennifer Stolzer and Craig Skaggs
Saturday, August 4 – **Resources for Indie Authors at St. Louis County Library** presented by Sarah Steele SLCL Reference Specialist for Reader's Advisory.
Saturday, September 8 – **Delve into Genres** with Camille Faye, Jo Hiestand, and Mia Silverton
Saturday, October 6 – **Writer Beware: "How Not to Get Published"** presented by Richard C. White, author, and part of the publishing watchdog group, Writer Beware.
Saturday, November 3 – **Surviving the Hike and Planning the Aftermath**, NaNoWriMo workshop presented by Amanda Wells
Saturday, December 4 – **Holiday Party with YWA Readings**

Brad R. Cook

The History of St. Louis Writers Guild

Young Writers Program Logo
designed by Jennifer Stolzer

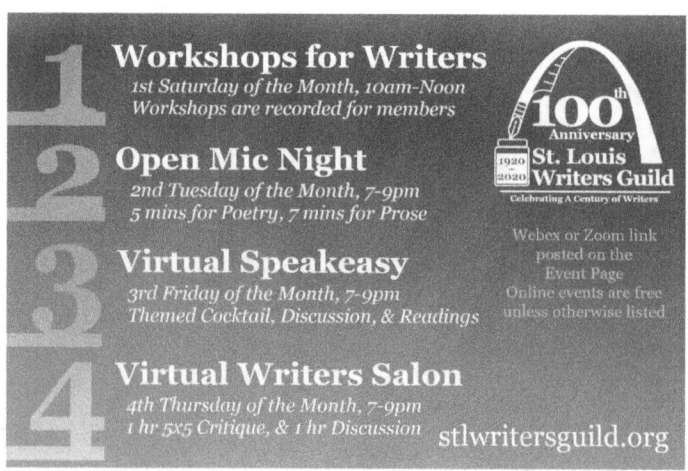

1, 2, 3, 4... Ad designed by Brad R. Cook

24 |
SLWG, 2019, 2020, and Beyond, Jessica Matthews, President

In the summer of 2019, St. Louis celebrated the St. Louis Blues first Stanley Cup victory, but as the new Season was about to begin, David stepped down as his Martial Arts career flourished, and he became the fight coordinator for a movie. At the August 2019 Board Meeting, Jessica Mathews was unanimously voted in as the new president. It was a wise decision because she dove in and began going through every corner of the organization, not only seeing what needed to be done, but also figuring out new ways to grow. She would be quickly tested as the world changed in 2020. COVID-19 shutdown the world one week after Writers in the Lodge. Within days everything including the Lodge was closed until further notice. Without a way to meet in person, the board, led by Jessica, decided to keep the literary community connected. SLWG created a number of online events that not only allowed people to reconnect as the world spun into isolation, but allowed people to start writing again.

Her first meeting as president was the September 2019 Editing Extravaganza, but unfortunately, she had to represent SLWG at Penned Con. In her stead, Jessica had me read this address to the membership.

Jessica Mathews' Address to the SLWG Membership
I know you have all heard the news that David Lucas is no longer the

The History of St. Louis Writers Guild

president of the St Louis Writers Guild. I want to thank him for his many years of service to our organization and I wish him the best of luck in his future endeavors. He is about to embark on an exciting adventure. My wish, as the new president of our organization, is that we can all learn enough in our lifetimes to be able to go on adventures of our own. I want us to be able to share our journeys with each other, to learn from each other and to guide each other on our many paths to success. I'm sorry I could not make it to the workshop today. I am representing SLWG at a conference. Promoting our organization and our values of teaching and helping others is one of my goals as president. I want to do more community outreach, especially with youth. If you have a suggestion for community events we could hold or contacts of other organizations that would benefit from our collective expertise as writers, readers and everything in between, please let me know.

I'm excited to be the president during our one hundredth year. We have some amazing programming coming up that I know you will enjoy. We will be having more workshops, pitch sessions and guest speakers than ever before. Not to mention our one hundredth anniversary t-shirt contest and the anthologies we are publishing for our young writers and Guild members.

I hope the next one hundred years turn out as well as the first hundred! If you want to see any changes to the Guild or additional programming, please let us know by speaking to a board member in person or emailing us at president@stlwritersguild.org.

Have a great workshop today!

Workshops for Writers

Meetings after a century would be familiar to a member from the 1920s, and that was pretty mind-boggling. A couple of board members arrived about 9:15 a.m. to set up the SLWG Members' Table, the projector, and raise the sign. The other board members and volunteers arrived by 9:45 a.m. Members and guests started to appear about 9:30 a.m. but most would come about ten minutes before 10 a.m. Jessica Mathews started the announcements with current news and what was coming soon. Then, as customary, she'd ask if anyone had submitted over the last month, and many people raised their hands. Next, she asked if anyone had been rejected, and several would keep their hands up. As always, these triumphs were applauded. Lastly, she would ask who had been accepted or newly published, and members shared their accomplishments. Then Jessica introduced the speaker.

The workshops lasted until about noon with a 10-minute break about 11 a.m. Some went over, but each meeting ended in a question and answer session, with the speaker sticking around afterward to sell books and answer questions.

SLWG Moves to Online Meetings

In the spring of 2020, COVID-19 spread across the country and caused the shutdown of every non-essential business. Conferences, conventions, book fairs, and more were canceled or rescheduled. The bookstores in town started curbside service, and increased the amount of shipping. St. Louis Writers Guild was able to hold Writers in the Lodge, but in a flash, everyone was working from home or had lost their jobs. From April on, meetings were held online. If anything, St. Louis Writers Guild is adaptable. As writers struggled with the chaos and stress, writing became difficult for some. In response, SLWG created the Virtual Writers Salon, which met every Thursday night from 6 - 9 p.m. CST during the quarantine. Using Webex or Zoom, both online meeting softwares, over a dozen members met online to discuss all things writing. The tag line was, *Join SLWG to Write, to Talk About Writing, and to Hang with Fellow Writers*. The first Virtual Writers Salon was held on March 26, 2020. Soon, Jessica instituted 1, 2, 3, 4, a throwback to advertising campaigns of a decade before.

The first Saturday was an online version of Workshops for Writers.

The second Tuesday of every month was the online Open Mic Night.

The third Friday was the Virtual Speakeasy. Bartender Steven Langhorst would make a featured cocktail while discussing a historical writing topic.

The fourth Thursday was the Virtual Writers Salon's 5x5 Critique. Hosted by Autumn Rinaldi, the time shrank to 7 - 9 p.m. and continued the tradition of five minutes of reading, followed by five minutes of a sandwiched critique. They met weekly for a time to discuss a topic, but the 5x5 event was held on the fourth week of the month.

This is the current monthly schedule of the Guild.

#YWSTL Young Writers STL

St. Louis Writers Guild began a new initiative, one aimed at supporting young writers in the community. The Young Writers Awards is a major part of this initiative, and now the contest winners and finalists were published in a collection every year.

Expanding the young writers' programming was a big part of this initiative. That included getting sponsors for new contests for high school-aged writers and offering writing classes at Writers at the Lodge and more.

In July of 2020, SLWG held the Gateway Con Summer Writers Camp. With all the summer camps shutting down because of the coronavirus, SLWG held its own, a week long camp where young writers wrote a story. This was one of several online events in the Gateway to Publishing Conference Series. The other events included The Publishing Evolution, 2nd Annual Editing Extravaganza, and Pitchfest.

Associate Membership

Associate Memberships were re-introduced but this time with a twist. Whereas before, it had defined professional writers vs. not-yet-a-professional writer, it now was used to classify the new young writers' memberships. Open to Middle School and High School writers, the associate membership was a way to be a part of St. Louis Writers Guild and offer services to writers in those age groups. It also gave them a space on the website with resources for young writers, something apart from all the information SLWG provides members.

SLWG had used interns from the colleges for years, but as those internships shifted to workforce starting positions, a new crop of interns came knocking: high school students who needed internships to get into their preferred university. These interns came to meetings and helped out, helping edit *Here's News!*, sitting in on critique groups, interviewing authors, and other duties.

St. Louis Writers Guild Published Books

In 2019, SLWG published the winners and finalists of the Young Writers Awards in the *Young Writers Collection*. With a colorful cover and the new #YWSTL logo designed by Jennifer Stolzer, the book was a hit with the children and their parents.

That was followed in 2020 with two anthologies. The first was the *SLWG 100th Anniversary Members Anthology*, which featured 34 short stories, poems, essays, flash fiction, and more. The cover featured the statue of St. Louis in front of the Art Museum, and the interior featured an arch and skyline on every page.

Lastly, there was *Love Letters to St. Louis,* which featured stories about St. Louis, the city, the landmarks, the people, and the history. The cover of the second anthology featured a colorized image of the arch during construction.

The covers for the two members' anthologies were selected by a vote of the membership when the books were announced. T.W. Fendley edited the pieces for format and punctuation, Jamie Krakover, Amy Zlatic, and Jennifer Stolzer proofread the book, while I handled the interior layout and cover design.

The President
2019, 2020 and beyond . . . Jessica Mathews

Board Members and Meeting Locations
St. Louis Bread Co. / Panera Bread on Manchester in Kirkwood
McAlister's Deli, Manchester, Des Peres
Kirkwood Library, Jefferson Ave., Kirkwood, Missouri
Online via Webex and Zoom

2020 Board Members
T.W. Fendley, VP of Programs and Publicity
Jennifer Stolzer, Secretary
Jamie Krakover, Treasurer
Brad R. Cook, Historian
Cherie Postil, VP of Contests
Amy Zlatic, VP of Membership

Committee Members
Michele Wicks - Social Media Coordinator
Autumn Rinaldi - Publicity and Host of the Virtual Writers Salon
Steven Langhorst - Bartender and Host of the Virtual Speakeasy

Workshops and Events
2019
Saturday, January 5, 10 a.m. to noon – Workshops for Writers: **Book Descriptions that Sell** presented by Karen Sargent, at The Lodge Des Peres, 1050 Des Peres Rd., St. Louis, MO, 63131.
Saturday, February 2 – Improving Characterization Across Gender and Sexuality with J. Rachel Clay and Kathleen Kayembe
Saturday, March 2 – Freelance Your Way to Success with Linda O'Connell
Saturday, April 6 – Get Conference Ready: Perfecting Your Pitch to Literary Agents and Publishers presented by Brad R. Cook
Saturday, May 4 – What to Expect When You're Expecting (A Book) with Jennifer Geist and Cynthia A. Graham
Saturday, June 1 – Fundamentals of Book Marketing with LaShaunda Hoffman & Tabitha Caplinger
June 14-16 – Gateway to Publishing Conference & Convention, *Writers of Tomorrow*, at the St. Louis Renaissance Airport Hotel
Saturday, July 13 – Bad Book Covers with Jennifer Stolzer and Brad R. Cook
Saturday, August 3 – Audiobook Production for Authors with George Sirois and Jennifer Jill Araya
Workshops and Events from the 100th Anniversary
September 14 – Editing Extravaganza, *a Workshops for Writers Event, and part of the 100th Anniversary Celebrations*. 10am to

Noon at The Lodge Des Peres.

October 5 — How to use Wattpad & Social Platforms to Kickstart Your Writing Career with Shelly X. Leonn & LL Montez

November 2 — Navigating the Wild, Wild West of Publishing with Cathy Davis

December 7 – Holiday Party, *with readings by the winners of the 2019 Young Writers Awards. Over 150 people attended the event, mostly parents and family.*

2020

Saturday, January 4, 10 a.m. to noon – Workshops for Writers: **The Writing Techniques of Jules Verne** presented by Ronald R. Van Stockum Jr., at The Lodge Des Peres, 1050 Des Peres Rd., St. Louis, MO, 63131.

February 1 – Perfecting Your Pitch: Get Conference-ready presented by Brad R. Cook at The Lodge Des Peres.

March 7 – Writers in the Lodge special event! Featuring presentations included: **Working with a Literary Agent** with Kortney Price, **Writing in Someone Else's Sandbox** with Guy Anthony De Marco, **Book Editing for Self-Published Authors** with Andrew Doty, **Young Writers Workshop – Show Don't Tell** with Cherie Postill, plus editing consultations and pitches to agents. Co-sponsored by the St. Louis Publishers Association. Held at The Lodge Des Peres.

April 4 — Freedom in Form: The Poetics of Haiku and Ghazal presented by Ben Moeller-Gaa and Jennifer Lynn: (Online webinar)

April 16 or 9, 7-9 p.m. – **First or Second Weekly Virtual Writers Salon**

May 2 — Workshops for Writers: **Contract Clauses: The Good, The Bad, and the Ugly** presented by Michael A. Kahn, author and attorney, in partnership with Volunteer Lawyers and Accountants for the Arts (VLAA) (Online webinar)

June 2020

June 6 — Workshops for Writers: **What Not to Do – Book Marketing Experiments** presented by Warren Martin, author and SLPA President. (Online webinar)

Tuesday, June 9, 7-9 p.m. – **SLWG Open Mic Night** (Now Online Monthly)

Friday, June 19, 7-9 p.m. – **First SLWG Virtual Speakeasy** with bartender and host Steven Langhorst

Thursday, June 25, 7-9 p.m. – **5x5 Critique at the SLWG Virtual Writers** hosted by Autumn Rinaldi

July 2020

July 11 — **Research For Writers (Or How to End Up On A Watchlist in 20 Minutes or Less)** presented by Dr. James Young (Online webinar)

July 13-17 – **Summer Writers Camp,** Story Structure with Cherie Postill and Jody Feldman,

Tuesday, July 14 – **SLWG Open Mic Night**
Friday, July 17 – **SLWG Virtual Speakeasy**
Thursday, July 23 – **SLWG Virtual Writers Salon**

August 2020

August 1 — Workshop for Writers: **How to Write About Encounters with the Extraordinary** presented by Karen Cavalli (Online webinar)

Tuesday, August 11 – **SLWG Open Mic Night**
Friday, August 21 – **SLWG Virtual Speakeasy**
Thursday, August 27 – **5x5 Critique at the SLWG Virtual Writers Salon**

August 22 – **The Publishing Evolution – Panel: Write, Publish, Promote & Profit in the Digital Age, Workshop: Empowering Your Writing** presented by Crystal Shelley, **Panel: Art for the Cause, Workshop: Locksmithing for Writers** presented by Tex Thompson. (Online webinar) *The second event of the Gateway to Publishing Conference Series in celebration of the 100th Anniversary.*

September 2020
Saturday, September 12 – Second Annual EDITING EXTRAVAGANZA with editors Andrew Doty of Editwright.com and Meghan Pinson of My Two Cents Editing. (Online webinar) *The third event of the Gateway to Publishing Conference Series in celebration of the 100th Anniversary.*
> **Tuesday, September 8 – SLWG Open Mic Night**
> **Friday, September 18 – SLWG Virtual Speakeasy**
> **Thursday, September 24 – SLWG Virtual Writers Salon**

October 2020 – A Century of Celebration!
October 10, 10 a.m. to 3 p.m. – **PITCHFEST** – *Ask the Expert Workshops and Pitch Sessions (Online webinar) The fourth event of the Gateway to Publishing Conference Series in celebration of the 100th Anniversary.*
> **Tuesday, October 13 – SLWG Open Mic Night** with a reading of the 1935 Short Story Contest Winner
> **Friday, October 16 – SLWG Virtual Speakeasy** Meet the Founders!
> **Thursday, October 22 – SLWG Virtual Writers Salon**
> **October 24 — SLWG 100th ANNIVERSARY special event! The Truth About Screenwriting** presented by Paul Guyot with online party afterward.

November 2020
November 7 — Taxes: Volunteer Lawyers and Accountants for the Arts (VLAA)
> **Tuesday, November 10 – SLWG Open Mic Night**
> **Friday, November 20 – SLWG Virtual Speakeasy**
> **Thursday, November 26 – SLWG Virtual Writers Salon**
> **Saturday, November 28 – December 31 – SLWG's 100th Anniversary Virtual Book Fair**

December 5: Holiday Party! Featuring readings by Young Writers Contest award winners. (Online event)

The History of St. Louis Writers Guild

Books by St. Louis Writers Guild

25 |
Where's the Apostrophe?

According to all the grammar rules, the proper way to write the organization's name was St. Louis Writer's Guild or St. Louis Writers' Guild. The problem comes when one needs to announce an event, such as St. Louis Writer's Guild's Workshops for Writers. Sure, it's grammatically correct, but it looks strange on a sign and no two volunteers ever wrote the name the same way. So, for branding purposes, they decided early in the 2000s to eliminate the apostrophe – to treat St. Louis Writers Guild as a proper name and not a sentence.

Oddly enough, the question—where's the apostrophe?—was often asked, and always received mixed responses. Editors tend not to agree, though, my favorite are the promotional people, the marketers, ad executives, or people from similar organizations who think it was brilliant to drop the apostrophe.

So, apologies to the editors and English teachers, but without the apostrophe, it was easier to brand SLWG's promotional material, and in the end made it simple to get everyone on the same page.

SLWG Style Guide

To make it easy for anyone to help with publicity, St. Louis Writers Guild maintained a standard design and style guide, one that had changed only a couple of times in the last thirty years.

The 1990s used the Arial font. Everything had a clean

The History of St. Louis Writers Guild

design. In the mid-1990s, the classic logo was created, and with the addition of the Edwardian font used in the new design, SLWG added some flair to their publicity material.

In the 1990s, the Guild stopped using "The" before, and thus it became simply, St. Louis Writers Guild. This was done for space and design issues on posters and signs, nowadays the organization was increasingly known as SLWG.

In the 2000s, the standard SLWG font became Verdana, which gave a clean design to all SLWG signs, forms, and flyers. Edwardian Script was used sparingly to add a touch of elegance to the signs, posters, and flyers, but the bolder Verdana was easier to read.

Around 2011, the Georgia font was added to SLWG's official fonts. It became the standard font as the Guild modernized online design. It brought back a bit of the elegance of the Edwardian font, but maintained the readability of the Verdana font. The new logo, created in 2015, used Georgia for the name and wording, and it became the current standard font.

In 2019, Arial returned as the standard font for the website.

Black and white remained the SLWG color scheme for many decades. This was probably, as today, used for practical purposes like making cheap copies, but they are both classical colors that will never become outdated.

St. Louis Writers Guild did use color. Maroon was common, especially during the SLWG bookmarks of the 2000s.

Scribe Blue, a.k.a., Cornflower Blue, became a dominant color in the 2010s. It was often used with white lettering, which made for a pretty design. The color helped to brighten the new version of *The Scribe* as it moved from newsletter to literary magazine. It even inspired The Blue Page in the back of each issue, which contained information on coming events. Scribe Blue was used for posters and other color designs but faded as *The Scribe's* emphasis waned. The tradition was retained in the current website, however, which used a gradient light-blue for much of its icons.

The Gateway to Publishing Conference & Convention represented the different parts of the conference with three colors. The Writer's Conference used blue, the Book Fair used red, and the Writer's Retreat was green. This allowed all promotional material to be color-coded, making it easy to know which aspect of the conference was being advertised, and hopefully avoiding any confusion among attendees. The third year, in 2019, SLWG used orange, green, and blue in the promotional posters created to showcase the different events and advertise the conference, but the conference still used the three-color pallet for the different parts of the conference. Technically, the name tags were also color coordinated, representing the Staff (orange), Conference Attendees (blue), Author Hall Authors (green), and those who only paid for Master Classes (white).

The Organization's Name Over the Years

St. Louis Writers Guild – current and proper

The St. Louis Writers' Guild – most often used in the newspapers

The Writers Guild of St. Louis – used in 1920s and occasionally in the 1970s and 1980s

The Authors' Guild of St. Louis – misuse of name by newspapers in the 1920s & 1930s

St. Louis Writers' Group – misuse of name by newspapers in the 1930s

The St. Louis Writers' Organization – occasionally used by the newspapers

The Writers of St. Louis – referenced in the 1920s and 1930s

The St. Louis Writers Guild – used for many years, it tends to come in cycles

St. Louis Writer's Guild – used in newspapers in the 1980s

Saint Louis Writers Guild – an official title for state and federal paperwork, grants, and book publishing

STL Writers Guild – used online

@stlwritersguild – used for all social media

SLWG – used for hashtags and to shorten the name as an anagram

* The Tuesday Writers Club of St. Louis – referenced in the 1920s. First used in 1927 to describe St. Louis Writers Guild, it eventually became its own group created by a former president.

SLWG vs. STLWG

It's a little thing, a "T," but it was a huge divide, and for some members, an impossible habit to break. The anagram of St. Louis Writers Guild was obviously SLWG, but St. Louis was so often abbreviated as STL that many people can't help but write STLWG. St. Louis Writers Guild has never officially used STLWG as a hashtag or an abbreviation, but a quick check of #STLWG will offer up some photos and posts. A few board members or members of the publicity committee used STLWG when they started, and we'd politely correct them. Eventually most changed, but it has remained an issue for my entire time with St. Louis Writers Guild.

SLWG was the standard set in the 2000s and used extensively on all the social media platforms. #SLWG lit up on Twitter during every meeting, and live tweets became a great way to follow events. As anagrams became increasing common, SLWG became shorthand for the organization in posters, flyers, online tweets, online banners, and other social media posts.

Membership Cards

A question often asked at St. Louis Writers Guild was if there were membership cards, permanent name tags, or web badges. In the end, the reality is they are very hard to maintain records of, and for the web badges, to make certain fakes were pulled down, or old members didn't keep them. It's always been a mess, without an easy, or inexpensive solution. However, David Lucas did more to further this cause than anyone. He tried several solutions for membership cards.

Brad R. Cook

The History of St. Louis Writers Guild

Author Series Logo 2016

26 |
The Story of the Lecture Series

St. Louis Writers Guild's third monthly event ended after a tortured run. This one event changed more in the last ten years than any other, but that doesn't mean it wasn't a great event. The lecture series began in the 2000s as the regular monthly meeting held at McNulty's Pub and Grill on the last Wednesday of the month. When the main monthly meeting switched to Saturday mornings at Barnes & Noble—Crestwood, the Wednesday night meeting started being held at the Barnes & Noble—Ladue. The first of the SLWG Lecture Series was held on Wednesday, September 19, 2001. The topic was "Writing the Query Letter and Synopsis" with Shirley Kennett, author and member of the Mystery Writers of America, 7 p.m. at Barnes & Noble, 8871 Ladue Road in Ladue. The fee was $3 for guests, free for members.

When I joined the Guild a few years later, the Lecture Series was held on the third Thursday of every other month, the odd months, and it was free for all to attend. Lectures differed from the monthly workshops in many ways, and they had a completely different format. The lecture was an hour long. An author talked about a topic but also about their books, and at the end people bought the author's books. Basically, it was a book signing with a specific topic to be discussed by the author.

Chairs were set up in the back corner of Barnes & Noble in Ladue, amongst the bookshelves. With audiences as large as thirty people, the event still felt very intimate. Many times, people were standing in the back or along the bookshelves, listening intently. And yes, occasionally a shopper would want a book from a section people were sitting in, though it was mostly the photography section and other sections that people rarely browsed.

Incredible authors spoke at the lecture series like Joanna Campbell Slan, Dianna Graveman, Claire Applewhite, and even the *St. Louis Post-Dispatch* Book Reviewer, Jane Henderson. I even held my first solo lecture here. I spoke about researching through online and offline resources. There is a great picture of me, but it's a total illusion. I'd already given my lecture and most people had headed home, when Rebecca realized we didn't have a picture of the event. At the time, we were using images for *The Scribe* and other publications. So, Peter Green sat down, I acted like I was talking, and we took the photo.

Eventually B&N decided that we could no longer set up amongst the stacks, and SLWG was given part of the café, the side of the counter. It only took a couple of lectures to realize SLWG needed more space. Around that time, Borders built a new store on Brentwood Boulevard, right at the intersection of Brentwood and Eager, Hwy. 64, and I-170. They had a huge upstairs, and when SLWG approached them, they were eager to host us.

Borders set rows of chairs, about forty of them, with aisles and even set up their sound system for SLWG. B&N had always discouraged SLWG from using sound because it would upset the shoppers, but Borders set up in the middle of store and encouraged shoppers to join. Borders even ordered the authors' books. SLWG was very reliable about selling books. Some great authors came through this part of the lecture series, including Antony John, whose British accent made everyone love him, and screenwriting legend David Trottier who drew the largest crowd.

With the change in location and all the rebranding going on at SLWG, the lecture series became the SLWG Author Series.

Sadly, within a year, Borders announced it was closing. The SLWG Author Series was the last event held at Brentwood Borders location. The debate on the board was where to head next, and by serendipity, we were working with Maryville University and the St. Louis Poetry Center on several events. SLWG inquired at

Maryville University, and they let us use Buder Hall for the lectures. The space was excellent. A student center, it had a stage and a nice sound system with wireless microphones. It could easily seat about 50 people and could have accommodated more. Marcel Toussaint spoke about poetry, his life, and awards. He was the first of many authors, like Cole Gibsen, Gerry Mandel, Robert Randisi, and more. The second SLWG Movie Night was also held at Buder Hall on July 19, 2012. SLWG showed Sam Hellman movies, and I talked about SLWG's First President and the founders. (The first SLWG Movie Night was on July 11, 2009 at the Engineers Club and showcased *Single White Female*, a movie based on John Lutz's novel. John spoke about the book and the movie was shown.) However, eventually SLWG ran into scheduling conflicts with the students, who obviously got first choice of their student lounge. The Thursday night time slot that was the SLWG Author Series was taken by the band, and once again, SLWG needed a new home.

All on the Same Page Bookstore had just opened up on Olive Boulevard in Creve Coeur. Robin Tidwell, who would go on to be President of Missouri Writers Guild, owned the small independent bookstore in a strip mall. Shelves lined the walls with a large open area in the middle. The crowds dwindled with the move. Where once forty people had attended, now the event was down to fifteen, and eventually, just a few. The speakers were still great: authors like Nicole Evelina, USA Bestselling Author of historical fiction, fantasy, nonfiction, and women's fiction, and Denise Elam Dauw, music educator and author of *If Music be the Food of Love*. With the sudden passing of Linda Houle, the owner and publisher of L&L Dreamspell, a heartfelt episode of the SLWG Author Series was held to honor her and discuss how her authors would continue.

A new feature of the SLWG Author Series was that it moved online. Partly this was a reaction to the shrinking crowds, but also, more and more, the internet was coming to dominate our lives. The web offered a much larger audience than those who came on a Thursday night. With the move to online, it also became more of an interview format, and the time shortened.

Sadly, All on the Same Page Bookstore would close as

well, but not the publishing side, Rocking Horse Publishing. The SLWG Author Series was one of the last events at the bookstore. However, as fate would have it, STL Books opened up in Kirkwood. Owned by Robin Moore Theiss, past-president of St. Louis Writers Guild, it was an independent bookstore on Jefferson Avenue.

The format of the SLWG Author Series was changed as well. The lecture format was completely replaced by an interview format. The 20-30-minute interview was broadcast live via Livestream and then the recording was posted to YouTube. People online could ask questions, either through Twitter or through Livestream. New York Times Bestselling Author Angie Fox was one of the guests, along with other authors like Claire Applewhite, Peter H. Green, Judy Moresi, Fedora Amis, Robin Tidwell, Denise Elam Dauw, LS Murphy, Nicole Evelina, and award-winning New York Times Bestselling author, Anne Leckie.

The SLWG Author Series was at STL Books for about a year when sadly the bookstore closed its physical location but remained online. With the loss of STL Books, the SLWG Author Series took a big hit. It had already lost its physical audience, and each show was watched by a bunch of members but not much beyond that. However, the board didn't want to let it go; there was still value in it. It has always been an excellent way of showcasing authors.

One other problem with moving the SLWG Author Series online, now the authors had to appear both live online and in a recording that would last for years. SLWG started to have authors turn down appearing on the SLWG Author Series. It became hard to find someone who had the time in their schedule and were willing to appear online. If it could have lasted a few more years, it might have made it. Now everyone has a vlog (video blog) or a podcast that is on YouTube, and some just livestream their life for fun.

For a couple of months after STL Books closed down, we tried to turn the SLWG Author Series into an interview of the speaker at the monthly Workshop for Writers. However, trying to film after the meeting meant clearing the room, and it took forever. The speaker had just talked for two hours and was done.

They lacked energy and therefore were not as interesting. However, they were still great interviews, each with insight and usually an extension of the topic presented at the meeting.

The quality never suffered; in fact, during this time, the SLWG Author Series had one of its biggest episodes with Ann Leckie, author of the New York Times Bestselling, multi-award winning, *Ancillary Justice*. She would be the last of the SLWG Author Series and its most watched episode.

After running into the same issue of speakers who were not interested in being interviewed, the SLWG Author Series was quietly retired. My hope was that it could be resurrected and re-envisioned, but we'll have to see. For over a decade it was stellar event and a feature of St. Louis Writers Guild, part of the 1…2…3… campaign.

Locations for the SLWG Lecture Series
Barnes & Noble Ladue, 8871 Ladue Road
Borders Books at Brentwood Boulevard and Hwy. 64
Buder Hall at Maryville University
All of the Same Page Bookstore, on Olive Boulevard
STL Books – Jefferson Avenue, Kirkwood
Online as the SLWG Author Series – YouTube

Why did the numbers decline?
It was a question I often pondered: why did some events succeed and others fail? My conclusion: it was the world that changed around SLWG. Not only were there more literary events in a month, but there were just more distractions for people's time. Netflix alone made a lecture or open mic more difficult to attend. People's evenings tend to be a coveted time; in fact, by the end of the SLWG Lecture Series, many of the city's literary events had moved to the weekend.

Historic Kirkwood Amtrak Station
photo by Brad R. Cook

27 |
The Epic Saga of the SLWG Open Mic Nights

Started in 2005, St. Louis Writers Guild's open mics had a roller-coaster history. As the Guild expanded, they added events and activities to each month, and the Open Mic was a popular addition. Originally called the St. Louis Writers Guild Open Mike Event, it was held on a Tuesday night from 7-9 p.m. at Kaldi's Coffee in Kirkwood, Missouri. The second open mike was held on Tuesday, October 11, 2005 at Sunset 44, a restaurant in Kirkwood, where the Guild held meetings as well.

As the open mic (see Open Mic vs. Open Mike at the end of this chapter) became a regular monthly event, now officially on the second Tuesday of every month, the location moved, first to PJ's Tavern in Kirkwood for June 2006, then up Lindbergh Boulevard to Wired Coffee, a colorful coffee shop in Sunset Hills. Now known as The Open Mic @ Wired Coffee, it was before the age when Twitter had changed the meaning of an ampersand. The first open mic at Wired Coffee was held on August 8, 2006. The brand-new sound equipment meant participants could not only be heard above the coffee grinders, but they stood behind a microphone, and Dwight Bitikofer often brought a music stand to set work upon.

The format of the night remained the same to the present day, five minutes for poetry and seven minutes for prose. Participants arrived at the event and signed up on the sheet to read. The MC called each person. Some MCs added bits between readers, others were just about the names. Everyone signed up got to read and if there was time at the end, people could finish their stories if time had run out or read another poem.

Huge crowds of 30 or more packed Wired Coffee at a series of small tables and comfy chairs surrounding a fireplace. Wired Coffee sat in a small strip mall and had good java, but the thing that everyone loved was the ice cream.

The Open Mic @ Wired Coffee lasted for several years. In a way, it was the glory days of the open mic and was remembered fondly by those who attended. However, when Wired Coffee closed, a new location had to be found. The Open Mic drifted back to Kirkwood to the Kirkwood Brewery, a restaurant in downtown Kirkwood that had a stage and seating aside from the restaurant and beer brewing.

The Family Friendly Open Mic as it was now known, still met on the second Tuesday, and was a popular venue. Members had dinner either before the open mic or during it. The place had good craft beer, too. As the restaurant began to change names, there became a problem with having the room every month. One month, they called on Tuesday and said we couldn't have the room that evening. After having to cancel several open mics, the board began looking for another venue.

Dwight Bitikofer, who had become the MC of the Open Mic, knew the people who ran the nearby historic Kirkwood Train Station. Still a stop for Amtrak trains, it remained in regular use. The Amtrak train didn't show up until 9 p.m. when the open mic ended. The volunteers who ran the station were willing to arrive a little early and let SLWG into the station a couple of hours before the train arrived.

The historic station was stunning. Built in 1892, the small stone building was separated into parts. One side had table and chairs, and that was where SLWG set up the open mic. The other half had rows of wooden benches to wait for the train, a ticket counter, and bathrooms. The ticket counter sat in between and was the office for the volunteers. It was a delightful setting for an open mic.

Freight trains rolled by on occasion; their screeching wheels interrupted the poets until it passed. As Dwight often explained, the trains were slowing down because of the slight hill that was Kirkwood. Several train poems were written, an affectionate term for any piece written during these pauses. Plus, many of the spur-of-the-moment poems were about trains. Steven Langhorst was one who often wrote these poems of the moment and then shared them. Then there was Dwight Bitikofer's *Train*, a poem that one must hear Dwight perform to truly understand. Calling out "Train!" as if he were a steam whistle on a locomotive, he performed it with passion and emphasis, a delight to all who heard it.

With a regular group of members coming monthly, and several new guests or audience/ listeners, the open mic had a rhythm. Linda O'Connell made everyone laugh and say "Aww" as she read one of her essays that had either just appeared in a *Chicken Soup for the Soul* book or would soon be in one of their anthologies. Dr. Rebecca Carron Wood shared her political opinions of the day in a well-worded limerick or other poetry form, but she wrapped it in other humorous pieces so no matter your politics, you were certain to laugh. Faye Adams, who was always accompanied by her husband Billy, read her latest award-winning poem. Then Marcel Toussaint stepped up to the microphone. An award-winning poet of note, Marcel began by talking about the poem, why he wrote it, or what had moved him to read this poem out of the countless he had written. He retained a French accent acquired during his upbringing in Morocco, and he often wore his latest medal from the awards he'd won. Always dressed impeccably, he recited his poem with reserved flair. Marcel hated the time-keeper, usually me, and constantly railed against the constraint of 5 minutes. What many, including Marcel, might not have known—most of the time, he got seven to nine minutes, and often, more like ten. Joyful memories. Sadly, Marcel passed away in 2018.

Dwight Bitikofer, the MC, invited each guest up, and was also welcoming and encouraging to new writers. SLWG made certain to be inviting. No one was forced to read, and audience members were always welcomed . . . coveted even. Audiences at any given Open Mic could hear Faye or Billy Adams, a poem from Evelyn Buretta, maybe the latest deeply touching piece from Kathleen Kayembe, the latest yarn from Jennifer Stolzer's fantasy world *Threadcaster*, or I might read something historical like a short story by Sam Hellman, Shirley Seifert, or "Stella for Star," the short story Tennessee Williams had written for the SLWG short story contest.

There were a couple of nights when the station volunteers forgot or couldn't make it over to unlock the station. Those who attended on these nights gathered on the park benches in a little garden adjacent to the station. In the twilight of a summer evening it made for fun, though with only a few benches, it was often standing room only. Luckily, during the summer months, a popup, soft-serve ice cream hut opened on the other end of the parking lot: a tasty treat to go with the poems.

Sadly, as downtown Kirkwood grew, so did its restaurants. Soon, parking, which had always been ample, was taken by diners, and one might have to park a block or two away for the open mic. For anyone with the sound equipment, this was an issue; luckily, the station allowed us one of the parking spots in front for the car carrying the equipment. Then a big renovation, several million dollars, was to begin on the building. With dwindling numbers, from a high of 40 on a regular night and as many as 60 on special occasions like the Young Writers' Award Winners reading, the SLWG Open Mic fell to a core group of about 12. Without a monthly space, it was decided to hold fewer open mics a year but to make them events members wanted to attend, even if they weren't reading.

The Open Mic Night became a quarterly event, and each took on a different atmosphere. The Novel Neighbor, an independent bookstore in Webster Groves, became the spot for the open mics. They have an open space beside the bookstore, an artsy room that is a fitting place for writers. The winners of the contests read, and then a regular open mic was held, too. There was even a fund raiser for the Young Writers Programs the Guild was holding and to support Gateway Con. Wine was served along with some food.

Loud Mouth Open Mic

After a time, members wanted an open mic that wasn't family-friendly, so SLWG created an adults' only version, an R-rated version of the open mic, where readers could drop an f-bomb, say a few "shits," or have a sex scene, and no one cared. In 2007, SLWG created the Loud Mouth Open Mic Night; the logo was a big mouth almost swallowing a microphone. The first event was held on March 27, 2007 at The Mack, a bar at 4615 Macklind Avenue in South St. Louis.

Another SLWG Open Mic Night – For Our Loud Mouths, A second open mic night for edgy writers, humor writers, out-of-the-box writers and push-the-envelope writers who want to share with others!

An MC still ran the event, only it was most often a comic named Mike McGuire. He performed a bit of comedy in-between readers. Sticking to the 5 minutes for poetry, 7 minutes for prose format of the other open mic, Loud Mouth became very popular, though the two open mics had very different crowds.

In 2010, The Mack began seating customers in the room SLWG used for its open mic. Soon, the readers were competing to be heard over the roar of the bar, and if a game was on, the noise was impossible. Several patrons complained about the language, and SLWG had to find a new location.

The Schlafly Tap Room on Olive Boulevard in St. Louis was nice enough to give SLWG one of their rooms for the open mic. It was closed off from the other sections of the restaurant, was a large space with plenty of tables and chairs, and the dark wood paneling and tall glass windows with the city behind provided a great backdrop.

Loud Mouth at the Schlafly Tap Room was a great success. A large crowd attended, everyone enjoyed the food and Schlafly beer, and some great stories and poems were told. Laughter filled the room, usually a raucous laughter brought on by the inappropriate limerick, or a funny take on everyone's favorite four-letter word.

However, then came the infamous day in 2012: what would be the final Loud Mouth. The night started off as a typical night. The number of people had dwindled over the years, but a handful of regulars attended every time, and one or two new people found the event. The Family-Friendly open mic had much bigger attendance, but Loud Mouth was still the cool open mic.

A young man entered, thin, with dark hair and wire-rimmed glasses. He sat at a table with a few of the regulars and signed up to read. The usual fare of essays, scenes from a manuscript, and poetry with curse words started off the evening, and then this man stepped up to the microphone. He proceeded to read a story that was vile, disgusting, and vomit-inducing: a graphic depiction of a bug entering a woman, then morphing to be borne by the woman. Within a minute, several people in the room got up and left. He was stopped after a couple of minutes. He protested, but the crowd joined in, saying that he was done. He had wanted to get a reaction, and he had. With a smirk, he headed off. The night continued, but everyone began to leave. The event barely lasted an hour.

A policy had been in place for people who abused the Loud Mouth rules. After the first offense, a person was spoken to about how their work hadn't been appropriate. The next time it happened, they were asked not to return. That night though, it was as if the very concept of Loud Mouth had been rejected.

Several regular Loud Mouth attendees wrote or spoke to the board to say they would not return, and the people who had walked out told others of the story. There wasn't a good way to vet stories ahead of the reading, and where was the line between good taste and bad? Who decided what was appropriate? There were discussions on how to improve the event, but without an audience, it didn't matter. The event ended, and the Family-Friendly open mic went PG-13. One or two questionable words were okay, but it prevented the truly disturbing from being read.

Loud Mouth, the not-so-family-friendly open mic, had a fiery end, one of the only SLWG programs to end so abruptly. It left a legacy of understanding why adult themes and language were important for writers, allowing them to be free in their creativity, and a heap of memories for everyone who attended.

Open Mic vs. Open Mike

The debate over Open Mic vs. Open Mike has more to do with age than the rules of English. In the beginning, the event was titled the St. Louis Writers Guild's Open Mike Night, then that changed to the SLWG Open Mic @ Wired Coffee. It remained the Open Mic ever since. At the time, the editors argued for Open Mike, but Open Mic reflected the common name used to refer to readings. Plus, the abbreviation of microphone became standardized in the computer universe as mic. However, if you go back to those early advertisements and blurbs, all refer to the Open Mike.

The History of St. Louis Writers Guild

Writers in the Park Logo

2013 & 2014 WitP Programs
"Buy a Book Get a Sandwich" Ticket
2011 WitP Ad

28 | Writers in the Park— The Festival for the Writer

Writers in the Park was created as part of the 90th Anniversary Year of Festivals. The idea was to combine a writer's conference and writer's festival, to bring a day of workshops and a book fair to members without the expense of traveling or having it at a hotel. We did try to hold the first one in a hotel, but the upfront cost was more than St. Louis Writers Guild could afford. Instead of tossing the idea aside, I thought about how to have a conference without a hotel. We had already been at The Big Read Festival and had a history of holding bigger events.

I was put in charge of making that first year happen and would end up coordinating them all. As Historian, I was coordinating the anniversary events, and even back then I had more experience with conferences than the other board members. Originally, I looked at Shaw Park, in Clayton, and their big pavilions for Writers in the Park, but they were far apart, which meant we couldn't use more than one. However, David Lucas, who lived in Kirkwood, mentioned Lions Amphitheater at Kirkwood Park. It seemed too good to be true—an amphitheater with a large picnic site at the top a wooded area next to it with tons of shade, plus Scout Shelter on the other side of the road. One last bonus: not one, but two parking lots, one of which was right behind the venue. Perfect. We also looked at Faust Park in Chesterfield. T.W. Fendley lived in Chesterfield at the time, and in order to use one of these parks, we needed a resident.

Kirkwood Park won the day. We learned we could get the amphitheater but only if we fit in to its very booked schedule. September was no good because Kirkwood had festivals almost every weekend, and it couldn't be in the middle of summer because of the concert series. However, a brief window of opportunity existed after the concert series ended and September's festivals began. Serendipity.

I had a uniform: every year, I wore shorts because it was summer, and my black SLWG polo, to identify myself with the organization. *Apparently, I had a death wish (why else would I wear black outside in the sun?)* Lastly, to be visible to anyone and easily identifiable, I wore a wide-brimmed floppy hat and sunglasses. I also carried a clipboard with everything like the schedule, the program, all the bios, notes, and other things I needed that day. Often, I heard, "Ask the guy in the hat," or "Talk to the man with the clipboard." I had a nametag on, but "the guy in the hat" was usually easier.

The biggest thing to come out of Writers in the Park was a promotional gimmick to sell more books and food. It might have started as way of encouraging sales, but it became more—one of the most spoken about and beloved features of Writers in the Park: "Buy a Book, Get a Sandwich!" People who purchased a book were given a ticket for a free sandwich. With the festival fully funded, even the food was covered.

2010—Writers in the Park: A Celebration of the 90th Anniversary, Schedule

The first Writers in the Park was held on Saturday, August 22, 2010 in the Lions Amphitheater and the Main Pavilion at Kirkwood Park. Food was provided by Big Bear Grill, and STL Books had a booth.

The first Writers in the Park was a nerve-racking affair because no one knew if it would be a success. Would writers want to go to park to learn about writing? Would writers sit outside in a park for hours of workshops? First, though, it had to be set up. SLWG had a couple of tables rented from Weintraub Rentals at the top of Lions Amphitheater.

SLWG had some old signs, laminated posters of the classic logo, in the storage locker. They had been used at the Writers Under the Stars event. There were also four collapsible shelves used at book fair events like The Big Read. There were even a couple of old yard signs with the posters taped inside. My wife and I made some large black arrows for the big signs, and a number of small signs to line the walkways. Thus, we had signs to lead people to the amphitheater and shelves to make the book fair look like a bookstore.

The first year we had a lot of food left over. There were so many wraps, but the big one was the chips. Big Bear Grill had made homemade chips to be handed out with the wraps. They delivered them in giant metal bowls, and at the end of the day, after selling a bunch of food, we still had several bowls of chips left. I gorged on chips for the rest of the day and the next, but eventually most were thrown out for getting too old. In future years, we adjusted the food order

About 85 people attended, and the day was an overwhelming success.

Writers in the Park 2010 Schedule:
10 a.m. – 11 a.m.
Y/A Writing with Cole Gibsen – Author of Katana
Mystery Writing with Judy Moresi – Author of Widow's Walk
Sci-fi/Fantasy Writing with Jaclyn Devey and David Lucas

11 a.m. – 12 p.m.
Querying a Literary Agent or Publisher with Cole Gibsen and Judy Moresi
Romance Writing with Dr. Rebecca Carron Wood – Author of The Full Moon Hotel
Memoir/Biography Writing with Peter Green –Author of Dad's War with the United States Marines

12 p.m. – 1 p.m.
Editing Tips with Mary Ward Menke – Owner, WordAbilities LLC
Writing for the Internet with David Lucas – Internet Columnist

Children's Workshop
10 – 11 a.m., Children's Writing with Faye Adams – Author of Chester the Lonely Crow
11 a.m. – 12 p.m. The Big Write Kids Contest Workshop

Readings in Lions Amphitheater from 12-2 p.m.
Five minutes per reader; Poetry, Prose, and Humorous Essays accepted.
Children, SLWG Members, and Non-Members are welcome to sign up.
Please keep it family friendly.
Emcee will be poet Dwight Bitikofer

2011—Writers in the Rain

After the tremendous success of the first Writers in the Park, each year took on its own personality and thus, after that, each Writers in the Park took on a mantle. The second Writers in the Park became known affectionately as Writers in the Rain. St. Louis weather has never been predictable; at best, it will rotate through the seasons in a week, and at worst it can seem like the vengeful gods of old. A host of storms led to days of showers, but forecasters kept hinting that a break would come that weekend.

When I arrived at the park to set up on Saturday, August 20, 2011, the dark skies above and smell of rain indicated the day would be a wet one. We gathered up everything in the park, and moved into the community center rooms, a last-minute adjustment that meant we owed more than we'd originally paid. Thankfully, the wonderful people over at the community center were incredibly helpful.

One thing that deserves to be mentioned were the volunteers, like David Lucas and T.W. Fendley, who busted their butts to move an entire writers' conference, people and all, from Lion's Amphitheater to inside the community center. Nothing was set up inside, either. I have a strong memory of flipping tables and slinging chairs like a poker dealer in Las Vegas.

It was also one of the first times I remember using social media to announce last-minute changes. When the rain started to pour, SLWG took to Twitter and Facebook to announce the move inside. It worked, too; most of the attendees came to the community center, though we did have to have someone stand outside under an umbrella to guide the few stragglers to the conference.

Writers in the Park 2011 Schedule:
9:30 a.m.
Registration – Lions Amphitheater

9:45 a.m. – 10 a.m.
Greetings and Announcements – Lions Amphitheater

10 a.m. – 11 a.m.
Seven Habits of New York Times Bestselling Authors with Angie Fox – Lions Amphitheater

11 a.m. – 12 p.m.
Developing Non-fiction Platforms with Dianna Graveman – Scout Shelter
Writing the Fight Scene with David Lucas – Site 13

12 p.m. – 1 p.m.
Poetry with Kim Lozano – Lions Amphitheater
Computer Tips For Writers with Peter Green – Site 13
Missouri Writers Guild's Warrior Writer Project – Scout Shelter

1 p.m. – 2 p.m.
Family-Friendly Open Mic – Lions Amphitheater
Tweet up and Social Networking – Lions Amphitheater
Missouri Writers Guild's Warrior Writer Project – Scout Shelter

2012—The Festival of the Writer
For the third year, and now that I was President, the board

decided to go after funding for Writers in the Park. Kickstarter.com was a new online fundraising platform, and St. Louis Writers Guild set up a 30-day campaign. The different donation tiers started at $10 for a tweet listing the person as a contributor, $25 SLWG Lanyard plus a tweet, $35 e-book of *St. Louis Reflections*, $50 Book Displayed on the Contributors' Table, plus a tweet, $75 *St. Louis Reflections* paperback plus a tweet, and the big prize: $100, 1 year SLWG Membership, name in the program, plus a tweet. SLWG raised $1294.25 after Kickstarter's and Amazon's fees. Then Missouri Writers' Guild pledged $300 and became an official sponsor that year. St. Louis Writers Guild still contributed about $300 to cover all the expenses.

We then created the tote bags, silicone bracelets, signs, and more. The tiered prizes were distributed, and the rest was used for gift bags and such for the speakers. Several general Writers in the Park Signs were created, but there were never enough. Ever. No matter how many were made, we always needed more. Plus, for the first time, we were able to pay speakers at Writers in the Park. We had a full line up, with award-winning children's authors Kate Klise, Jody Feldman, Shawntelle Madison, and Jeannie Lin, plus, W. E. Mueller and Kelly Cochran from Sisters in Crime of Greater St. Louis, Bob Baker from St. Louis Publishers Association, Margo L. Dill from Saturday Writers, Niki Nymark from Loosely Identified Poets, Ben Moller-Gaa from St. Louis Poetry Center, Faye Adams from the Writers Society of Jefferson County, and Jennifer Stolzer, T.W. Fendley, and David Lucas from St. Louis Writers Guild.

The third Annual Writers in the Park, the true Festival of the Writer, was held on August 25, 2012 at Lions Amphitheater at Kirkwood Park. In my opinion, it was the greatest of them all, not that the others weren't great. One could argue we had bigger speakers at other events, but the weather was perfect. We had a huge crowd, and everything went smoothly. From a logistical standpoint, it was the easiest to put on.

This was also the year when the greatest SLWG sales technique came into fruition. We were looking for a way to increase book sales and also bring people to the park for this pop-up book fair. We had bought sandwiches from 6 North Café, and since they were already paid for, we didn't need to sell them to raise money for the event. Thus, "Buy a Book, Get a Sandwich" was created. I made a small ticket, and with every book sold, the author handed the buyer a ticket which they redeemed for a sandwich. They were really good—turkey, ham, and a veggie, on good bread with all gourmet ingredients. The promotion worked. The authors sold a ton of books, and SLWG sold a ton of chips and drinks along with the sandwiches. This worked so well, that not only did we do it every year, but it continued with the "Buy a Book, Get a Raffle Ticket" promotion at Gateway Con.

Writers in the Park 2012 Schedule:
9:30 a.m. – 10 a.m.
Greetings and Announcements—Lions Amphitheater

10 a.m. – 11 a.m.
Shawntelle Madison & Jeannie Lin – Finding an Agent and Publisher – Lions Amphitheater
Kate Klise – Calling All Young Authors! Come Learn How to Write a Book! – Scouts' Pavilion

11 a.m. – 12 p.m.
W. E. Mueller and Kelly Cochran of Sisters in Crime Greater St. Louis Chapter
Crime & Mystery, Writing the Novel or Short Story – Lions Amphitheater
T. W. Fendley & Jennifer Stolzer of St. Louis Writers Guild
Spec Fiction: From the Final Frontier to Middle Earth – The Grove
Kate Klise – the award-winning children's author continues – Scouts' Pavilion

12 p.m. – 1 p.m.
Margo L. Dill of Saturday Writers
Everything You Need to Know You Learned in Elementary School: Improve With the Basics
Niki Nymark of Loosely Identified Poets – Poetry – Big Tree
David Lucas of St. Louis Writers Guild – Writing the Fight Scene –

The History of St. Louis Writers Guild

The Grove
    Jody Feldman – Secrets to Writing a Potential Winner – Scouts' Pavilion

    1 p.m. – 2 p.m.
    Bob Baker of the St. Louis Publishers Association
    10 Things I've Learned After 20 Years as a Published Author – Lions Amphitheater
    Ben Moeller-Gaa of St. Louis Poetry Center – Haiku – The Grove
    Faye Adams of Writers Society of Jefferson County and Loosely Identified Poets
    Young Writers Awards Contest and Kids Poetry Workshops – Scouts' Pavilion

    We encourage you to share your experience and network with other attendants by either commenting on our Facebook page, or on Twitter @ stlwritersguild using the hash tag #SLWG
    Sponsored by the Missouri Writers' Guild and many contributors through Kickstarter.com
    Thank You to STLBooks.com and Six North Café

2013—Young Writers in the Park

SLWG didn't hold another Kickstarter campaign. The idea wasn't to go bigger every year but to figure out the best way to provide the writers' conference experience. With the continued success of Writers in the Park, it was not hard to find sponsors, and SLWG sold ads in the program to fund the next several years, paying for the park, the speakers, the handouts and more. Young Writers in the Park had a budget of about $700, which was used to bring in award-winning author Susan Grigsby for a young writers' workshop. At the time, SLWG offered the writing contest for young writers, but that was about it. However, one of the most asked questions at SLWG is about kids' writing programs. Writers in the Park became a way of adding kids' workshops into the programming.

Writers in the Park 2013 Schedule:

9:30 a.m. – Registration in Lions Amphitheater

10 a.m. – Querying a Literary Agent with Nicole Evelina, represented by Jen Karsbaek of Forward Literary - Lions

11 a.m. – Editing Tips with Mary Menke, owner of WordAbilities – Lions

11 a.m. – Designing a Book with Robin Tidwell, author, and co-owner of All on the Same Page Bookstore and Rocking Horse Publishing – The Grove

12 p.m. – Your Nonfiction Book: How to Shortcut the Process and Save Time, Energy, and Dollars with Nancy Baumann, the Book Professor – Lions

12 p.m. – Writing for Children with Tim Hill, author of the Joe the Crab Series – The Grove

1 p.m. – Genre Talk, round table discussions of book genres, presented by SLWG's Cycle Critique Groups – The Grove

1 p.m. – Winners of the 2013 Deane Wagner Poetry Contest – Lions

Young Writers Workshop
Susan Grigsby, author, poet, and educator, presents
Kids Writing Poetry for young writers in 4th-8th grade
11 a.m. to 12 p.m. – The Grove

2014—Writers Melting in the Park

In 2014, my wife, Amber, won an award at her job and was given $750 to donate to an organization of her choice. She donated it to St. Louis Writers Guild for Writers in the Park. When Commerce Bank found out what she had donated the money to, they added $500. Thus, that year needed no additional funding. The donation couldn't buy good weather, though, and it was extremely hot that day.

The fifth Writers in the Park became known as Writers Melting in the Park. Saturday, August 23, 2014 was a scorcher, the hottest day of the month. St. Louis in August can be intense, one of the reasons we'd chosen the end of the month. That day, the temperature reached 98 degrees and SLWG was outside in the concrete amphitheater that didn't have any shade. David and I knew we had to do something. Our solution was to have two cooling stations: one in the shaded recess of the amphitheater's stage, and a second in the community center's air-conditioned building. We also had plenty of water and ice on hand.

Writers Melting in the Park was a great success; despite the heat, there was a large crowd. Yes, everyone complained about the heat, and we joked about never knowing what St. Louis weather would bring.

We did have a few heat issues, but no one had to go to the community center. I was one of them. I had to go into the shade, pour water over my head and sit in front of one of the many fans we'd set up at every station.

We did notice a funny phenomenon that made some of the photos give a skewed view of attendance: people sat in the shade, but the shade moved throughout the day. In Lions Amphitheater, the shadows fell on one side and moved up until only the top couple rows were still in shade. So, people sat in the middle of one side and then move back as the day went on. The speaker remained on the stage, with a microphone, but the photos make it look like no one attended. In reality, over 100 people braved the day. For Writers Melting in the Park, we did have a large beach umbrella providing shade on stage, and eventually the speakers moved out of the concrete amphitheater and gathered under the trees around the venue.

Writers in the Park 2014 Schedule:

10 a.m. – Her Writing, Her Fans, and the Less than Three Conference with Heather Brewer, New York Times Bestselling Author - Lions

11 a.m. – Self Editing with Angie Fox, New York Times Bestselling Author – Lions

11 a.m. – Working with a Bookstore with Robin Theiss, owner of STL Books – The Grove

12 p.m. – Writing the Western with Sarah M. Anderson, Award Winning Western Romance Author – Lions Amphitheater

12 p.m. – Working with an Illustrator with Jennifer Stolzer, Writer, Illustrator, and Cover Artist – The Grove

1 p.m. – Genre Talk, round table discussions of book genres, presented by SLWG's Cycle Critique Groups – The Grove

1 p.m. – Write Pack Radio Recording – Submissions: Handling Rejection, Worry and Regret – Lions Amphitheater

Young Writers Workshop – Scouts' Pavilion

11 a.m. – Build-A-Story with Margo L. Dill, Middle Grade and Young Adult Author – for 4th-8th grades

12 a.m. – Writing Young Adult with Cole Gibsen and Sarah Bromley for high school aged writers

11 a.m. to 1 p.m. – Make-A-Book with Carol McAdams Moore

2015—Writers Freezing in the Park

The sixth Writers in the Park became known as Writers Freezing in the Park. As Saturday, August 29, 2015 rolled around, the temperature was once again in the hundreds, and we knew no one would come if we held it outside. People had suffered through the year before, and we'd promised to make the experience a pleasant one. The announcement went out: The sixth Writers in the Park would be held inside the Kirkwood Community Center.

SLWG took over an entire floor of the community center making one room for books, and three for workshops. The budget exploded as we had to pay for each room used. It was the first year that Writers in the Park had gone into the red since 2010, but you can't put a price on air-conditioning in a scorching heatwave. The air-conditioning was set by the facility, and the heat caused it to work overtime which made inside quite chilly, so much so, that people went outside during the 10-minute breaks between workshops to warm up.

SLWG tested out a new way of making money for the event: renting tables in the book room for authors to come and sell their books. We'd had SLWG members' books on a table the whole time, but now we were opening it up to authors.

One room was for book sales, and once again we had sandwiches from 6 North Café which meant the return of "Buy a Book, Get a Sandwich." We then had three other rooms for programming. We also continued the Young Writers' workshop which had become a popular event.

Writers in the Park 2015 Schedule:
10 a.m. – Writing YA vs Writing NA with Marie Meyer, author of Across the Distance – Hellman

11 a.m. – Writing for the Causes, like Denise's fight for Alzheimer's Research with Denise Elam Dauw, author of If Music Be the Food of Love – Hellman

11 a.m. – Building your Brand: Developing Your Visual, Verbal and Virtual Author/Book Platform with Cathy Davis, Davis Creative LLC – Seifert

12 p.m. – How to Host a Successful Critique Group with L.S. Murphy, author of Pixilated – Hellman

12 p.m. – Researching your Novel, your Life, and Everything in Between with Brad R. Cook, author of Iron Horsemen – Seifert

1 p.m. – Genre Talk – Hellman & Seifert

1 p.m. – Write Pack Radio Live Recording Topic: Writing Communities – Conf

Young Writers Workshops
11 a.m. – Young Writers Writing Workshop with Kathleen Kayembe – Conf

12 p.m. – Paws for Puzzles at the Park with Debbie Manber Kupfer – Conf

2016—The Last Writers in the Park
By 2016, SLWG already was planning the first Gateway to Publishing Conference & Convention that would take place the following year. It was too much work, and strained too many resources to hold both events. In order to save costs, the event replaced the August workshop, and we cut the number of workshops to make it streamlined for attendees. We still had a book room, and two rooms for programming. The event was sponsored by Rivendell Books. Twenty-sixteen was the swan song, a great way to end this successful event.

Writers in the Park 2016 Schedule:
9:30 a.m. – 10 a.m.
Greetings and Announcements – Hellman

10 a.m. – 11 a.m.
Audiobooks, ACX, DIY and Everything in Between – George Sirois, author of Excelsior,
and T.W. Fendley, author of The Labyrinth of Time – Hellman
Young Writers Workshop for those in 4th – 8th grade:
3 by 3, The Parts of a Story – Brad R. Cook, author of The Iron Chronicles – Conference Room

11 a.m. – 12 p.m.
Constructing a Story: The Seven Story Structures – David Lucas, Executive Producer, Winding Trails Media – Conference Room

12 p.m. – 1 p.m.
YA vs. NA – Meredith Tate, Author of Missing Pieces – Hellman
Social Media Marketing – Barry Coziahr, President, RESPONSE! Target Media – Seifert

1 p.m. – 2 p.m.
Book Design – People REALLY DO Judge a Book by its Cover – Peggy Nehmen,
Book designer, Nehmen-Kodner – Hellman
Facebook for Authors – Sarah Coziahr, VP of Operations at RESPONSE! Target Media – Seifert
The Pros and Cons of Heroes and Villains – Write Pack Radio – Conference Room

We encourage you to share your experience and network with other attendants by either commenting on our Facebook page, or @stlwritersguild on Twitter using the hash tag #SLWG

Visit the Book Room with novels by local authors,
SLWG Members, and the Speakers at Writers in the Park!

The History of St. Louis Writers Guild

Sponsored by
A generous gift from Sir EJ Drury II of Rivendell Books

Thank You to
Six North Café
And the Authors who are featured in the Book Room

What we created was not lost. I, for one, consider it a great honor to have planned and executed seven writers' conference that were free to attendees. However, everything that was Writers in the Park was upscaled to create the Gateway to Publishing Conference & Convention. The core values of this and every event are clearly rooted in Writers in the Park and the numerous writing conferences and festivals that St. Louis Writers Guild has been involved in since its creation.

2020—Writers in the Lodge

A good idea is too hard to let go of. In 2020 for the 100th Anniversary, Writers in the Park resurfaced with a different venue, format, and name. All the lessons learned with the Gateway to Publishing Conference and Convention were applied to the Writers in the Park model, and Writers in the Lodge was born. There were a few changes and additions, like charging non-members the usual $5 fee, and bringing editorial consultations and pitch sessions. It also became half a day, or three hours long. However, it still delivered the conference-feel and was a great experience for writers.

Held at The Lodge Des Peres on Saturday, March 7, 9:30 a.m. to 12:30 p.m. it had two rooms, one for the three workshops, and then a second room for pitching to literary agents, editing consultations, and a young writers workshop.

Writers in the Park 2020 Schedule:

9:30 a.m. Working with an Agent presented by Kortney Price, literary agent

10:30 a.m. Writing in Someone Else's Sandbox presented by Guy Anthony De Marco, author

11:30 a.m. Editing for Self-Publishing Authors presented by Andrew Doty, Editwright.com

11:30 a.m. Show Don't Tell presented by C.L. Postill

Editing Consultations
Kortney Price, Andrew Doty, and Meghan Pinson

Pitch Sessions
Lauren Miller, Metamorphosis Literary Agency

The History of St. Louis Writers Guild

The Scribe Logo 2004

The Scribe Logo 2013

29 | The Scribe: A Changing Newsletter

St. Louis Writers Guild produced a newsletter or similar publication for decades. Currently, SLWG has *Here's News!*, an electronic monthly newsletter that has been going out to members and the literary community since the early 2000s.

The current run of newsletters began in the 1990s. *Ins + Outs* was a paper newsletter consisting of several pages with a staple binding that was mailed to members. There weren't enough issues remaining to know how often they were sent out, but it was most likely quarterly, like *The Scribe*.

One thing that *Ins + Outs* did do was publish the winners of the Short Story Contest and Poetry Contest winners. With the emergence of *The Scribe* in the 2000s, this practice ended to preserve the publication rights of the stories and poems entered. At the time, there was still a market for short stories in journals and other publications. By preserving entrants' first publication rights, several stories that placed or won the SLWG contests went on to be published or win other contests.

I believe it was in the 2000s, during David Motherwell's presidency, when *The Scribe* was created. For a time, they tried to save money by only producing a single page version of *The Scribe*. By 2007, *The Scribe* was a quarterly printed newsletter that was mailed to each member's home. Mary Menke was the Managing Editor, in charge of collecting all the articles and other materials, plus checking each article. Mary was a board member, VP of

Operations, and an editor, the owner of WordAbilities.com. The layout of *The Scribe* was handled by Katie Shanahan, the Associate Editor.

These teams developed a standard format for *The Scribe*, features that would appear in each issue. *The Scribe* continued *Ins + Outs'* design with 11x17 pages bound in the middle with staples, and then folded over and closed with a sticker for mailing.

In 2010, as the cost of stamps was rising every year or even every couple of months, and the price of printing was increasing, the expenses were getting out of control. At the end, *The Scribe* represented over half of SLWG's yearly budget, and that was only on stamps and printing, not the content. No one was paid for the articles in *The Scribe*.

The other drawback was the sheer labor that went into *The Scribe*. Four times a year, Mary Menke gathered and edited all the articles, then she sent them off to the printer. Once it was printed, Mary, Robin, and several volunteers—sometimes those volunteers were family and not members—had to fold, sticker, and address each issue. At this time, SLWG was booming and membership was close to 200 – there was a lot of folding.

Something had to be done or *The Scribe* would become the only thing SLWG did in a year. *Here's News!*, the electronic newsletter, got a makeover, a flashy new graphical look, and it easily went out each month. There was less of a need for both a quarterly newsletter and a monthly one. So, *Here's News!* became SLWG's monthly communication, and *The Scribe* became a literary magazine.

From Newsletter to Literary Magazine

In 2011, the old newsletter ended its run, and a quarterly magazine was produced. Originally, the hope was that it could be a monthly magazine, but no one was paid, everyone had other jobs and other writing to attend to, and there wasn't enough time. *The Scribe: A Literary Magazine by St. Louis Writers Guild*, had a shiny new graphical look and new articles on a variety of topics, but it continued the traditions of *The Scribe* newsletter, and for over a year, it was definitely a magazine. The new *The Scribe* continued the tradition of showcasing a member, the president's address, articles about writing, and news on the latest SLWG events.

T.W. Fendley became the editor of *The Scribe* and continued the excellence that had always defined the publication. An intern, Mohnish Soundararajan, helped design the new logo for *The Scribe*. It had never really had a proper logo. Each issue simply had a black banner at the top with *The Scribe* in bold lettering. Beside it was the classic logo. Mohnish was the one who chose the sky blue for the logo and offset it, and I added the tag, *A Literary Magazine by St. Louis Writers Guild*.

Scribe Blue, as it became known, was used for posters and other color designs.

For almost three years, *The Scribe: A Literary Magazine by St. Louis Writers Guild* thrived, though the pressure to produce each issue was intense. Laying out *The Scribe* took at least a week; it was produced in Word. InDesign would have been easier, but SLWG couldn't afford the expensive Adobe software. Collecting and editing the articles took two weeks at least, and most of the time the editor was hounding the contributors for articles. I know the President's Announcements I wrote for each issue were always late, but I themed the President's Announcements based on the content of the issue.

From E-Magazine to E-book

Much like a time of peace and prosperity between World Wars, the magazine could not last. It took so long to produce each issue, especially for volunteers with other jobs and writing projects. The publication looked great and had so much good information inside, but it was a dream that ended too soon. It began as all these stories do, with a missed issue. Then came the inevitable scramble to get two issues out. It took weeks to collect and edit the stories, and then at least a week, but more like two weeks, to lay out the magazine and get it into a publishable pdf. I was using Word at the time to layout each issue, which worked but took a lot of time.

The decision was made to do away with the graphics and keep the content, to produce an e-book on a monthly basis. At this point, *The Scribe* became both a monthly reporter of the events, with write-ups on each workshop, and a place for essays, poems, and stories. *The Scribe* continued for a couple of years in this format. Each month a new cover was created, and at first SLWG opened up cover creation to anyone. We had a couple of members submit covers, and it went well for a short time, but eventually time constraints and a lack of being able to pay for each cover meant fewer submissions. I made many of the covers, using shots of St. Louis Landmarks for one year, and historical black and white images for another year.

At the end of each year, 2015 and 2016, the issues of *The Scribe* were collected into a single book that was published and printed. This book was sold for $10 at workshops and events. *The Scribe* worked well in this format, but after several years, similar problems returned. People weren't turning their articles in on time and fewer started coming in.

The Scribe Blog

When Lauren Miller came onboard as the Director of Communications, she took over as editor of *Here's News!* and *The Scribe*. She had the idea of creating a literary journal instead of the literary magazine, and work was started on *1764*. SLWG couldn't sustain both, and since people were paid to submit to *1764*, the decision was made to end *The Scribe* in 2018.

For a brief time, *The Scribe* was a blog, reporting on each month's event, but finding a reporter was getting difficult, and it fell on a couple of dedicated members coordinated by T.W. Fendley. With the audio recordings of each workshop posted on the website, the written account was less important and was replaced.

The Scribe has had an incredible run, and I do hope that it returns or is revitalized one day.

Brad R. Cook

The History of St. Louis Writers Guild

30 |
Writing Contests—
A Long History of Supporting Writers

An important part of St. Louis Writers Guild's year were the writing contests. From honoring current writers to encouraging tomorrow's authors with the Young Writers' contests, the idea of having a judge, a professional writer, editor, or educator select the best and validate their efforts has always been a foundation of the organization.

Why St. Louis Writers Guild Created Writing Contests

One of the gems discovered while researching the history of St. Louis Writers Guild was the reason why the organization started holding writing contests. The 1929 *Globe-Democrat* newspaper article wrote, *To stimulate interest in their own club and as a means of exercising their pens for very love of the work, they hold an annual contest. The prize is nominal, $25. One year it is a short story the members of the Guild write, the next a one-act play, another year it may be a poem or essay or short-short story. The manuscripts submitted are shipped off to several judges of acknowledged rank in letters, and the winner selected. Many of these manuscripts later have been sent to editors and accepted. And, on the other hand, any which were considered good enough even to rank in the $25 contest have been sold for five or six times that amount.*

Nothing changed in the 90 years since the article. The contests still spread the word about St. Louis Writers Guild, and members continue to exercise their pens.

The St. Louis Writers Guild Members Contest – The First SLWG Writing Contest

Started in 1920, and for the reasons stated above, St. Louis Writers Guild created a contest to honor the efforts of its members. Announced at the opening of the Season in September, the deadline was a month later in October, and the winner was announced in November. This eventually changed, and the winner was announced at the gala diner in December. This contest was only open to St. Louis Writers Guild members, all of whom were professional writers, and came with a prize of $25 dollars (about $300 in 2019).

The contest rotated every year, focusing on a different form of writing. It started with short stories, but in 1921, the members insisted on a poetry contest. This was followed by an essay contest, a character sketch, and a one-act play. In 1927, they held a contest for the best one-act play, and the winner was produced by the Little Theater Company later that Season. Shirley Seifert won with her one-act play, *My Adda*. This rotation lasted until the end of the decade when they began holding multiple contests in a single year. It's uncertain how long this format lasted, but by the 1960s and 1970s, this contest transformed into the contest SLWG still holds to this day.

The First Contest for Unpublished Writers

In November 1933, St. Louis Writers Guild announced a writing contest that was open to any unpublished writers. The call went out for short stories, limited to 1000 words, with two prizes: $20 and $15. Manuscripts had to be mailed prior to January 1. They were requested to be mailed to the current president, Rebeka Deitz, in the 5000 block of Chamberlain Avenue. She was the Chairman of the Contest Committee. She also hosted the November meeting at her house, where this contest was announced. Information about the contest was included in the newspapers, putting the call for submission out to all of St. Louis.

This contest was only held the one year, but the foundation was used for the contests that followed. Apparently, the Guild changed up how it approached contests and teamed with members, authors of the day, to sponsor the contests.

The Winifred Irwin Writing Contest— the First "kids'" Contest

Some stories are too good not to pass on, but often history has a way of morphing the details. The story when I first joined St. Louis Writers Guild about the kids' contest was that in the 1920s, the Winifred Irwin Writing Contest was created in response to tragedy. Winifred Irwin was allegedly a young woman who received rejection letters on her story and committed suicide from despair. This greatly affected the members of the Guild, and they created the contest to encourage young writers . . .

However, the truth was a little different, as will soon become clear.

Today, St. Louis Writers Guild celebrates rejection at every meeting. Whoever presided over the meeting asks who has submitted and who has received a rejection. Rejection's never fun, but it's a major part of this industry. I've met plenty of kids through the contests and workshops, and watched frustration take over when the words won't flow. I understand all too well the despair of having your writing rejected. All writers do. Encouraging young writers is important; it fosters not only a life of reading and writing, but the confidence success inspires can have lasting effects.

Encouragement was what the Winifred Irwin and the Young Writers Awards were always about.

Here's the real story about Winifred Irwin:

Winifred Irwin was an author of children's literature. She was a member of St. Louis Writers Guild in the 1930s and lived with her husband and children here in St. Louis. In those days, the writing contests were sponsored by both an author and St. Louis Writers Guild. The author put up the money for the first prize or for half the prize money; it wasn't clear. However, they did get naming rights, and it was publicity for the author. The poetry contest at the time was called the Florence Seidlitz Poetry Contest.

In 1935, Winifred Irwin sponsored a contest for unpublished writers. We know the contest was also held in 1936 and 1937, but we don't know exactly how long it lasted.

Most interesting was the true answer to the riddle of the Winifred Irwin Short Story Contest being targeted to children. The "kids" they were trying to encourage were college students, writers in their twenties who were trying to enter the market. Today, the "kids" are elementary-school-aged and it's about encouraging future storytellers.

Oh, the part about the suicide wasn't entirely made up either. In the 1920s and early 1930s, Hollywood was experiencing a rash of suicides, most famously the young actress, Peg Entwistle, who jumped to her death from the Hollywood sign in September 1932. This national tragedy was undoubtedly one of the catalysts for the contest and encouraging new writers.

In the end, it's good to know that Winifred didn't have to die to inspire a contest.

The Winifred Irwin Short Story Contest was open to any unpublished writer in the St. Louis metropolitan area. The contest was announced at the October 1934 meeting, and had a deadline of midnight on January 10, 1935. Contestants had to deliver their manuscripts to either Mrs. George S. Malone, two thousand block of Bellevue Avenue, in Maplewood, or A. E. Satterthwait, on Waverly Place, in Webster Groves. About 100 writers entered the contest. Two cash prizes were awarded and two honorable mentions were named. First place received $10, $5 went to second place, and there was no award for the honorable mention. The winners were announced on January 31, 1935 at the Cabanne Branch Library, 1106 Union Boulevard, Cabanne Avenue and Union Boulevard, in a meeting attended by contest officials, participants and their friends.

The winner of the first Winifred Irwin Short Story Contest was Tennessee Williams. *Heck of a first pick!* He was a student at Washington University and worked at the Brown Shoe Company. Still Thomas Lanier, he turned in a story titled, "Stella for Star," a wonderful short story, and one where you can see his genius emerging. The tale of Tennessee Williams winning St. Louis Writers Guild's contest also stuck around. It was mentioned in almost every history that was written along the way, and once the letter announcing his win was discovered, it became an official part of the legacy.

Second prize was awarded to Joseph D. Nolan Jr., 24-year-old salesman, who received $5. Honorable mentions were given to Mrs. H. B. Tinker, McCausland avenue, and Miss Dorothy Angove of Mexico, Missouri.

Technically, the short story contest St. Louis Writers Guild holds today is the contest started by Winifred Irwin. The Short Story Contest that St. Louis Writers Guild held in 1920 and almost every year following was only for members, for published authors. The yearly contest was a way of acknowledging the efforts of members; it was not open to non-members. There's no evidence of when the contest switched. By the 1970s, the contest was open to all writers, published and unpublished, within a 50-mile radius of St. Louis. The annual St. Louis Writers Guild Short Story contest today is a mix of the Winifred Irwin Short Story Contest and the Short Story Contest started in 1920.

Tennessee Williams and the Short Story Contest (Written in 2010 for The Scribe)

As St. Louis Writers Guild still advertises to this day, Tennessee Williams won the short story contest in 1935. He was known as Thomas at the time, and was attending Washington University. His story, "Stella for Star," won first place (The St Louis Globe Democrat; November 10, 1929; pg 14 & (University of Delaware library, Special Collections Department, Tennessee Williams Collection, 1939-1994; www.lib.udel.edu/ud/spec/findaids/williams_t/willtenn.htm.)

In 1935 Tennessee Williams entered the St. Louis Writers Guild's Short Story Contest—the oldest in the Midwest—and won the grand sum of ten dollars. This is what we advertise, though to be truthful, we didn't have the story. It was lost.

Robin Moore Theiss had talked to Dakin, Tennessee's brother, at the presentation ceremony of the bust of Tennessee Williams in the Central West End. She found two clues, one was a letter that was written by the Writers Guild to tell him he had won and another was a listing at the Harry Ransom Center at the University of Texas at Austin.

As the new Historian, I turned my attention to finding this story that was such a part of the *Writers Guild's* legacy. I found the Ransom Center and spent a few hours going through the catalog of their archives, and then in Box 43, Folder 5 I found a title, "Stella for Star." I immediately inquired about the folder and asked to hire a proxy researcher to see exactly what it contained. Jean Cannon wrote me back and explained that there were two manuscripts and a number of fragments. That was when I jumped for joy, and yelled "I found it!" which sent both my cats scurrying for the other room. We decided to copy the entire file, all the fragments and both manuscripts, about 70 pages in all.

Then just before June, an ordinary white box arrived at my door. It wasn't in order, which has made discerning the final draft a bit difficult, but it has been a joy to go through. Most of the pages are annotated by his hand, and it is amazing to see his mind at work. It's typed, so when he made a correction, he started a separate piece of paper and then later included them in a draft. That is one reason why there are so many fragments and has made me appreciate my computer. You can see where he made his corrections and how he struggled with plot and characters just like we writers do today, but even then, it is still excellently written and amazing to read. It is classic Tennessee Williams; his incredibly deep and complex characters are expressed with an artful, poetic detail.

What arrived was magic. Not only is there a copy of the story with creases from where it was folded in thirds and put in an envelope, but included were edited pages with handwritten notes in the margin and scrap pages with alternate paragraphs typed out.

A writer's mind laid out the process for a young Tennessee Williams. I'm not going to lie, it felt like treasure, the same feeling as opening a chest of gold. *Stella for Star* is not a direct prequel to his famous work *A Street Car Named Desire*, but it does have that same feeling and his use of flowing language. It remains unpublished, and due to copyright laws, I'm not allowed to include it in this book. I did hold a reading at one of the Wired Coffee Open Mic Nights. Because there isn't a list of winners from all the years, we'll never know how many young writers became best-selling authors, but I have to imagine there have been a few. I've never won, but I have placed in the annual short story contest. So, I feel a bit of a kinship with all those who have placed over the decades.

When researching this book, there was one thing that stuck

out as not making sense. The prize money Thomas won. He was awarded a $10 first prize, but in the 1920s, the short story winners earned $25. There was no reason for the discrepancy, and in the end, I assumed they had adjusted the prize money after a decade and a half of contests. Such was not the case, and the newspapers revealed all. I found the announcement in the *St. Louis Post-Dispatch*, which listed the winner of the first Winifred Irwin contest.

With the truth revealed, it led to some odd answers. Yes, Thomas did win the first Winifred Irwin contest, but it turned out that the contest held by St. Louis Writers Guild today, the Short Story Contest, is more like the Winifred Irwin contest than the original SLWG short story contest.

The Florence Seidlitz Poetry Contest

Starting in 1932, Florence Seidlitz sponsored a poetry contest with St. Louis Writers Guild. The contest had an October 30th deadline and the winner was announced month later at the end of November. Florence was an author and poet and a member of St. Louis Writers Guild. She and her husband hosted several Guild meetings.

At the November 30, 1932 meeting, Mrs. Edwa Robert Moser and Miss Josephine Johnson served as joint hostesses at the home of Mrs. Moser, in the 7000 block of Northmoor Drive. The meeting had been postponed from the night before as a courtesy to Anita Knight, whose prize-winning play, *More Latitude*, was produced at the Wednesday Club. The winners of the Florence Seidlitz Poetry Contest were announced. Mrs. Otis Turner won for her poem, "Transmigration," and Alice Lippmann won second place for her poem, "Rebirth." Honorable mentions were given to poems by Mrs. Frank W. Schaberg, Mrs. Clyde Robertson, and Mrs. May Wilson Todd, but they did not receive any money.

St. Louis Writers Guild announced the contest would be held again in 1933.

In 1934, the Florence Seidlitz Poetry Contest had a deadline of October 30, and the winners were announced on November 27.

On November 28, 1935, the *St. Louis Post-Dispatch* announced that Alice Lippmann won the Florence Seidlitz Poetry

Prize. Her prize of $15 included her picture along with the article in the newspaper. Mrs. Alice Lippmann, wife of Dr. Gustave Lippmann, physician, lived on Alexander Drive.

Prize Money

The prize money for the contest varied greatly over the years, rising and falling with the times and the state of short stories. In the beginning, first prize was an impressive $25 ($300), and within a decade, SLWG was offering more than one contest a year, with the new contests having a first prize of $10 and a second prize of $5. In the 2000s, the prize money had risen to a high of $300, but that changed the year before I joined the board. The problem became a lack of enough entries to justify such a high prize. Eventually, the board decided to adjust the prize money. At first, there was pushback from writers in St. Louis who had made the SLWG short story contest part of their yearly income, but it turned out SLWG was simply following the rest of the industry. Many contests failed or ended at this time, and fewer literary journals, periodicals, and magazines paid for short stories from unknown authors. For a long time during the 2000s and 2010s, the prize money breakdown was $100 for First Place, $75 for Second Place, $50 for Third Place, and $10 to each of the Honorable Mentions. However, as the entries dwindled from the high near 100 to about 25, and then fewer, the prize money was cut to $50 for First Place, $30 for Second Place, and $20 for Third Place. Prize money was generally determined by how many entries were received, and an unofficial rule became that if fifty percent of the entry fees were not covered by the contest entry fees, then the deadline was extended.

It is impressive, but as far as I can tell, every era of St. Louis Writers Guild held the short story contest.

The Deane Wagner Poetry Contest

The Deane Wagner Poetry Contest began in 1994 after the tragic death of a beloved member of the St. Louis literary community. It opens in April of every year to honor National Poetry Month, and has a June 1 deadline. A different area poet or academic is chosen each year to judge the contest.

Any topic is allowed, but each poem has to be the author's original work and previously unpublished. Poems are intended for an adult audience but must not contain blatant sexual, violent, religious, political, or other content that is not appropriate for a general audience composed of persons of all ages and sensitivities.

The entry fee is $10 for the first poem and $5 for each additional entry, with a limit of five entries per person. The poem cannot exceed two pages. Two copies of each poem are to be mailed together in one envelope, along with one typed cover sheet indicating the poems' titles, and the poet's name, address, telephone number, and email address. Poems must be typed in single-spaced format on standard white paper (8-1/2 x 11) in black ink, using a standard typeface or font, such as Courier, Times New Roman, Georgia, or Arial. If the poem exceeds a single page, page numbers must appear in the lower right corner. The poem's title has to appear on each entry. DO NOT INCLUDE THE POET'S NAME ON ANY ENTRY.

The current prize money is $50 First Place, $30 Second Place, and $20 Third Place, and $10 for the Honorable Mention.

Deane Wagner Poetry Contest and the James H. Nash Short Story Contest

In 1994, St. Louis Writers Guild honored fallen members who had greatly impacted the organization. With the annual poetry and short story contests now memorializing these members, the contests became known as St. Louis Writers Guild Memorial Writing Contests. Both were popular contests. They had been before, and after being named for these members, their popularity only grew. Many presidents and contest coordinators over the years had tried to rename the St. Louis Writers Guild Annual Short Story Contest.

The James H. Nash Memorial Short Story Contest was named after a popular president of the 1970s, and lasted into the 2000s.

Deane Wagner was a popular poet, beloved by the local writing community. Those who knew her still talk fondly about her, and because her death was a tragedy, it appeared as though naming the contest after her allowed many to heal.

During my time on the board, it was suggested to rename the contest, at first, because no one remembered her, and it had been over two decades, then another member passed away and it was suggested that it could be renamed for a modern member. However, I argued that history is important. I researched Deane, wrote her history in an article for **The Scribe**, and included a bit about her on the contest form. The Deane Wagner Poetry Contest is at least 26 years old now, and it doesn't appear to be changing anytime soon.

SLWG Sponsored Missouri Writers Guild Writing Contests

For many years, starting in the 1920s, and definitely throughout the 1930s and for the next couple of decades, St. Louis Writers Guild sponsored a contest for the best journalistic article of the year. The Missouri Writers' Guild conference was held at the end of Journalism Week, and St. Louis Writers Guild counted several newspaper employees as members. St. Louis Writers Guild hosted the journalism contest until the modern era, even outlasting the reign of journalists in the SLWG ranks.

As St. Louis Writers Guild entered the modern era, it sponsored the free form poetry contest. Faye Adams championed the poetry contest for Missouri Writers' Guild and though it always puled in the least number of entries, SLWG was pleased to support Missouri Writers' Guild. The poetry contest ended when another writers guild in the state wanted to hold a poetry contest, and the board of Missouri Writers' Guild chose that organization to hold the contest. SLWG held a few different contests after that. After the next proposed contest was rejected, SLWG did not submit another proposal and had not sponsored a Missouri Writers' Guild Conference Contest in a couple of years.

James H. Nash and the Memorial Contests of the 1990s and 2000s

Shortly after the passing of James H. Nash in 1980, St. Louis Writers Guild renamed the annual short story contest the James H.

Nash Memorial Short Story Contest. By 2002, the contest was still being held, with rules that were similar to the previous contests.

It opened in September at the beginning of the Season, and had a maximum 5000-word count. The deadline was October 31. First place received $150.

Each manuscript had to have a 3-by-5-inch card attached to the front, with the writer's name, address, phone number, title, and number of words. The title had to appear on the front page. The entry fee was $15 per manuscript, with a maximum of three per writer. In 2002, entries were sent to Donna Springer via the Guild's P.O. Box.

The contest ended its run in 2005 or 2006 as the name reverted back to the St. Louis Writers Guild Annual Short Story Contest.

St. Louis Writers Guild's Kids' Writing Contests
The Big Write Contest

The Big Write Contest was the children's writing contest held by the Big Read Festival and sponsored by St. Louis Writers Guild and Cultural Festivals. There were two categories, one for fourth and fifth graders, and another for sixth, seventh, and eighth graders. Cultural Festivals operated off grants and were able to advertise the contest in several countries. Most of the entries came from schools that had whole classes submit. I think some of the schools made every student participate. In 2009, over 700 entries came from five or six different countries, the farthest of which was Columbia, South America.

The contest began with a sentence, and then the kids wrote the next 500 words. The board had several readers who vetted the entries, and then two members volunteered to read the entries and select the winners. St. Louis Writers Guild never had a problem finding people who wanted to help. The winners read and were awarded their prizes at the festival. Robin Moore Theiss and Faye Adams, and then Rebecca Carron Wood and Faye Adams announced the winners to the delight of onlookers and parents in the audience.

The Big Write ended when The Big Read Festival ended. A

cut in funding caused the Cultural Festivals to focus elsewhere; they still hold the Clayton Art Fair to this day. As difficult as it was to see that festival cease, St. Louis Writers Guild's real concern was all the young writers. No one on the board wanted to see the contest end.

It was 2011, and I had recently become the President of St. Louis Writers Guild. At one of the board meetings we discussed ways to continue. We couldn't use The Big Write: that name was owned by the festival. But St. Louis Writers Guild had designed and created the contest, so we could use the bones of the contest. Thus, the Young Writers Awards were created. There were a couple of names tossed around, but no one wanted to say kids' contest, or anything like that; we simply wanted to honor future writers.

Young Writers Awards – 2012 to present

The Young Writers Awards appears to have been the first kids writing contest entirely held by St. Louis Writers Guild. It kept the structure of the 500-word count and opening sentence. This gave the entries a similarity, yet because of imagination, each was so unique. One new feature was the requirement of a title. The Big Write had never required one, which led to a massive headache if they got out of order before you had numbered them all. Titles really helped with logistics. Another new feature was opening the contest up to not just schools, but also individuals and the home-schooled as well.

Jennifer Stolzer facilitated contests after me, and she has now passed the torch to Cherie Postill. The first year we received a handful of entries and one year, we didn't advertise it very well and we had a struggle reaching out to the schools. We only had a few entries, and everyone who entered won a place, but we treated them all like rock stars. Soon though, word got out, we advertised better, and were able to get the contest entry forms to district representatives, and now the contest has well over two hundred entries every year. Not quite the seven hundred from before, but in truth, that pushed the limits of SLWG's logistical strength.

The Young Writers Awards opens in August: for one reason, because that is when The Big Read and Writers in Park were held, but also, we did a poll of teachers and found out that due to all the required testing at the end of the year, our writing contest was better at the beginning of the year. Many teachers use the contest as a way of getting kids back into the swing of writing and working in class. The entries are collected, and a first wave of readers, usually a board member, will vet the stories and then the board reads them, and we assign first through sixth to the ones we like. Then Jennifer adds up all our numbers and the winners are decided. The winners are then invited to read and be honored at the annual holiday party and book fair held in December.

I say it often, but the Young Writers Contests will renew you as a writer. Kids have no limitations on their imaginations. These stories are brilliant and imaginative. They push into places adult writers would never go. Sure, some aren't the most technically sound, and grammar might be a bit off, but they are the best stories. And I have found the best ones are always recognizable. We usually agree on the winners. It's easy to spot the future authors.

One more note about contests, an observation as someone who has honored a lot of young writers: many different types of kids enter the contest from the writer with pushy parents, or the parents who clearly helped them, but then there is the gifted writer in a house that doesn't understand. I see them in every contest: young writers, usually very good writers, intellectuals who live in houses with parents who value sports over education. Their older brother or sister sits beside them in their jersey, having just come from practice to the award ceremony. However, put that kid in front of a room full of professional writers cheering their words, give them an award, mention their accomplishment of having completed a story and won an award for it. Suddenly, that mom or dad who jumps at trophies looks at the bookish kid and feels that same pride. The parents' epiphany is visible as is their pride, and I know they'll be more supportive of that young writer. It is one of my favorite things to see in the contest.

The Gateway Con Writing Contests

In 2019, St. Louis Writers Guild held three new contests: 1) For young writers, The Young Writers CON-test, 2) For adults, the Storyteller Award, and 3) For the author hall attendees, a Best Booth Award!

As part of the Gateway to Publishing Conference & Convention, the contests were free to attendees to enter. For the adult contest, there was a fee if the entrant wasn't attending the conference. The Best Booth award was voted on by everyone who attended the book fair. The votes were tallied at the Book Party and the prize, a cool little dish for a writing desk with a typewriter on it was awarded.

They made the Book Fair fun, and despite the Blues Stanley Cup Parade taking place that day, several kids and families attended the award ceremony.

Readings at the Open Mic Nights

Since the creation of the open mic nights in the mid-2000s, the winners of the Deane Wagner Poetry Contest, Young Writers Awards, and the Short Story Contest have been invited to read at the next open mic night. Usually, winners are excited to read, and SLWG had several winners in other states come in for the reading and award ceremony.

The readings became a way of sharing the winning entries without compromising the publication rights. The event was popular among the audiences and members, too. The stories and poems never failed to entertain. Often, the judges came to hear the entries and speak with the participants. These were always the highest-attended open mics. When the open mic moved to a quarterly event, the nights selected were the ones the winners usually read at, and thus the tradition continued and the open mic remained a successful event.

Modern Contests

The entry fees from the Short Story Contest and Poetry Contest used to be fundraisers for St. Louis Writers Guild. Each year, the contests raised more funds than the prize money paid out. Earning between a hundred or a couple hundred dollars, St. Louis Writers Guild relied on this money, especially the short story contest, which came at the end of the calendar year and covered any shortfalls until membership renewals in June. In 2006, the contest winnings were a percentage of the overall entries, and the winner won hundreds of dollars.

However, it wouldn't last. As journals shut down, and the market for short stories and poems dwindled, fewer entries came in every year. There was a time in the 2010s when scam contests became a problem, and writing contests with entry fees were seen as troublesome, but SLWG relied on its history and its legacy to ensure writers of its legitimacy. Plus, the entry fee on the contest remained low, usually $10-$15. Since 2010, the writing contests have not made money for the Guild. The one thing no one wanted to do was to stop holding the contests. The writing contests have never been about the money made, or the prizes awarded; St. Louis Writers Guild has always believed in supporting and encouraging writers.

Contest Coordinators

A group of dedicated St. Louis Writers Guild volunteers had always been the backbone of the writing contests. They represent the most work, that can be done by a member, beyond the president. There are multiple contests a year, sometimes five or more. They all require promoting, collecting the entries, logging the entries in a database, vetting the entries to see which qualify, numbering them, sending them to the judge, contacting the winners, printing the certificates, and MCing the reading and award ceremony. All that for every contest, and two of them overlap: the Young Writers Awards, and the SLWG Short Story Contest.

A.F. Satterthwait, Rebeka Deitz, Norah Morgan, Donna Springer, Faye Adams, Brad R. Cook, Jennifer Stolzer, Cherie Postill, and the many more to come . . . Thank You.

Classic Logo color reversed. Used for t-shirts, journals, and business cards.

31 |
A Changing World

I have to say, I was witness to a profound change not only in St. Louis Writers Guild, but in the whole publishing world: the modernization and electronification of the publishing industry and St. Louis Writers Guild as well.

I mentioned the calendars in an earlier chapter, and they along with the newsletter, The Scribe, optimized this change.

When I joined the board of St. Louis Writers Guild, the biggest expense SLWG had was its printing and mailing costs. Every month a dual-sided calendar was printed, and quarterly, hundreds of Scribes were created, printed, address labels would be applied, they would be folded, stickered closed, and then stamped. The board used to get together and have mailing parties to get everything ready. Then during renewals, a letter and membership form were sent to every member.

The system had worked since 1920, but every year the price was skyrocketing. Plus, at the time, everyone was focused on saving trees, and every month you'd look at this chunk of forest and wonder if there was a better way.

The world was changing, too. Email had taken over. SLWG had started *Here's News!* a few years before. *Here's News!* was an email newsletter that they had problems getting people to sign up for, much less open and read.

(A bit of historical context: at the time, huge weekly or daily emails came from everyone, from your crazy aunt or uncle to major companies, and included sales, jokes, memes, and more. The epically long email was how cat memes made their way through the world before the modern social media. Think of a day's worth of Facebook posts sent via email to every contact you know.)

The Scribe went digital and became a monthly magazine. The monthly calendar moved online, and *Here's News!* grew into the main way St. Louis Writers Guild connected with its members and the community. Progress.

With the money that had been freed up, the board ran off to Mexico – kidding! St. Louis Writers Guild focused on programming, and moved into newer and better locations. It would be a fortuitous move, too. Gone were the free meeting spaces of the past. Every venue started charging for their rooms.

The first big change for St. Louis Writers Guild was the software needed to send out an electronic newsletter. Thus, Donna Springer's run brought about the first e-newsletter, and a website; then came the need for sound equipment. Robin Moore Thiess raised money to acquire two speakers, an amp, and center console. Two microphones were purchased: a regular wired mic for panels or readings, and a lapel mic that allowed the speaker to be hands-free. The sound equipment was very nice for the time, and was held by the president or one of the board members and brought to all events—the workshop, the lecture, the open mics, Writers in the Park, and more.

With the new speakers came odd requests—"Do you have a projector?" When I first started, every speaker had roughly the same setup. They arrived with a tote or briefcase, and that is not a statement of gender. There must have been limited carrying options. The author had a few books, either in a bag or small box. The first big author I met had a small rolling carrying case. The presentation consisted of everyone following along with a handout, usually a couple of pages long and stapled in the upper right-hand corner – though some would just be loose and inevitably someone didn't get all the pages. To be clear, I have no issue with handouts, love them, but it was a different time. Now most authors show up with a small cart. They have their laptop, copies of every title they sell, signs, SWAG, and promotional material. Plus, they may still have handouts.

At the time, SLWG didn't have a projector, and the speaker generally had their own. Then came 2009 and the year of requests. Seven speakers, over half the year, asked for a projector. Several people on the board looked into them. I remember researching how to rent one. At the time, a projector could cost $1000-$2000, but to rent one cost about $300 for the day. Math can be difficult for some writers—we're right-brainers—but even this was an easy one. So, we scoured the papers and ads. Seriously, describing this sounds like the Dark-Ages or something compared to the simple Google searches and Amazon deals of today. Eventually, one was found on sale for $400 at Micro Center, a computer and electronic device retailer. It was the fourth largest purchase in SLWG history at that time – the software, the website, the sound equipment, and the projector.

Now, St. Louis Writers Guild is a well-oiled and modern machine. The website's huge and visually stunning. Here's News! is a gorgeous newsletter that has all the up-to-date information a member needs and news from around the literary community. *The Scribe* transformed into a digital journal that published a collection every year and became a couple of published books. The Facebook group is an online forum of over 1400 members where authors can get answers, and people can promote events and releases. Twitter is now a way of connecting with the world, and Instagram allows the Guild to show off its events. All of this content is generated by members for members and writers all over the world.

St. Louis Writers Guild had always shifted with the times, from the domination of newspapermen to novelists and freelance writers. Even in my own time, memoirists became fiction authors, and now there's a shift to nonfiction. And bloggers became vloggers before transforming into podcasters with YouTube channels.

On a quick note, SLWG can't teach you how to be a writer. SLWG does have workshops on dialogue, world building, imagery, and more; we provide in-depth knowledge on specific topics. But a workshop to make you a great writer . . . that isn't how it works. The Presidents are often asked for the phone number of the Guild's literary agent, or for publishers that produce members books, by people who don't understand how the industry works. SLWG isn't a gatekeeper of the publishing industry. It's a collective of writers helping each other avoid the pitfalls and point out the paths in this industry. To show authors how the industry works, prepare them, and help them gain access. It has never and will never be a rubber stamp into bookstores.

Changes to the Publishing Industry

The publishing industry has changed, too, with the rise of Print-on-Demand and the hybrid author. When I started, self-publishing was a dirty word, and now, it's transformed the industry. It used to be that the Big Five, or the Big Six as they used to be known, were the only ones on the block that published books for the mass market. They owned a number of imprints that published specifically romance, science-fiction, Westerns, and every other genre. Writers built up interest and a portfolio by publishing short stories, one-act plays, character sketches, essays, or poems in the leading magazines of the day. After a couple of publications, publishers and literary agents started paying attention, and soon a book deal would be offered. Payment was by the word, and a writer could make hundreds of dollars off a short story. If it were big enough and went through enough reprints, a short story could earn thousands.

As the money dried up and publications shut down, the industry handed much of the market to smaller presses, which exploited these niche markets, and to self-published authors who could find their own markets. Self-publishing used to be the domain of the rushed and unprofessional authors who demanded total control, countermanding expert advice, but with the rise of independent publishing and hybrid authors, the publishing industry was now more author-driven than ever before.

Print-on-Demand, the ability to print small runs of books instead of having to print thousands of books at once, drove this change, along with the computerization of the world, which allowed the tools of the publisher and cover artist to be available to every author. Instead of working for projects within a single publishing house, freelance editors, cover artists, and layout designers were free to take on any client, which brought a professionalism to the indie-publishers. Where the industry goes from here is anyone's guess, but writers will adapt.

Changes to Querying

The Querying Process has completely changed as well. When I started querying, the process was for authors to buy a book that was published every year, *Publishers Marketplace*. It listed every literary agent and publisher. Query letters would be printed and stuffed into envelopes with the submission packet, along with a SASE (Self-Addressed Stamped Envelope). Weeks would pass until the creased envelope returned with a ribbon of paper cut from a full page with the form rejection printed on it. The industry has progressed, going from stacks of pages sent through the mail to an all-electronic process of emails.

An organization that started gathering in living rooms with announcements in the newspaper had become email blasts, websites, and community centers. Progress. With meetings broadcast over the internet, and speakers who remote in from far-off lands where will St. Louis Writers Guild be in another century? Perhaps the future will be meetings held through holograms in our living rooms.

The History of St. Louis Writers Guild

SLWG Brochures, bookmarks, and postcards

32 |
The Secret to
St. Louis Writers Guild's Success

I've been a member of several groups and known many more, but St. Louis Writers Guild's success is no surprise. It is the community of writers that has kept the Guild alive. St. Louis is a focal point for writers and has been for a century. This organization has not only survived but thrived because of the outstanding writers that make up the membership.

Out of these members come those who give of themselves and their time. The strength and success of St. Louis Writers Guild comes not from one person, but a collective of writers who truly want to help their fellow wordsmiths.

Often, critics of St. Louis Writers Guild say, "The Board is just a group of pompous-asses who promote their friends and control who succeeds and fails . . ."

There have been some creative insults in various forms over the years, not only during my own time with the Guild. I found this sentiment popped up throughout its history. What people never understand is, yes, the board of St. Louis Writers Guild were friends, but... they didn't start out that way.

I knew no one when I joined the board. I hadn't previously been friends with any board member except for T.W. Fendley, whom I had been in a critique group with before she joined the board. David Lucas and I were often seen as interchangeable. We'll answer to each other's names, and I had the honor of being best man at his wedding, but I didn't know him before meeting him through St. Louis Writers Guild. I really got to know David at The Big Read, when we both set up and worked the SLWG booth for several hours.

The secret of the board is that they become friends. I get the feeling it has been that way since Sam Hellman and Elinor Maxwell McCord played bridge together. It was that way when Charles Guenther served three decades on the board, and it was that way with many of the board members I've had the honor to serve with.

St. Louis Writers Guild's success is simple – a robust group of volunteers, people willing to give of themselves to help other writers. Publishing is a huge industry, but in a way, it's a small community. Writers live through computers, or by pen and paper, but as humans, we need people, too. Writers must come together, to remember that each of us face the same issues, the same problems, the same setbacks. Together, writers thrive.

St. Louis Writers Guild did have a system to fill positions. People who were interested in helping out were given some responsibility, and if they did that well, came to events, and helped, plus hung around for more than a few months, then more duties were added. Before long, a board position opened up and the volunteer was offered that role. People tend to find something they can bring to SLWG, from editing, to graphic design, or handling email, contacting speakers or media, and as the presidency opened, someone who had already been working with the Guild and knew its operations stepped up and led the organization. The board voted on all new volunteers and board members. It had been that way for almost two decades, and worked well.

The question was often asked, why not hold elections? SLWG used to hold elections every year, but it took a couple of months to run those elections, and they often led to a rotating board, or the same people being shuffled around positions. Nothing against board of directors that change every year, but that limited the amount of planning time. St. Louis Writers Guild was usually planned many months out: six months to a year. A person who only served a single year would not be able to schedule and execute it all. Members who serve at their leisure are there because they want to be and can leave at any time. Most board members serve three to five years. It allows for more planning and execution of programs and services.

Plus, as a writers' guild, the average member was a part of the organization to learn about writing and improve their craft. The inner workings of the SLWG are less important than the programs it hosts, and the services it offers. Those who do care tend to volunteer, to get involved, and thus, eventually become part of the structure of the organization. I've remained a part of SLWG because I strongly believe in providing good information to writers. I've known too many who have been scammed. I also wanted to learn more of the history.

St. Louis Writers Guild Programs were scheduled about 6-8 months ahead of time, and bigger speakers could take even longer. Gateway Con took about a year and a half to plan, and even Writers in the Park took six months to a year to organize. *The Scribe* and other publications also took a long time to plan, execute, and publish. Having a board that served multiple years allowed people to plan these events in a way that fits into their schedules. Remember, every one of them was a volunteer with not only their own writing career but also their own jobs, too.

The other secret to St. Louis Writers Guild's success is that the board voted on everything. Every decision St. Louis Writers Guild ever made was done by quorum. Even though the president sets the tone and direction for the Guild, everything was voted on with only the majority moving forward. The president did have a vote and a half to break ties, but usually the vote was unanimous because if a board member didn't agree with something it was discussed and issues were addressed. So, the final product presented to members and the public was usually well thought out, reviewed, and had a consensus on how to proceed. It really was an effective way of ensuring that only the best ideas moved forward.

If there isn't a writers' group in your area, create one. Start small; help each other grow. If there is a writers' guild or group in your area, join, be a part of it, make it the best it can be, and help one another.

Writers need each other.

The History of St. Louis Writers Guild

A quick Q & A . . .
How does SLWG spend membership money?

First, every spending decision is by board vote and getting 5-7 people to agree usually kept costs down. Plus, SLWG has had some incredible Treasurers who have all kept a close eye on spending.

Basically, here is the breakdown:

The majority, probably about 70%, is spent on event locations and speakers

15% is spent on prize money and judging fees
10% is spent on the website, PayPal, and other services
5% is spent on handouts, brochures, and signage
0% is spent on paying volunteers

Does SLWG seek grant funding?

Yes, St. Louis Writers Guild has solicited funds for all the large events like Writers in the Park, the Young Writers Awards, The Night of 3 Missouri Poet Laureates, the Gateway to Publishing Conference & Convention, and more. SLWG also sought corporate and author sponsorship for events and programs to help cover costs and provide opportunities to advertise books and author services. Matching funds, budget limitations, and other logistical issues usually prevented SLWG from obtaining grants and foundation money but raising money had always been a way of doing more without constantly expecting members to burden the cost. The biggest issue remained getting volunteers to take care of this kind of endeavor. Grants took time, required additional materials, and usually were due a year to a year and a half before the event.

Are there rules for board members?

Yes, all board members and volunteers are subject to the bylaws of St. Louis Writers Guild. This includes mandatory attendance of meetings, maintaining one's conduct within the industry, and a variety of other commonsense rules. However, the biggest rule wasn't written down. Since well before David Motherwell, and certainly since his presidency, the focus of St.

Louis Writers Guild has been on what the organization could do for writers.

How do you choose the speakers or topics?

I can't speak for every era, but I can say that while I've been a board member, the speakers were chosen by committee or after a board member met the speaker at a different literary event. Some were requests or suggestions by members. Often, it was the personal connections that the board members formed with other authors that caused them to come and speak with St. Louis Writers Guild and remain a member afterward.

The History of St. Louis Writers Guild

Classic Logo adjusted for 2013

New SLWG Logo created in 2015
Designed by Brad R. Cook & Steven Langhorst,
illustrated by Jennifer Stolzer

33 | The Historians of St. Louis Writers Guild

This book would not be possible without the efforts of those members who passed along the history of St. Louis Writers Guild. Not only did they ensure that the legacy of SLWG continued, but having so much history ignited the imaginations of those who followed to dig deeper. St. Louis Writers Guild has always touted its history, mentioning its founding in 1920, Tennessee Williams winning the short story contest, the writers conferences it's held, and all the top authors that have been members. The ability to showcase this history was only possible because of several dedicated St. Louis Writers Guild members.

The Historians

Louis Dodge was the first to record the history. In 1921, he wrote a piece for the *St. Louis Globe-Democrat* describing the founding of the organization. Finding the article confirmed much of what had been researched for this book.

Hamilton Thornton gets an honorable mention because not only was his article in 1929 the source material for many historians to come, but he included such detailed information. By mentioning the members, and including both what the Guild did as well as the reasons they held contests or created this literary community, he provided a wealth of information.

The History of St. Louis Writers Guild

Robert Hereford was the first researcher for St. Louis Writers Guild. As a newspaperman, he had access to all their records and could comb the archives, but he also interviewed members from the 1920s to find out more. He wrote the history in 1948.

Marcella Thum cared about sharing the legacy of St. Louis Writers Guild. She compiled the SLWG history from the accounts of Hereford and Dodge. Her historical account was one of the first to be found.

King McElroy was president in 1970, the 50th Anniversary of St. Louis Writers Guild. He wrote a history that definitely pulled from Robert Hereford's earlier work. He also had the first recorded historian on his board. Coming three years after Marcella Thum, I have to assume the history of SLWG was on the minds of many members.

Carolyn Wood was the first recorded Historian of St. Louis Writers Guild. She was Historian in 1970 for the Guild's 50th Anniversary.

David Motherwell researched the history and discovered the 1929 St. Louis Globe-Democrat article written by Hamilton Thornton.

Robin Moore Theiss (now Robin Moore) could be called the collector of St. Louis Writers Guild history. As a lover of old books, she obtained several novels by past St. Louis Writers Guild presidents and members, many of which are signed. Her impressive collection was displayed in a glass case at her bookstore, STL Books. Robin also created the Legacy Project, which dedicated interns and the historian to researching SLWG's history.

Peggy Haldeman was historian before me. She and Robin Moore Theiss tracked down the letter announcing Tennessee

Williams had won the short story contest, proving a long-held legend of St. Louis Writers Guild. She served as membership chairman for a number of years and was instrumental in planning the 85th Anniversary.

Brad R. Cook, Historian of St. Louis Writers Guild for the 90th, 95th, and 100th Anniversaries. I started extensively researching the founders and the early days of the Guild, and tracked down a number of items, beginning with Tennessee Williams' "Stella for Star." However, it was recording the personal stories from members that I consider my biggest contribution to the legacy of St. Louis Writers Guild.

University Interns who worked on the Legacy Project
Danya Shaik from St. Louis University
Alexis Operle from the University of Missouri—St. Louis

The History of St. Louis Writers Guild

34 |
The Presidents of
St. Louis Writers Guild

The list of presidents was kept by the Guild for decades. It was a way of displaying SLWG history without recording every detail, and in the end, was instrumental in preserving the legacy. The list, featured since the 85th Anniversary, was compiled from bits and pieces of histories that came before. Most of it was accurate, which is amazing given the timespan.

This list is coded, an asterix means the name was found through my research. A double asterix means the name was changed to correct the list. Bold lettering means that I have confirmed this information and know it to be accurate.

1920 – Sam Hellman
1921 – Shirley Seifert
***1922 – Louis Dodge**
***1923 – Shirley Seifert**
***1924 – Ralph Mooney**
1925 – No record
***1926 – Irvin Mattick**
1927 – No record
***1928 – Elizabeth Allen Satterthwait**
1929 – Dr. Alfred F. Satterthwait
1930 – Elinor Maxwell McCord
***1931 – Elinor Maxwell McCord**
***1932 – Rebeka A. P. Deitz**

*1933 – Rebeka A. P. Deitz
*1934 – Mable H. Malone – 10th SLWG president
*1935 – Mable H. Malone
*1936 – Elinor Maxwell McCord
1937 – Dr. Harvey J Howard
1938 – Anita Knight
1939 – Robert Hereford
1940 – Bert Hoffman
1941 – Ralph Mooney
*1942 – Emily Pope
1943 – James Worsham
*1944 – Clare Fleeman Alger
*1945 – Clare Fleeman Alger
1946 – Ruth Rodgers Johnson
*1947 – Norah Morgan
*1948 – James A. Worsham
*1949 – Franklin E. Poindexter
1950 – Ruth Grosby – 20th
1951 – Ruth Grosby
1952 – Florence Armstrong
1953 – Dr. Jerome S. Grosby, DDS.
1954 – Marion O'Brien
1955 – Marion O'Brien
1956 – Charles Norton
1957 – Nicolette Stack
1958 – Caroline Ward
1959 – Charles Guenther
*1960 – Bernice Roer
*1961 – Lois Rea
1962 – Devere Stephens – 30th
1963 – Merna Lazier
1964 – Janet Neavles
*1965 – Mrs. Bessie Megee
*1966 – Mrs. Bernice Peukert
1967 – Marcella Thum
1968 – Dorothy Sappington
1969 – Richard Lynch

1970 – King McElroy
1971 – Elizabeth Mulligan
1972 – Antonio Betancourt – 40th
1973 – Art Hoglund
1974 – James H. Nash
1975 – Virginia McCarthy
1976 – Charles Guenther
1977 – Charles Guenther
1978 – Joyce Flaherty
1979 – Mary Gorman
1980 – Dorothy Nash
1981 – Ron Lightle
1982 – Gwen Lowder
1983 – Marcella Holloway
1984 – Linda Madl – 50th
1985 – N. Paul Dusseault
1986 – Carolyn May
1987 – Linda Sage
1988 – Cynthia Georges
1989 – Sandy Palmer
1990 – Chuck Hardwick
1991 – Frank Foley Jr.
1992 – Julie Keleman
1993 – Jan Shafferkoetter
1994 – Mary Schirmer – 60th
1995 – Mary Schirmer
1996 – Terry Gibson
1997 – Terry Gibson
1998 – Terry Gibson
1999 – Terry Gibson
2000 – David Motherwell
2001 – David Motherwell
2002 – David Motherwell
2003 – David Motherwell
2004 – David Motherwell
2005 – David Motherwell
2006 – Robin Moore Theiss

2007 – **Robin Moore Theiss**
2008 – **Robin Moore Theiss**
2009 – **Dr. Rebecca Carron**
2010 – **Dr. Rebecca Carron Wood**
2011 – **Dr. Rebecca Carron Wood**
2012 – **Brad R. Cook**
2013 – **Brad R. Cook**
2014 – **Brad R. Cook**
2015 – **David Alan Lucas II**
2016 – **David Alan Lucas II**
2017 – **David Alan Lucas II**
2018 – **David Alan Lucas II**
2019 – **David Alan Lucas II**
2019 – **Jessica Mathews** – 67th SLWG President
2020 – **Jessica Mathews**

Have a St. Louis Writers Guild Memory or Story?

First, write a couple of details in YOUR copy, so if some future researcher finds the book, it will be there. *(use the blank pages, it's ok, but only in your copy... don't add it to the ones in bookstores)*

Second, consider writing it down as a short story, essay, or poem. SLWG can be a great source of material. Then submit it, or maybe publish it as an article. It will help future researchers find information about the Guild.

Third, let me know. I love SLWG Memories, Myths, and Lore. Contact me at bradrcook.com, through SLWG, or tap me on the shoulder at an event, many of the stories in this book came from conversations over the years.

| Index

Symbols

5+5 - 39, 86, 203, 210, 211, 212, 213, 264, 292
5x5 - 315, 320

A

Billy Adams - 230, 252, 253, 274, 298, 337
Faye Adams - 229, 230, 252, 253, 257, 261, 263, 274, 285, 286, 290, 337, 346, 348, 350, 374, 375, 379
Clare Fleeman Alger - 125, 126, 134, 398
All on the Same Page Bookstore - 291, 292, 331, 351
Fedora Amis - 291, 292, 299, 309, 332
Claire Applewhite - 229, 252, 262, 267, 278, 291, 292, 330, 332
Florence Armstrong - 131, 133, 135, 398
Associate Membership - 316
Auditor - 90, 140, 141
Author Series - 277, 278, 279, 281, 284, 290, 291, 292, 330, 331, 332, 333

B

Temple Bailey - 11, 34, 42, 56, 59, 67, 71, 72, 73, 96, 123
Walter Bargen - 203, 240, 275, 276, 277, 290
Barnes & Noble - 2, 200, 207, 208, 209, 210, 211, 212, 213, 214, 218, 220, 228, 234, 235, 236, 239, 241, 244, 250, 260, 262, 264, 284, 285, 329, 333
Guy Bates - 185, 186, 196, 206, 211
The Big Read - 226, 227, 238, 241, 253, 254, 255, 261, 264, 282, 343, 345, 375, 376, 388
The Big Write - 226, 230, 240, 241, 253, 282, 283, 346, 375, 376
Dwight Bitikofer - 219, 221, 238, 240, 246, 247, 248, 252, 257, 258, 272, 274, 285, 286, 288, 335, 336, 337, 346
Marianne Blake - 2, 221, 229, 231, 235
St. Louis Blues - 305, 313

Susan Boogher - 11, 42, 71, 123
Bookmarks - 216, 227
Borders Books - 197, 285, 333
Frederick Hazlitt Brennan - 35, 97, 98, 106
William Brennan - 9, 35
Buder Hall - 264, 288, 289, 331, 333

C

St. Louis Cardinals - 117, 153, 158, 165, 186
Martha Carr - 151, 166, 167
Rebecca Carron - 223, 227, 229, 240, 243, 244, 248, 249, 252, 256, 261, 269, 274, 284, 337, 345, 375, 400, 414
Castlereagh Tea Room - 132, 137, 145
Charter Members - 9, 41, 42, 48, 88
Chase Park Plaza - 117
Cheshire Inn - 165, 175
Classic Logo - 182, 183
David Clewell - 275, 276, 290
Louis Cochran - 74, 115, 123
Contest Coordinator - 90, 230, 285, 286, 306
Brad Cook - 3, 240, 264, 266, 285, 286
Brad R. Cook - 3, 4, 229, 248, 252, 257, 264, 269, 285, 287, 289, 290, 291, 292, 306, 307, 308, 309, 310, 317, 318, 319, 354, 355, 379, 395, 400
Fannie Cook - 98, 115, 119, 121, 124, 125
Crestwood - 2, 196, 200, 207, 208, 209, 210, 211, 212, 213, 214, 218, 220, 228, 233, 239, 241, 244, 250, 260, 329
Critique Groups - 86, 87, 225, 237, 238, 264, 351, 353
Pearl Curran - 38, 42, 77

D

Denise Elam Dauw - 291, 331, 332, 354
De Giverville Avenue - 11, 20, 59
Rebeka A. P. Deitz - 99, 397, 398
Rebeka Deitz - 93, 97, 99, 107, 108, 109, 110, 111
Director of Communications - 90, 303, 306, 362
Louis Dodge - 11, 30, 36, 41, 42, 46, 48, 49, 55, 56, 57, 68, 71, 74,

75, 90, 100, 112, 123, 393, 397
Margery Doud - 71, 75, 106, 108, 111, 114
N. Paul Dusseault - 169, 170, 399

E

Suzann Ledbetter Ellingsworth - 290
Nicole Evelina - 291, 308, 331, 332, 351

F

Rev. William Barnaby Faherty - 152
T.W. Fendley - 278, 285, 286, 289, 301, 305, 317, 343, 346, 348, 355, 361, 362, 387
Grace Reeve Fennell - 42, 52, 60, 71
Flaming Pit Restaurant - 86, 149, 150, 159, 160, 161
Frank Foley - 185, 186, 192, 399
Angie Fox - 261, 265, 266, 278, 292, 299, 332, 347, 352
Ryan P. Freeman - 302, 306

G

Garavelli's Restaurant - 165, 175, 176, 180, 192
Gateway Con - 86, 302, 303, 304, 305, 306, 316, 338, 349, 377, 389
Gateway to Publishing Conference & Convention - 39, 86, 287, 294, 298, 300, 303, 304, 305, 309, 310, 318, 324, 354, 356, 378, 390
Jay Gelzer - 9, 31, 32, 56, 104, 105, 106
Genre Talk - 87, 351, 353, 354
Cynthia Georges - 169, 399
Cole Gibsen - 263, 266, 288, 291, 304, 331, 345, 353
Terry Gibson - 182, 185, 186, 399
Glen Echo Country Club - 85, 86, 95, 103
St. Louis Globe-Democrat - 9, 12, 13, 14, 18, 24, 27, 30, 34, 45, 57, 58, 59, 62, 66, 67, 70, 75, 76, 82, 92, 93, 95, 97, 100, 101, 102, 103, 104, 105, 119, 120, 121, 122, 124, 125, 134, 135, 155, 158, 189, 393, 394
Dianna Graveman - 221, 235, 245, 257, 289, 330, 347
Peter H. Green - 242, 246, 247, 252, 257, 274, 278, 285, 286, 306, 332
Dr. Jerome S. Grosby - 133, 134, 398

Ruth Grosby - 118, 119, 126, 133, 134, 135, 398
Charles Guenther - 85, 133, 134, 136, 139, 146, 149, 152, 154, 155, 156, 157, 160, 175, 176, 197, 203, 388, 398, 399

H

Peggy Haldeman - 203, 205, 221, 229, 235, 394
Emily Hall - 308
Hannibal Writers Guild - 302, 306
Chuck Hardwick - 185, 187, 399
June Hartman - 141
Sam Hellman - 9, 11, 12, 13, 14, 15, 16, 40, 41, 43, 45, 49, 51, 55, 56, 63, 64, 67, 68, 71, 96, 101, 105, 123, 331, 338, 388, 397
Historian - 3, 89, 152, 223, 229, 257, 285, 298, 306, 317, 343, 369, 394, 395
Marcella Holloway - 169, 170, 399
Harvey J Howard - 96, 398
Doreen Hulsey - 221, 225, 229, 231, 235

I

Ins + Outs - 182, 188, 359, 360
Winifred Irwin - 94, 97, 110, 111, 112, 113, 114, 115, 184, 367, 368, 369, 371

J

Ruth Rodgers Johnson - 118, 120, 125, 127, 398
Joplin - 141, 146, 266, 273

K

Kathleen Kayembe - 299, 301, 318, 338, 354
Julie Keleman - 185, 399
Kirkwood Amtrak Station - 244, 267, 274, 275, 288
Kirkwood Community Center - 187, 233, 244, 251, 262, 264, 267, 270, 289, 291, 292, 295, 296, 307, 308, 353
Anita Knight - 93, 96, 101, 115, 371, 398
Ted Kooser - 247, 264, 272, 275
Jamie Krakover - 286, 287, 306, 317

L

Steven Langhorst - 287, 315, 318, 320, 337
Louis Lanier - 182, 185, 186, 188, 190, 192
Margaretta Scott Lawlor - 42, 57, 72, 75, 82, 105, 111
Merna Lazier - 140, 398
Ann Leckie - 278, 307, 333
Lecture Series - 220, 233, 235, 236, 238, 239, 247, 259, 260, 262, 263, 264, 265, 275, 277, 283, 284, 288, 289, 290, 329, 333
Suzann Ledbetter - 220, 237, 245, 290
Left Bank Books - 206, 210
Ron Lightle - 167, 169, 170, 399
Jeannie Lin - 289, 348, 349
Literary Colony - 41
The Lodge Des Peres - 283, 292, 296, 309, 310, 318, 319, 356
Loud Mouth Open Mic - 226, 237, 238, 239, 240, 241, 260, 261, 262, 277, 339
Robertus Love - 11, 42, 56, 60, 72, 75, 123
Gwen Lowder - 169, 171, 399
David Alan Lucas II - 285, 289, 295, 400
David Lucas - 223, 246, 249, 251, 257, 263, 281, 284, 291, 292, 295, 297, 298, 299, 305, 308, 313, 326, 343, 345, 346, 347, 348, 349, 355, 387
Richard Lynch - 140, 398

M

The Mack - 226, 238, 239, 240, 241, 244, 260, 261, 262, 339
Shawntelle Madison - 266, 289, 309, 348, 349
Linda Madl - 169, 171, 175, 399
Main Street Books - 308
Mable H. Malone - 76, 92, 96, 97, 398
Gerry Mandel - 229, 232, 240, 261, 263, 274, 288, 289, 308, 331
Corinne Harris Markey - 45, 57, 72
Warren Martin - 272, 290, 320
Maryville University - 247, 253, 264, 272, 275, 277, 288, 289, 290, 330, 331, 333
Jessica Mathews - 304, 305, 306, 307, 313, 314, 317, 400

Irving Mattick - 55, 56, 59, 60
Carolyn May - 169, 399
Elinor Maxwell McCord - 14, 42, 68, 72, 76, 93, 95, 96, 97, 101, 102, 103, 104, 106, 107, 108, 109, 388, 397, 398
King McElroy - 36, 149, 151, 152, 158, 159, 394, 399
McNulty's Irish Bar - 200, 206, 207
McNulty's Irish Pub - 181, 196, 197, 209, 210
Leonora McPheeters - 9, 35, 36
Bessie Megee - 398
Membership Chairman - 90, 203, 257, 306, 307
Membership Coordinator - 2, 205
Mary Ward Menke - 229, 232, 249, 251, 252, 345
Susie Meyer - 85, 205
Midwest Mystery Writers of America - 231, 302
Lauren Miller - 291, 303, 306, 357, 362
Missouri Writers Guild - 9, 10, 26, 41, 44, 56, 136, 143, 145, 146, 151, 158, 172, 183, 232, 239, 255, 258, 262, 263, 265, 281, 290, 331, 347, 374
Ralph Mooney - 9, 11, 24, 25, 26, 27, 28, 43, 55, 58, 59, 60, 63, 68, 85, 104, 123, 125, 131, 397, 398
Dorothy O. Moore - 133, 135
Norah Morgan - 85, 125, 126, 127, 128, 131, 133, 379, 398
MORWA - 180, 272, 302
David Motherwell - 69, 70, 118, 199, 200, 201, 203, 204, 205, 217, 221, 229, 235, 284, 297, 359, 390, 394, 399
Motor Vogue - 51, 63, 64
Alice Curtice Moyer-Wing - 72, 76
Elizabeth Mulligan - 149, 151, 152, 158, 159, 399
MWG - 10, 44, 45, 100, 147, 229, 233, 237, 240, 257, 272, 273, 281, 285, 286, 290, 303, 304, 306

N

Dorothy Nash - 169, 171, 172, 298, 399
James H. Nash - 152, 172, 183, 184, 373, 374, 399
Janet Neavles - 140, 398
Nelson's Café - 131, 132, 135, 136
Charles Norton - 133, 398

Novel Neighbor - 338

O

Lynn Obermoeller - 248, 259
Marion O'Brien - 133, 398
Linda O'Connell - 252, 258, 274, 289, 291, 318, 337
Open Mic Night - 226, 234, 237, 238, 240, 241, 260, 264, 277, 289, 315, 320, 321, 338, 339

P

Sandy Palmer - 169, 399
J.D. Parran - 242, 245
Ridley Pearson - 236, 249, 267
Bernice Peukert - 398
Poets Laureate - 275, 290
Franklin E. Poindexter - 125, 126, 128, 132, 398
Joe Pollack - 168
Emily Pope - 125, 398
St. Louis Post-Dispatch - 9, 13, 14, 19, 26, 45, 94, 97, 110, 115, 120, 122, 128, 142, 150, 151, 153, 155, 158, 159, 160, 161, 166, 168, 169, 170, 175, 176, 190, 191, 192, 193, 194, 195, 207, 208, 248, 265, 280, 330, 371
Cherie Postill - 302, 306, 319, 320, 376, 379
Joan and Ferd Potthast - 189
President - 3, 4, 8, 12, 13, 18, 19, 24, 25, 30, 45, 49, 50, 56, 57, 58, 62, 69, 70, 73, 76, 78, 79, 88, 89, 92, 93, 94, 96, 97, 99, 100, 101, 108, 110, 112, 118, 127, 128, 133, 134, 140, 141, 142, 147, 152, 154, 156, 169, 170, 171, 185, 186, 187, 188, 189, 199, 200, 203, 204, 205, 217, 228, 229, 232, 243, 244, 249, 250, 251, 256, 258, 269, 273, 285, 286, 288, 289, 295, 303, 305, 306, 313, 317, 320, 331, 347, 355, 361, 376, 400

R

Robert Randisi - 245, 263, 331
Catherine Rankovic - 246, 263, 290, 291, 307
Lois Rea - 140, 398

Harlan Eugene Read - 72, 76, 82, 96, 106, 108
Chris Richman - 248, 264
Autumn Rinaldi - 315, 318, 320
Mrs. Dr. H. H. Rodgers - 38, 77
Bernice Roer - 140, 141, 142, 145, 146, 398

S

Linda Sage - 169, 173, 399
Dorothy Sappington - 140, 398
Dr. Alfred F. Satterthwait - 56, 78, 397
Elizabeth Satterthwait - 47, 60, 68, 97
Saturday Writers - 255, 272, 302, 348, 349
Mary Schirmer - 181, 185, 187, 193, 195, 196, 399
Schlafly Tap Room - 244, 339
The Scribe - 182, 184, 202, 203, 204, 217, 229, 232, 245, 272, 298, 301, 303, 324, 330, 358, 359, 360, 361, 362, 369, 374, 381, 382, 383, 389
Season - 57, 58, 60, 83, 84, 85, 86, 88, 90, 93, 94, 106, 107, 114, 125, 140, 149, 165, 180, 181, 183, 189, 252, 284, 313, 366, 375
Secretary - 25, 36, 89, 97, 99, 133, 134, 140, 141, 152, 185, 188, 229, 232, 257, 259, 282, 285, 286, 305, 309, 317
Florence Seidlitz - 60, 94, 109, 110, 112, 114, 367, 371
Shirley Seifert - 6, 9, 11, 18, 19, 20, 21, 22, 41, 42, 43, 45, 50, 55, 56, 58, 59, 83, 94, 104, 120, 121, 123, 125, 338, 366, 397
Jan Shafferkoetter - 185, 399
Harold Shumate - 25, 43, 57, 79
Sisters in Crime - 180, 231, 255, 258, 272, 348, 349
SLPA - 170, 186, 272, 283, 288, 292, 320
Donna Springer - 85, 202, 203, 206, 212, 229, 253, 375, 379, 382
Nicolette Stack - 133, 137, 398
Harvey Stanbrough - 228, 240, 245
St. Louis Star-Times, - 9, 13, 154
Devere Stephens - 140, 398
STLBooks - 217, 279, 350
St. Louis Community College - 180, 181, 184, 187, 193, 194, 243
St. Louis Publishers Association - 170, 186, 258, 272, 283, 302, 319, 348, 350

St. Louis Reflections - 203, 206, 251, 252, 267, 274, 348
St. Louis Writers' Guild - 49, 57, 59, 93, 95, 104, 113, 117, 122, 123, 151, 161, 192, 323, 325
StlWritersGuild - 217, 243
stlwritersguild.org - 225, 250, 255, 271, 314
Jennifer Stolzer - 282, 286, 288, 292, 299, 301, 302, 305, 307, 309, 310, 312, 317, 318, 338, 348, 349, 352, 376, 379
Sunset 44 - 203, 214, 225, 233, 335

T

Robin Moore Theiss - 3, 70, 94, 205, 217, 222, 223, 225, 228, 229, 234, 244, 248, 249, 251, 274, 284, 332, 369, 375, 394, 399, 400
Hamilton Thornton - 14, 27, 36, 67, 68, 69, 71, 72, 73, 393, 394
Marcella Thum - 36, 139, 140, 142, 143, 146, 150, 174, 176, 394, 398
May Wilson Todd - 38, 42, 46, 48, 55, 56, 58, 72, 79, 80, 110, 112, 371
Marcel Toussaint - 248, 252, 253, 259, 289, 331, 337
Louise Travous - 72, 144
Treasurer - 89, 97, 133, 134, 140, 141, 152, 154, 185, 190, 202, 206, 229, 257, 258, 274, 285, 286, 306, 317
William Trowbridge - 275, 276, 290

V

J. Lillian Vandevere - 72, 80
Vice President - 73, 89, 97, 100, 133, 140, 141, 152, 200, 229, 244, 258
VLAA - 300, 319, 321
Voices of Valhalla - 248, 264, 267, 279, 280

W

Deane Wagner - 183, 184, 185, 190, 191, 194, 206, 233, 237, 238, 263, 351, 372, 373, 374, 378
Caroline Ward - 133, 134, 137, 398
Webster-Kirkwood Journal - 181
Michele Wicks - 318

Tennessee Williams - 94, 136, 161, 223, 224, 227, 338, 368, 369, 370, 393, 394, 395
Carol Winkler - 192
Winston Churchill Apartments - 110, 115, 117, 128, 130
Winter Gala - 248, 249, 265, 267
Wired Coffee - 225, 226, 232, 234, 235, 237, 238, 239, 240, 241, 244, 260, 261, 262, 285, 335, 336, 341, 370
Carolyn Wood - 152, 159, 394
Workshops for Writers - 87, 88, 187, 243, 251, 270, 277, 284, 288, 289, 290, 291, 296, 297, 298, 299, 314, 315, 318, 319, 320, 323
James A. Worsham - 118, 120, 121, 124, 125, 126, 128, 131, 398
Patience Worth - 47, 50, 54, 71, 77, 78, 95, 96, 103
Donald Wright - 11, 42, 56, 97, 110, 111, 112, 113, 123
Write Pack - 299, 300, 308, 353, 354, 355
Writers' Conference - 118, 121, 122, 125, 132, 135, 145, 150, 161, 228, 276
Writers Guild of St. Louis - 39, 325
Writers in the Garden - 245, 263
Writers in the Lodge - 313, 315, 319, 356
Writers in the Park - 247, 254, 255, 263, 266, 270, 280, 281, 289, 291, 292, 307, 308, 342, 343, 344, 345, 346, 347, 348, 349, 350, 351, 352, 353, 354, 355, 356, 382, 389, 390
Writers Under the Stars - 221, 234, 235, 274, 345

Y

Casper Yost - 60, 97, 106, 107, 114, 124
Young Writers Awards - 86, 90, 282, 283, 293, 302, 309, 316, 317, 319, 350, 367, 376, 378, 379, 390
YWSTL - 316, 317

Z

Amy Zlatic - 306, 307, 317

| Announcements

A couple of things to remember when reading this book...

Biographies and lists of published work may not be complete but come from verified listings of their work. Most biographies relate to their time in SLWG, they may come from Amazon or the author's website. Some biographies were solicited.

Apologies for the past-tense with people who are in fact, still alive. It was odd to write about everyone I know in the past-tense – I just talked to some of them the other day.

I did not include the addresses of private residences that still exist today. They are all maintained in a database, but no reason to annoy the people living there now.

What's up with my wording? In places, I kept the original language from the newspapers and occasionally used the commonly referred to name of the organization. It's a way of trying to incorporate the decade without hitting people over the head with information. Yes, sometimes it makes for a super-formal sentence and varies from my casual interjections, but it's how they talked. (Discussionistic was their word not mine.)

What's up with all the names? One of my goals for this book was to track down the first names of all the women involved with the organization. It was common practice to list women in the newspaper as Mrs. (husband's name). This was a problem for multiple reasons and led to inaccuracies. At some point, the Mr. and Mrs. were clipped from the President's List meaning for one year it was the husband listed as president. I have kept all the name iterations for future researchers. Records for SLWG and members were listed under these different names, in fact, often it was one of these alternatives that were pivotal in discovering more.

What's up with the dates? If you want to get specific, most of the dates are correct, the actual day that the event was held. I tried hard to figure out the real date of the events, but for some of the workshops and such, the date refers to when the article ran in the newspaper. If I couldn't find the real date, rather than guess or make one up, I left the date it appeared in the newspaper which was usually within a week of the real date.

There might be one or two inaccuracies. In the course of my research, I found many stories that had been passed down were not entirely accurate. Most of the information in this book came from research, things I know to be true, and can verify. Any inaccuracies are unintentional, but a few tidbits and stories did come from previous board members, my memory, or the memories of others, and I have to go by that. If there was something factually wrong, or if I don't know the whole story, please let me know.

Also, if there was a story I missed or didn't include, please contact me.

There are plenty of blank pages, add your SLWG memories.

Lastly, If I couldn't say anything nice, I might not have mentioned it.

A final thought… I have to wonder given everything we've gone through with COVID-19 and its similarities to the 1918 Flu epidemic if St. Louis Writers Guild was started from a need to connect after all the isolation. Was the need to be together in the wake of the pandemic the real catalyst in the formation of St. Louis Writers Guild? Having written this whole book before the pandemic shut everything in the country down, I can see how isolation has affected the writers of St. Louis. We'll have to see as the country gets a handle on COVID-19 what will the future bring.

| Acknowledgements

First, to my wife Amber, thank you for putting up with losing me on the first weekend of every month, and for the pile of SLWG records in the office, but mostly for the sound equipment. I need to apologize... I mean thank her, for tolerating the sound equipment.

To Sam, Shirley, Ralph, Jay, and all the Charter Members who started St. Louis Writers Guild. A century and more of helping writers is the legacy they started, and it has been a part of so many people's publishing journey, including mine.

Thank you to the board members I've served with at St. Louis Writers Guild, not only did we keep up a wonderful legacy, but we had fun doing it. Robin, Mary, Peggy, Marianne, Alicia, Dianna, Faye, David, Peter, Ashley, Dwight, Jamie, Jennifer, Jessica, Lauren, Amy, Cherie, and Teresa.

Thank you to the members of SLWG, especially the long-time members who truly carried the organization over the years. Without all of us, this writers guild would not exist, and we writers would be lonelier without it. Shout out to the short-term or occasional members too! Without you, we'd never see a new face at meetings.

A very humble thank you to Robin Moore Theiss for taking a chance and bringing me onto the board, little did she know what she was starting.

To Dr. Rebecca Carron Wood for our shared love of classic literature and funny poetry with a message. I had a great time during your era, and remember those days fondly.

To David Alan Lucas II, for all the sword fights. Together we helped a lot of writers – with sword fights – and along their publishing journeys. It was an honor to run this organization with you.

To Jessica Mathews, I know SLWG is in good hands. The future looks good.

To Mary Ward Menke, thank you for editing this book it turned out great and you had a lot to do with keeping me on the right track. Also, for handing over all your records to me when you left the board. It was a treasure trove of information.

To Jennifer Stolzer for not only being my friend, my illustrator, fellow animation aficionado, and best of all – bad book cover preventer. Hopefully, we saved a bunch of books from a horrible cover.

To Peter H. Green, not only the first person I met at SLWG but a great guy and a wonderful author. The memory I shared in this book is just one of many I think of often. Plus, an added thank you for letting me use your sketches.

To Steven Langhorst, who has been a friend for many years. Your enthusiasm at events is always welcome and for this book especially. In part, I wrote this for you to read. I hope it was worth the wait and lived up to all my hype.

I wouldn't be where I am without my critique group partners, first to T.W. Fendley. Teresa has been not only a writing partner but also a friend and dedicated volunteer with a passion for St. Louis Writers Guild. She is always a joy and I cannot imagine St. Louis Writers Guild without her. They say life is an unexpected path and I'm glad we got to walk along this part together. Nicole Lanahan (Cole Gibsen) is a gifted writer who wears her emotions on the page, and she also founded Got Your Six Support Dogs, giving trained service dogs to veterans and first responders. Her success in all things is astounding, and she wrangles chaos better than many I know. In life we all meet people we want to emulate and I can only hope to be more like her. Jennifer Lynn is a healer, and her vision of the world is one I hope everyone can embrace. It's a vision that has made her a success. With a detailed eye, she always improves my writing. I met all of them through the Guild. I credit them with all the good words, and thank them for not only years of writing together, but also, years of friendship. Go read their books. Seriously, you just read how cool they are, now seek them out.

The History of St. Louis Writers Guild

I have to acknowledge the St. Louis County Library, specifically their online research portals. Otherwise, I would have needed to spend too many hours in the library's stacks. Seriously, I have worked with some amazing librarians through this whole project and this book would not be possible without their efforts. Add to that the unsung heroes who have been digitizing the old newspapers and other records. Often this book felt like a race against their work as if I was coming in behind them every week and seeing if they had digitized any more information for me.

To everyone who didn't make it into this book. There are a million stories from St. Louis Writers Guild. So many people have their own experiences, their own stories, their own perspectives of events. I do wish I could include them all, but they can't all fit in a single book. Apologies if your story didn't make it into this account, it wasn't out of malice.

One more, to you, the reader, especially if this some years in the future. Thank you for taking a moment to find out about this amazing organization, and carry on the memory of St. Louis Writers Guild.

Brad R. Cook

St. Louis Writers Guild

---

founded in 1920

St. Louis Writers Guild is a 501©3 nonprofit organization with the mission to further Missouri's literary heritage, connect, support, and promote writers and literary organizations in the community.

stwritersguild.org
@stlwritersguild

You have friends here!

About the Author |

Brad R. Cook
Author and SLWG Historian
I see things that never were and say, "Why not?"

Brad R. Cook, is the author of historical fantasy, and award-winning short stories. He began as a playwright, dipped into the corporate writing world, and served as co-publisher and acquisitions editor for Blank Slate Press. He currently serves as Historian of St. Louis Writers Guild after three and half years as President. He learned to fence at thirteen, and never sets down his sword, but prefers to curl up with a centuries' old classic.

Books
The Iron Chronicles
  Iron Horsemen
  Iron Zulu
  Iron Lotus

Steamtree: The Airdrainium Adventures

Short Stories
A Clockwork Heart
The Dragon Slayer
Doomed Flight of the Majestic
Touch the Stars

bradrcook.com
@bradrcook

www.ingramcontent.com/pod-product-compliance
Lightning Source LLC
Chambersburg PA
CBHW070418010526
44118CB00014B/1798